The Responsibility to Protect in Libya and Syria

This book offers a novel and contemporary examination of the 'responsibility to protect' (R2P) doctrine from an international legal perspective and analyses how the doctrine was applied within the Libyan and Syrian conflicts as two recent and highly significant R2P cases.

The book dissects each of R2P's three component pillars to examine their international legal underpinnings, drawing upon diverse legal frameworks – including the laws of the UN, laws of international organisations, international human rights law, international humanitarian law, international criminal law, international environmental law, and laws of State responsibility – to extract conclusions regarding existing and emerging host and third-State obligations to prevent and react to mass atrocity crimes. It uses this legal grounding to critically examine specific aspects of the Libyan and Syrian R2P cases, engaging with some of the more traditional debates surrounding R2P's application, most notably those that pertain to the use of force (or lack thereof), but also exploring some of the less-researched non-military methods that were or could have been employed by States and international organisations to uphold the doctrine. Such an analysis captures the diversity in the means and actors through which R2P can be implemented and allows for the extraction of more nuanced conclusions regarding the doctrine's strengths and limitations, gaps in enforceability, levels of State support, and future trajectory.

The book will be of interest to scholars and students in the field of international law and human rights law.

Dr Yasmine Nahlawi is Research & Policy Coordinator at Rethink Rebuild Society through which she serves as an analyst and expert commentator on the Syrian R2P situation. She has presented in both UK and EU Parliaments and appears regularly on television and radio forums, including Channel 4 and various BBC programmes, to comment upon developments within the conflict. She holds a PhD in Public International Law and an LLM in International Legal Studies from Newcastle University, as well as a BSc in Political Science from Eastern Michigan University.

Routledge Research in International Law

For a full list of titles in this series, visit https://www.routledge.com/Routledge-Research-in-International-Law/book-series/INTNLLAW

Available:

Transnational Terrorist Groups and International Criminal Law
Anna Marie Brennan

Confronting Cyberespionage Under International Law
Oğuz Kaan Pehlivan

International Law and Revolution
Owen Taylor

Russian Discourses on International Law
Sociological and Philosophical Phenomenon
Edited by P. Sean Morris

Backstage Practices in Transnational Law
Lianne J.M Boer and Sofia Stolk

International 'Criminal' Responsibility
Antinomies
Ottavio Quirico

The Future of International Courts
Regional, Institutional and Procedural Challenges
Edited by Avidan Kent, Nikos Skoutaris and Jamie Trinidad

The Far-Right in International and European Law
Natalie Alkiviadou

The Responsibility to Protect in International Law
Philosophical Investigations
Natalie Oman

The Responsibility to Protect in Libya and Syria
Mass Atrocities, Human Protection, and International Law
Yasmine Nahlawi

The Responsibility to Protect in Libya and Syria

Mass Atrocities, Human Protection, and International Law

Yasmine Nahlawi

Routledge
Taylor & Francis Group
LONDON AND NEW YORK

First published 2020
by Routledge
2 Park Square, Milton Park, Abingdon, Oxon OX14 4RN

and by Routledge
605 Third Avenue, New York, NY 10017

First issued in paperback 2021

Routledge is an imprint of the Taylor & Francis Group, an informa business

Publisher's Note
The publisher has gone to great lengths to ensure the quality of this reprint but points out that some imperfections in the original copies may be apparent.

British Library Cataloguing in Publication Data
A catalogue record for this book is available from the British Library

Library of Congress Cataloging-in-Publication Data
Names: Nahlawi, Yasmine, author.
Title: The responsibility to protect in Libya and Syria : mass atrocities, human protection and International law / Yasmine Nahlawi.
Description: Abingdon, Oxon ; New York, NY : Routledge, 2020. |
Series: Routledge research in international law |
Based on author's thesis (doctoral - Newcastle University, 2016) issued under title: The Responsibility to Protect : An Examination of Host and Third-State Obligations in Preventing and Reacting to Mass Atrocity Crimes in Light of the Libyan and Syrian Conflicts. |
Includes bibliographical references and index.
Identifiers: LCCN 2019036246 (print) | LCCN 2019036247 (ebook) |
ISBN 9781138618657 (hardback) | ISBN 9780429461101 (ebook)
Subjects: LCSH: Responsibility to protect (International law) |
Syria--History--Civil War, 2011---Law and legislation. |
Libya--History--Civil War, 2011---Law and legislation.
Classification: LCC KZ4082 .N34 2020 (print) |
LCC KZ4082 (ebook) | DDC 341.4/8--dc23
LC record available at https://lccn.loc.gov/2019036246
LC ebook record available at https://lccn.loc.gov/2019036247

Typeset in Galliard
by Taylor & Francis Books

ISBN 13: 978-1-03-223971-2 (pbk)
ISBN 13: 978-1-138-61865-7 (hbk)

DOI: 10.4324/9780429461101

This book is dedicated to the Syrian people and their valiant struggle for freedom and democracy.

Contents

List of cases

Permanent Court of International Justice

- *The Case of the S.S. "Lotus" (France v Turkey)* (Collection of Judgments) PCIJ Rep Series A
- *The Panevezys-Saldutiskis Railway Case (Estonia v Lithuania)* (Judgment) PCIJ Rep Series A/B No 76

International Criminal Tribunal for the Former Yugoslavia

- *Prosecutor v. Tadić* (Decision on the Defence Motion of Interlocutory Appeal on Jurisdiction) ICTY-94–1 (2 October 1995)
- *Prosecutor v. Tadić* (Opinion and Judgment) ICTY-94–1-T (7 May 1997)
- *Prosecutor v. Kupreškić et al.* (Judgement) IT-95–16-T (14 January 2000)
- *Prosecutor v. Delalic* (Judgement) IT-96–21-A (20 February 2001)
- *Prosecutor v. Krstić* (Judgement) ICTY-98–33T (2 August 2001)

International Criminal Tribunal for Rwanda

- *Prosecutor v. Akayesu* (Judgement) ICTR-96–4-T (2 September 1998)
- *Nahimana et al. (Media Case)* (Judgement) ICTR-99–52 (28 November 2007)

International Court of Justice

- *Reparations for Injuries Suffered in the Service of the United Nations* (Advisory Opinion) [1949] ICJ Rep 174
- *Competence of the General Assembly for the Admission of a State to the United Nations* (Dissenting Opinion of Judge Alvarez) [1950] ICJ Rep 12
- *Reservations to the Convention on the Prevention and Punishment of the Crime of Genocide* (Advisory Opinion) [1951] ICJ Rep 15
- *Certain Expenses of the United Nations* (Advisory Opinion) [1962] ICJ Rep 151
- *Case Concerning The Barcelona Traction, Light and Power Company, Limited (Belgium v. Spain)* (Judgment) [1970] ICJ Rep 3
- *Legal Consequences for States of the Continued Presence of South Africa in Namibia (South West Africa) Notwithstanding Security Council Resolution 276* (Advisory Opinion) [1971] ICJ Rep 16

- *Case Concerning the Military and Paramilitary Activities in and Against Nicaragua (Nicaragua v. United States of America)* (Jurisdiction of the Court and Admissibility of the Application) [1984] ICJ Rep 392
- *Case Concerning Military and Paramilitary Activities in and Against Nicaragua (Nicaragua v. United States of America)* (Merits) [1986] ICJ Rep 14
- *Legality of the Threat or Use of Nuclear Weapons* (Advisory Opinion) [1996] ICJ Rep 226
- *Legal Consequences of the Construction of a Wall in the Occupied Palestinian Territory* (Advisory Opinion) [2004] ICJ Rep 136
- *Legal Consequences of the Construction of a Wall in the Occupied Palestinian Territory* (Separate Opinion of Judge Elaraby) [2004] ICJ Rep 246
- *Case Concerning Armed Activities on the Territory of the Congo (Democratic Republic of the Congo v. Rwanda)* (Judgment) [2006] ICJ Rep 6
- *Case Concerning Application of the Convention on the Prevention and Punishment of the Crime of Genocide (Bosnia & Herzegovina v. Serbia & Montenegro)* (Judgment) [2007] ICJ Rep 43
- *Case Concerning Application of the Convention on the Prevention and Punishment of the Crime of Genocide (Bosnia & Herzegovina v. Serbia & Montenegro)* (Separate Opinion of Judge Tomka) [2007] ICJ Rep 310
- *Case Concerning Application of the Convention on the Prevention and Punishment of the Crime of Genocide (Bosnia & Herzegovina v. Serbia & Montenegro)* (Declaration of Judge Skotnikov) [2007] ICJ Rep 366
- *Accordance with International Law of the Unilateral Declaration of Independence by the Provisional Institutions of Self-Government of Kosovo* (Advisory Opinion) [2010] ICJ Rep 403
- *Jurisdictional Immunities of the State (Germany v. Italy: Greece Intervening)* (Judgment) [2012] ICJ Rep 99
- *Legal Consequences of the Separation of the Chagos Archipelago from Mauritius in 1965* (Advisory Opinion) 2019 <https://www.icj-cij.org/files/case-related/169/169-20190225-01-00-EN.pdf>

European Court of Human Rights

- *Osman v UK* (App no 23452/94) ECHR 28 October 1998
- *Behrami and Behrami v. France and Saramati v. France, Germany and Norway* (App no 71412/01, 78166/01) ECHR 2 May 2007
- *Case of Al-Jedda v. The United Kingdom* (App no 27021/08, 78166/01) ECHR 7 July 2011

Inter-American Court of Human Rights

Velásquez Rodríguez v Honduras, Judgment of July 29, 1988, Inter-Am.Ct.H.R. (Ser. C) No. 4 (1988)

Acknowledgements

This book is based on my PhD dissertation, which I defended at Newcastle University in December 2016. Many of the arguments have been refined and updated to take into account developments that have occurred since my thesis submission. It is with sadness, however, that I note that the mass atrocity situations of both Libya and Syria – the two case studies of this book – are still ongoing.

The production of this book would not have been possible without the help and support of colleagues, friends, and family. Special thanks must first be made to my three doctoral supervisors, Elena Katselli, Rob Dickinson, and the late James Upcher. To Elena I owe infinite gratitude for her wise and warm supervision and for investing her time above and beyond what was required to offer highly nuanced feedback on several drafts of each chapter. I was truly blessed to work under her supervision. Special thanks must also be made to Rob who lent his expertise throughout the first two years of my PhD journey. His detail-oriented approach to my work made me more attentive to the finer implications of my writing. Unfortunately, Rob left Newcastle Law School two years into my PhD. Where he left off, however, James very gracefully stepped into his shoes, and I am extremely grateful to James for making the supervisory transition so smooth and positive. The shocking news of James's death in May 2017 left a devastating impact on me, although James's clever insights and his striking observations continue to ring through my head to this day when I consider the 'bigger picture' implications of my work and when I seek to integrate multiple legal issues with each other.

Thanks must also be given to James Pattison, Jorge Núñez, Vassilis Tzevelekos, Ibrahim Olabi, Aidan Hehir, Nigel White, and Ole Pedersen for reading and commenting on draft chapters. I am especially grateful to Sana Sekkarie for offering feedback on the entire manuscript. Thank you also to the editors at Routledge, most particularly Nicola Sharpe, Siobhan Poole, and Sarahjayne Smith, for their warm and efficient support throughout the publishing process, and to the anonymous reviewers at Routledge for their constructive feedback.

Unless otherwise specified, all web links referenced in this book were last accessed on 1 July 2019. Also important to note is that some of the material within this book was published elsewhere in previous form. Sections 5.3 and 7.2 derive from 'Overcoming Russian and Chinese Vetoes on Syria through Uniting for Peace' (2019) 24/1 *Journal of Conflict and Security Law* 111. Section 6.5 originates from 'The Legality of NATO's Pursuit of Regime Change in Syria' (2018) 5/2 *Journal on the Use of Force and International Law* 295. I am grateful to the publishers of both articles for allowing me to use the material in this book.

Finally, I must attempt to give proper due to my family, to which I owe my underlying strength and motivation. Special thanks to my parents, Khaled and Mysa, for being my unrelenting support team. Thank you also to my husband, Majed, who has stood by my side throughout this publishing journey, and to our beautiful children, Maryam and Abdullah, who have taught me that the greatest joy in life often comes in this smallest of forms.

To many I owe thanks for the completion of this book. Any shortcomings remain my own.

List of acronyms

API	Additional Protocol I
APII	Additional Protocol II
ANF	Al-Nusra Front
ASR	Articles on State Responsibility
AU	African Union
DARIO	Draft Articles on the Responsibility of International Organisations
GCC	Gulf Cooperation Council
HRC	Human Rights Council
IAC	International Armed Conflict
ICC	International Criminal Court
ICCPR	International Covenant on Civil and Political Rights
ICESCR	International Covenant on Economic, Social and Cultural Rights
ICISS	International Commission on Intervention and State Sovereignty
ICJ	International Court of Justice
ICRC	International Committee of the Red Cross
ICTR	International Criminal Tribunal for Rwanda
ICTY	International Criminal Tribunal for the Former Yugoslavia
IHL	International Humanitarian Law
IHRL	International Human Rights Law
ILC	International Law Commission
ILO	International Labour Organization
ISIS	Islamic State
JIM	Joint Investigative Mechanism
LAS	League of Arab States
NATO	North Atlantic Treaty Organization
NIAC	Non-International Armed Conflict
NSA	Non-State Actor
OIC	Organisation of Islamic Cooperation
OPCW	Organisation for the Prohibition of Chemical Weapons
P5	Permanent Five
PCIJ	Permanent Court of International Justice
R2P	Responsibility to Protect

UforP	Uniting for Peace
UK	United Kingdom
UN	United Nations
UNGA	United Nations General Assembly
UNIMI	United Nations Independent Mechanism of Investigation
UNSC	United Nations Security Council
UNSMIS	United Nations Supervision Mission in Syria
US	United States
VCLT	Vienna Convention on the Law of Treaties
WWII	World War II

1 Introduction

The 'responsibility to protect' (R2P) doctrine was developed in 2001 in response to a question posed by then-UN Secretary-General Kofi Annan to States: 'If humanitarian intervention is, indeed, an unacceptable assault on sovereignty, how *should* we respond to a Rwanda, to a Srebrenica – to gross and systematic violations of human rights that offend every precept of our common humanity?'[1] Here, Annan was referring to the international community's failure to react in a timely and effective manner to the genocides perpetrated in Srebrenica (in the former Yugoslavia) as well as in Rwanda in the 1990s.[2] Equally significant in this respect was the North Atlantic Treaty Organization's (NATO) military intervention in Kosovo in 1999 in response to ethnic cleansing committed by Serb forces against Kosovar Albanians, conducted without United Nations Security Council (UNSC) authorisation given the threat of the impending Russian veto.[3] Together, these cases exposed compelling weaknesses within the international legal system – and within the UNSC framework in particular – to respond effectively and consistently to gross breaches of human rights norms. R2P thus emerged to put words to deeds regarding the international community's commitment to 'never again' allow mass atrocities to occur. With a central purpose of ensuring human protection from mass atrocity crimes (defined as genocide, war crimes, crimes against humanity, and ethnic cleansing[4]), the doctrine has succeeded in stirring a

1 Report of the Secretary-General, 'We the Peoples: The Role of the United Nations in the Twenty-First Century' (2000) UN Doc A/54/2000 Para 217.
2 On the international responses to the Srebrenica and Rwanda genocides, *see* Fernando R. Tesón, 'Collective Humanitarian Intervention' (1995–1996) 17 *Michigan Journal of International Law* 323, 362–69; Thomas H. Lee, 'The Law of War and the Responsibility to Protect Civilians: A Reinterpretation' (2015) 55 *Harvard International Law Journal* 251, 279–81.
3 On NATO's unauthorised intervention in Kosovo, *see* Bruno Simma, 'NATO, the UN and the Use of Force: Legal Aspects' (1999) 10 *European Journal of International Law* 1; Louis Henkin, 'Kosovo and the Law of "Humanitarian Intervention"' (1999) 93 *American Journal of International Law* 824; Christopher Greenwood, 'International Law and the NATO Intervention in Kosovo' (2000) 49 *International and Comparative Law Quarterly* 926.
4 *See* 2005 World Summit Outcome, UNGA Res 60/1 (24 October 2005) UN Doc A/RES/60/1 Para 138.

significant amount of international debate surrounding the roles that host States (those in which the atrocities are perpetrated) and third-party States (those that have no direct link to an atrocity situation) can or should assume in preventing and responding to mass atrocity situations.[5] It is within these debates that this book emerges.

1.1 This book at a glance

R2P was endorsed unanimously by States in the United Nations General Assembly (UNGA) as part of the 2005 World Summit Outcome document, although there is widespread agreement that it does not (yet) represent an international legal norm.[6] Nevertheless, analysing R2P as a purely political or 'soft law' tool short-changes the legal value that the doctrine possesses or has the potential to impart. This book seeks to unpack R2P's basis within international law and to situate its tenets within wider existing and emerging norms, drawing upon diverse legal regimes – including the laws of the UN, laws of international organisations, international human rights law, international humanitarian law, international criminal law, international environmental law, and laws of State responsibility – to determine which aspects of this doctrine are grounded within existing international legal norms, and those which require further development in order to fully actualise the doctrine's ideals and aspirations.

This book furthermore examines the doctrine's application in the two contemporary and highly significant case studies of Libya and Syria, in which non-violent anti-government protests within each of these States beginning in February and March 2011, respectively, deteriorated into mass atrocity situations following brutal government crackdowns. The choice of these case studies stems from two primary considerations. First, both conflicts are widely recognised as compelling R2P situations with far-reaching ramifications with respect to the doctrine's operationalisation. Namely, they appealed to the doctrine's full scope so that robust measures, including the use of force, were required to counter seemingly deliberate and gross failures of the respective governments to protect their populations. These cases can be asserted, perhaps boldly, to challenge the very viability of R2P, namely, whether this is a doctrine that can or does indeed deliver upon the promise of 'never again' allowing mass atrocity crimes to be committed. As such, the Libyan and Syrian cases can be branded as contemporary watershed moments for R2P with the potential to impart a distinct trajectory upon the doctrine's future progression (or lack thereof).

The second reason for the choice of Libya and Syria is that they share a number of fundamental similarities that make them prime situations for comparison: both

5 *See* 'Key developments on the Responsibility to Protect at the United Nations from 2005–2017' (*International Coalition for the Responsibility to Protect*, 2018) <http://www.responsibilitytoprotect.org/index.php/about-rtop/the-un-and-rtop>.

6 *See*, for example, S. Pandiaraj, 'Sovereignty as Responsibility: Reflections on the Legal Status of the Doctrine of Responsibility to Protect' (2016) 15 *Chinese Journal of International Law* 795.

emerged within Arab States with similar histories of repressive governments.[7] Both commenced within a month of each other and within the wider context of the Arab Spring,[8] meaning that the international community was, generally speaking, reacting to two relatively similar cases at roughly the same time.[9] Most importantly, in both situations, the governments failed in their responsibilities to protect their populations by committing war crimes and crimes against humanity against them.[10] As per the R2P doctrine, this then shifted the responsibility for the protection of these populations upon the international community. However, as detailed throughout this book, the international reactions to these two situations were widely inconsistent. An analysis of these differing reactions helps to extrapolate legal conclusions regarding the doctrine's strengths, limitations, gaps in enforceability, acceptance by States, and anticipated future trajectory.

This book adopts a distinct approach to examining the Libyan and Syrian R2P cases. First, it endeavours to highlight the multitude of actors that were (or could have been) involved in the doctrine's implementation. A significant set of scholarly works, for example, focus upon the UNSC (and its role in authorising the use of force) when assessing international responses to the Libyan and Syrian crises.[11] Other pieces restrict their investigations to the reactions of individual States or regional or international organisations.[12] In exploring the actions of a diverse set

7 *See*, for example, Tarik Kafala, 'Gaddafi's Quixotic and Brutal Rule' (*BBC News*, 20 October 2011) <http://www.bbc.co.uk/news/world-africa-12532929>; Martin Asser, 'The Muammar Gaddafi Story' (*BBC News*, 21 October 2011) <http://www.bbc.co.uk/news/world-africa-12688033>; HRC, 'Report of the United Nations High Commissioner for Human Rights on the Situation of Human Rights in the Syrian Arab Republic' (15 September 2011) UN Doc A/HRC/18/53 Para 22; Ghayath Naisse, 'A Revolution on the March' (*International Viewpoint*, 2011) <http://www.internationalviewpoint.org/spip.php?article2272>.

8 The term 'Arab Spring' refers to a wave of popular anti-government protests that emerged within the Middle East and North Africa region (specifically, in Tunisia, Egypt, Libya, Bahrain, Yemen, and Syria) beginning in December 2001 which led to the overthrow of dictatorships in Tunisia, Egypt, Libya, and Yemen.

9 The Libyan uprising began on 15 February 2011 while that of Syria began on 6 March 2011. HRC, 'Report of the International Commission of Inquiry to Investigate all Alleged Violations of International Human Rights Law in the Libyan Arab Jamahiriya' (12 January 2012) UN Doc A/HRC/17/44 Para 27; 'Bashar al-Assad: Criminal against Humanity' (International Federation for Human Rights, July 2011) at 6 <http://www.fidh.org/IMG/pdf/reportsyria2807eng.pdf>.

10 As further detailed in Sections 6.1 and 7.1 of this book.

11 *See*, for example, Justin Morris, 'Libya and Syria: R2P and the Spectre of the Swinging Pendulum' (2013) 89 *International Affairs* 1265; Andrew Garwood-Gowers, 'The Responsibility to Protect and the Arab Spring: Libya as the Exception, Syria as the Norm?' (2013) 36 *University of New South Wales Law Journal* 594.

12 *See*, for example, Colin Warbrick, 'British Policy and the National Transitional Council of Libya' (2012) 61 *International and Comparative Law Quarterly* 247; Alex de Waal, 'African Roles in the Libyan Conflict of 2011' (2013) 89 *International Affairs* 365; Tilman Rodenhäuser, 'Human Rights Obligations of Non-State Armed Groups in other Situations of Violence: The Syria Example' (2012) 3 *International Humanitarian Legal Studies* 263; Kurt Mills, 'R2P and the ICC: At Odds or in Sync?' (2015) 26 *Criminal Law Forum* 73; Olivia Flasch, 'The Legality of the Air Strikes against

of international actors, however, this book allows for an analysis of each actor's unique contributions to the implementation of R2P in Libya and Syria, respectively, as well as an understanding of how their joint responses through various international legal frameworks (could have) facilitated a reaction that transcended any one of their individual contributions. This is important as it emphasises that R2P's enforcement is not contingent upon any single actor within the international system, but that it rather integrates the actions of a range of entities and requires collective and wide-ranging responses in order to present an effective front against mass atrocities.

Second, this book devotes extensive consideration to non-military means through which R2P can be invoked, whereas the traditional approach has been to assess R2P's success or lack thereof in Libya and Syria through the lens of military intervention.[13] Importantly, the book does engage with some of the more traditional debates surrounding R2P's application, most notably those pertaining to the use of force (or lack thereof), but it also, crucially, investigates some of the less-researched non-military methods that were or could have been pursued by States and international organisations to uphold the doctrine. Such means include, for example, the suspension of States from regional and international institutions,[14] use of third-party countermeasures,[15] restrictions to the use of the permanent veto,[16] reactions to the use of chemical weapons,[17] overcoming barriers to humanitarian access,[18] and the application of R2P to non-State actors (NSAs).[19] In examining these wide-ranging facets, this book illustrates that R2P's invocation in the Libyan and Syrian cases could have been more extensive and, perhaps, more effective.

Finally, this book pinpoints particular shortcomings with respect to the international community's responses to the Libyan and Syrian R2P cases that in turn expose limitations within the doctrine itself. Such observations are coupled with concrete suggestions regarding means of enhancing R2P's enforceability to render it capable of delivering upon its central vision of eradicating mass atrocity crimes. Most important in this respect is that R2P must come to represent an obligation upon third-party States to react to the commission of mass atrocity crimes, which

ISIL in Syria: New Insights on the Extraterritorial Use of Force against Non-State Actors' (2016) 3 *Journal on the Use of Force and International Law* 37; Alex Whiting, 'An Investigative Mechanism for Syria: The General Assembly Steps into the Breach' (2017) 15 *Journal of International Criminal Justice* 231.

13 *See*, for example, Garwood-Gowers (n11); Morris (n11); Spencer Zifcak, 'The Responsibility to Protect After Libya and Syria' (2012) 13 *Melbourne Journal of International Law* 59; Michael Small, 'An Analysis of the Responsibility to Protect Program in Light of the Conflict in Syria' (2014) 13 *Washington University Global Studies Law Review* 179.

14 *See* Sections 6.2.1, 6.3, and 7.3 of this book.

15 *See*, in particular, Sections 2.2, 5.2, 6.2.1, 7.2.5, and 7.3.

16 *See* Sections 5.3.1 and 7.2.2.

17 *See* Section 7.2.4.

18 *See* Section 7.2.5.

19 *See* Sections 7.4 and 7.5.

would remove the element of discretion that plagues the international community's current responses to R2P situations. Should such an obligation to react fail to materialise, then the doctrine should at least come to formally recognise and incorporate means of circumventing the UNSC – as the only international body that can adopt binding measures upon all UN member-States and that can authorise the use of force absent self-defence – in the event that the body is deadlocked from responding to a mass atrocity situation due to the exercise of the veto by one or more of its permanent members.[20] R2P's development in one of the above manners is a prerequisite to achieving the international community's promise – 'never again'.

1.2 Book structure

Chapter 2 of this book offers an overview of the R2P doctrine. It first details some of the trends within the international legal system that facilitated its emergence, including the move from bilateralism to community interests as well as the push to impart obligations – rather than allowing discretion – upon third-party States to react to mass atrocity crimes. It then discusses R2P's core tenets through the separate examination of each of the major documents that contributed to its formulation, including through an analysis of the legal value and levels of State support for each of these documents. The chapter ties these observations together to cast an overall picture of R2P as an emerging umbrella norm of various sub-norms which the doctrine seeks to pull together, repackage, and build upon.

Following this overview, Chapters 3–5 are devoted to an in-depth analysis of each one of R2P's three component pillars as identified within a 2009 report published by the UN Secretary-General titled 'Implementing the Responsibility to Protect'.[21] These chapters thus situate each of R2P's pillars within existing international legal norms and identify gaps, if any, that exist with respect to their enforceability. As such, Chapter 3 undertakes a critical legal examination of R2P's Pillar 1 obligation for host States to protect their populations from mass atrocity crimes through analysing the legally prohibited status of each of these four crimes, drawing upon relevant treaty law, customary international law, and international case law. This analysis is complemented with an overview of *opinio juris* with respect to R2P's Pillar 1 to reflect upon this Pillar's acceptance by States as well as its normative gaps.

Chapter 4 engages in a similar examination of the international legal underpinnings of R2P's Pillar 2 responsibility for the international community to provide assistance and support to host States in meeting their Pillar 1 obligations. Noting that international norms and *opinio juris* underlying this pillar are

20 Some of the potential means discussed within this book by which this can be achieved include through the invocation of lawful measures, third-party countermeasures, and the Uniting for Peace mechanism. *See* Sections 2.2 and 5.3.2.1 of this book.

21 Report of the Secretary-General, 'Implementing the Responsibility to Protect' (12 January 2009) UN Doc A/63/677 Para 11.

significantly less developed than those of Pillar 1, this chapter considers emerging trends within international human rights law and international environmental law regarding a duty to cooperate and stipulates whether and how such obligations can come to be accepted as part of R2P.

Chapter 5 analyses R2P's third and most controversial pillar, which calls upon the international community to react to the commission of mass atrocity crimes when host States fail in their protection responsibilities. As such, this chapter investigates the legal underpinnings of and States' attitudes towards this pillar to situate it within existing obligations and norms, including through the consideration of relevant provisions of the Genocide Convention, the four Geneva Conventions, and the Articles on State Responsibility. This analysis is complemented with a discussion of how R2P's Pillar 3 must be strengthened or developed with view to achieving a robust R2P framework that is not employed on a case-by-case basis, but rather serves as an effective and legally grounded tool to bring an end to all mass atrocity crimes. Recognising that the full enforceability of Pillar 3 is contingent in many respects upon overcoming abusive vetoes within the UNSC, this chapter devotes significant consideration to investigating legal dimensions of the permanent veto, focusing upon means through which its abusive invocation can be curtailed or even circumvented in mass atrocity situations.

Following the detailed study of each of R2P's three pillars, Chapters 6 and 7 are dedicated to the examination of the doctrine's implementation within the Libyan and Syrian conflicts, respectively. Chapter 6 evaluates legal texts, State practice, and *opinio juris* to assess how the Libyan conflict both reflected and affected R2P's development, interpretation, and application. In addition to engaging with some of the major debates that have permeated discussions on Libya and R2P, namely, on military intervention and regime change, this chapter furthermore analyses some of the more 'under-researched' aspects of this conflict in order to emphasise the doctrine's versatility and broad spectrum of applicability. The specific angles explored within this chapter include Libya's suspensions from the UN Human Rights Council and the League of Arab States (LAS), the UNSC's imposition of sanctions and an arms embargo, the referral of the Libyan situation to the International Criminal Court, NATO's military intervention in Libya (with particular focus on the role of regime change), and the post-conflict rebuilding of Libya.

Chapter 7 adopts a very similar approach to analysing the Syrian R2P case. In addition to engaging with some of the more prominent debates on R2P's application in Syria (most particularly, regarding the employment of the veto and the consequences of non-intervention), it also explores other aspects pertaining to the doctrine's invocation, including the use of third-party countermeasures by the LAS (in the form of economic sanctions, asset freezes, a civil aviation ban, and the suspension of Syria from its seat); the international reaction towards chemical weapons use and how this reconciles with R2P; the relationship between R2P and humanitarian access, as well as how such access could have been ensured in the Syrian case; the pursuit of accountability outside the purview of the UNSC for perpetrators of international crimes in Syria; the applicability of R2P to

NSAs; and the role that R2P could have or should have played in the US-led coalition's intervention against the Islamic State and Al-Nusra Front terrorist groups in Syria.

Chapter 8 reflects upon the Libyan and Syrian case studies and extrapolates general trends and conclusions regarding the role that R2P played in both of them, with view to assessing the doctrine's overall applicability, strengths, weaknesses, and acceptance by States. These findings are considered alongside other contemporary developments pertaining to R2P, most particularly from other mass atrocity situations, to gauge whether and how the Syrian and Libyan cases are likely to impact upon the doctrine's future invocation or on the means of its implementation. The chapter concludes by tying together the various themes of the book, reflecting upon R2P's overall standing in international law as well as its likely future trajectory given the Libyan and Syrian precedents.

2 Contextualising the emergence of the Responsibility to Protect

2.1 Introduction

R2P is premised upon the notion that each State has the primary responsibility to protect its population from mass atrocity crimes.[1] If a State fails in this responsibility – either through an act attributable to it (e.g. it perpetrates such a crime itself) or through an omission (e.g. it is unwilling or unable to protect its population[2]) – then the responsibility to protect is transferred to the international community. The latter should then react by employing a range of measures, the final and most extreme being the use of force, to bring an end to the situation and to ensure human protection.[3] R2P thus seeks to impart a multi-layer system of responsibilities to ensure that outbreaks of mass atrocities are prevented or, in the second instance, are promptly and effectively ceased.

This chapter begins with a discussion of two general trends that have long been manifesting within the international legal system and which facilitated R2P's emergence, namely, the move from bilateralism to the recognition of community interests, as well as the move from a discretion of third-party States to react to mass atrocity crimes towards an obligation upon them to do so. Following this historical contextualisation, this chapter explores R2P's emergence and development through the separate examination of each of the major documents that advanced it. These documents are evaluated with respect to their legal value and contents with analysis of how together, they contributed to R2P's currently-accepted formulation.

1 Although the 2001 ICISS report suggested that R2P should apply to 'situations of compelling human need', the subsequent formulation of the doctrine through the 2005 World Summit Outcome document restricted the doctrine's scope to the four mass atrocity crimes. 'The Responsibility to Protect: The Report of the International Commission on Intervention and State Sovereignty' (International Commission on Intervention and State Sovereignty, December 2001) at xi <http://responsibilitytoprotect.org/ICISS%20Report.pdf> [hereinafter 2001 ICISS Report]; 2005 World Summit Outcome, UNGA Res 60/1 (24 October 2005) UN Doc A/RES/60/1 Para 138 [hereinafter 2005 World Summit Outcome].

2 For some analysis on the 'unwilling and unable' doctrine, *see* Section 7.5 of this book.

3 *See* 2001 ICISS Report (n1) Para 4.1.

2.2 Ongoing trends in the international legal system

Understanding the significance of R2P's (potential) contributions to international law requires an appreciation of some of the major trends out of which it arose as well as the gaps that it was created to fill. The next two sections discuss some of these trends and gaps.

2.2.1 From bilateralism to community interests

Although international law has come a long way, the traditional (Eurocentric) international legal system (also, the Westphalian system, often attributed to the signing of the Peace of Westphalia in 1648) was primarily founded upon unquestioned and uncompromising State sovereignty.[4] Externally, the State was the exclusive subject of international law,[5] bound by no other authority other than obligations that it assumed voluntarily (for example, through entering into treaties with other States).[6] This state of affairs was captured by the Permanent Court of International Justice's (PCIJ) landmark judgment in the 1927 *Lotus* case that the 'rules of law binding upon States … emanate from their own free will'.[7] In line with this, inter-State relations were predominantly bilateralisable in nature, as States entered into obligations on the basis of perceived national rather than collective interests.[8] The lack of recognition of collective interests restricted the emergence of formal frameworks of cooperation between States, which in turn limited collective responses to shared threats such as war.

Under this traditional Westphalian model, a State's sovereignty also maintained it as the sole and supreme authority within its territorial boundaries.[9] This meant that, in theory, it retained exclusive control over all matters within its jurisdiction, and that its policies could not be questioned or interfered with by any other

4 For critiques of this traditional view, *see* Luke Glanville, *Sovereignty and the Responsibility to Protect: A New History* (University of Chicago Press 2014); Stephen Carley, 'Limping toward Elysium: Impediments Created by the Myth of Westphalia on Humanitarian Intervention in the International Legal System' (2008–2009) 41 *Connecticut Law Review* 1741; Wayne Hudson, 'Fables of Sovereignty' in Trudy Jacobsen, Charles Sampford and Ramesh Thakur (eds), *Re-Envisioning Sovereignty: The End of Westphalia?* (Ashgate Publishing Limited 2008) 28.

5 As stated by Oppenheim and Lauterpacht, 'the subjects of the rights and duties arising from international law are states solely and exclusively'. L. Oppenheim and Hersch Lauterpacht, *International Law: A Treatise.* Vol. I, *Peace* (8th edn, Longmans, Green 1955) 16.

6 This represents a positivist reading of international law. On the distinction between positivism and naturalism in international legal theory, *see* Emer de Vattel, *Law of Nations; Or Principles of the Law of Nature, Applied to the Conduct and Affairs of Nations and Sovereigns* (6th American edn, Merriam and Cooke 1884) lxv–lxvi.

7 *The Case of the S.S. 'Lotus' (France v Turkey)* (Collection of Judgments) PCIJ Rep Series A No 10, 18 [hereinafter *Lotus* case].

8 *See* Jonathan I. Charney, 'Universal International Law' (1993) 87 *American Journal of International Law* 529, 529.

9 *See* W. Michael Reisman, 'Sovereignty and Human Rights in Contemporary International Law' (1990) 84 *American Journal of International Law* 866, 869.

power.[10] As such, a State was not required to observe human rights practices within its domestic sphere unless it specifically assumed such obligations upon itself. It could treat its 'subjects' as it wished; it could theoretically persecute a group, repress its people, or wage war to defend its territorial integrity (for example, against secessionist ambitions) while claiming these to be sovereign acts.[11] The only situation in which it forfeited this claim to internal sovereignty was if it violated the rights of another State (for example, by compromising that State's nationals or property within its borders), thus giving that State a right to react through self-help or diplomatic protection.[12] As such, human rights-related claims brought forward on behalf of individuals were asserted as States' rights for the protection of their nationals rather than as individual rights.[13] The PCIJ, for example, stated in its 1939 *Panevezys–Saldutiskis Railway* case that 'in taking up the case of one of its nationals … a State is in reality asserting its own right, the right to ensure in the person of its nationals respect for the rules of international law'.[14] Essentially, as long as a State did not infringe upon other States' rights, the Westphalian model of sovereignty bestowed upon it virtually unlimited and unchecked authority within its borders to enact and enforce its own codes and laws and made it immune from foreign interference.

This international legal regime was increasingly challenged – particularly in the aftermath of World War II (WWII) – as it became recognised that there are some interests, termed 'community interests', that cannot be achieved through the traditional bilateralist state of affairs, but rather require the cooperation of all States (i.e. a multilateral approach) in order to be fully attained. These interests represent areas of shared international concern whereby their violation by a single State can impart ramifications upon the security and wellbeing of all States (for example, with respect to the protection of the environment).[15] Critical to the development

10 *See*, however, Glanville (n4).

11 *See* Lois Henkin, 'Human Rights and State "Sovereignty"' (1995–1996) 25 *Georgia Journal of International and Comparative Law* 31, 32; Pärtel Piirimäe, 'The Westphalian Myth and the Idea of External Sovereignty' in Hent Kalmo and Quentin Skinner (eds), *Sovereignty in Fragments: The Past, Present and Future of a Contested Concept* (Cambridge University Press 2010) 93–94.

12 *See* Richard B. Lillich, 'Forcible Self-Help by States to Protect Human Rights' (1967–1968) 53 *Iowa Law Review* 325, 326–27.

13 *See* Lois B. Sohn, 'The New International Law: Protection of the Rights of Individuals Rather than States' (1982–83) 32 *American University Law Review* 1, 2.

14 *The Panevezys–Saldutiskis Railway Case (Estonia v Lithuania)* (Judgment) PCIJ Rep Series A/B No 76 at 16. *See*, however, Giorgio Gaja, 'The Position of Individuals in International Law: An ILC Perspective' (2010) 21 *European Journal of International Law* 11 (highlighting the International Law Commission's departure from this approach to recognise the rights of injured individuals in the exercise of diplomatic protection).

15 On community interests, *see* Elena Katselli Proukaki, *The Problem of Enforcement in International Law: Countermeasures, the Non-injured State and the Idea of International Community* (Routledge 2009) Chapter 2; Santiago Villalpando, 'The Legal Dimension of the International Community: How Community Interests are Protected in International Law' (2010) 21 *European Journal of International Law* 387.

of R2P, human rights norms have become accepted as a category of community interests given that human rights violations within a single State can provoke international consequences such as spills-over of violence, proliferation of weapons, refugee crises, and decreased international peace and security more generally.[16] This recognition in turn spurred the progressive development of responsibilities for both host and third-party States in preventing and reacting to their gross abuse, often at the expense of the traditionally untouchable State sovereignty.

The first major development with respect to the promotion of human rights as community interests in the post-WWII era came through the establishment of the United Nations (UN) in 1945. At its core, the UN Charter safeguards State sovereignty through provisions such as Article 2(4), which maintains that '[a]ll Members shall refrain in their international relations from the threat or use of force against the territorial integrity or political independence of any state',[17] as well as Article 2(7), which holds that '[n]othing contained in the present Charter shall authorize the United Nations to intervene in matters which are essentially within the domestic jurisdiction of any state'.[18] Alongside such protections for States, however, the UN framework is also vested in the promotion of human rights. For example, Article 1(3) of the Charter lists one of the purposes of the UN as '[achieving] international cooperation … in promoting and encouraging respect for human rights and for fundamental freedoms for all'.[19] Article 55 furthermore maintains that the 'United Nations shall promote … universal respect for, and observance of, human rights and fundamental freedoms for all'.[20] These Articles placed human rights on the international agenda for the coming decades, although it should be noted that they neither specified concrete standards by which States should abide, nor did they stipulate how these human rights commitments should be enforced.[21] Even Article 56, through which States pledged to 'take joint and separate action in cooperation with the Organization for the achievement of the purposes set forth in Article 55',[22] did not identify the means through which such action would occur. Together, however, Articles 1(3), 55, and 56 of the UN Charter paved the way for the future codification and greater enforceability of international human rights norms.

In addition to the above, also worth noting is how the UN Charter's collective security system contributed (albeit indirectly) to the promotion of human rights,

16 Ibid.
17 Charter of the United Nations (adopted 24 October 1945) 1 UNTS XVI Art 2(4) [hereinafter UN Charter].
18 Ibid., Art 2(7).
19 Ibid., Art 1(3).
20 Ibid., Art 55.
21 *See* Ed Bates, 'History' in Daniel Moeckli, Sangeeta Shah, and Sandesh Sivakumaran (eds), *International Human Rights Law* (2nd edn, Oxford University Press 2014) 30; Christine Chinkin, 'Sources' in Daniel Moeckli, Sangeeta Shah, and Sandesh Sivakumaran (eds), *International Human Rights Law* (2nd edn, Oxford University Press 2014) 77.
22 UN Charter (n17) Art 56.

particularly through the UNSC's Chapter VII powers. Specifically, Article 42 of the Charter allows the UNSC to 'take such action by air, sea, or land forces as may be necessary to maintain or restore international peace and security',[23] which encompasses the UNSC's right to authorise the use of force should non-forceful measures prove inadequate to address threats to or breaches of international peace and security, or if matters are otherwise deemed urgent in responding to such cases. The UNSC traditionally interpreted the term 'international peace and security' in an inter-State context, in which case it would invoke its Chapter VII powers to preserve and uphold a State's external sovereignty.[24] However, the body's interpretation of this phrase gradually expanded, particularly in the aftermath of the Cold War and the collapse of the Soviet Union in 1991,[25] to apply to intra-State conflicts including situations of gross human rights violations. This development came as a result of the increased recognition that such violations, even if committed within a State's borders, impinge upon international peace and security as a whole.[26] Throughout the 1990s, the UNSC employed its Chapter VII powers to authorise the use of force to respond to domestic mass atrocity situations in Somalia, Srebrenica, and Rwanda.[27] State sovereignty thus came to encompass a State's responsibility to uphold the basic human rights of its people, and, by default, sovereignty and human rights came to represent inextricable concepts that must be upheld and preserved together.

The aspirations embedded within the UN Charter with respect to the promotion of human rights as fundamental community interests, particularly within Articles 1(3), 55, and 56, paved the way for the emergence of multilateral human rights treaty frameworks, including the 1948 Convention on the Prevention and Punishment of the Crime of Genocide; 1966 International Covenant on Civil and Political Rights; 1966 International Covenant on Economic, Social and Cultural Rights; 1984 Convention Against Torture and Other Cruel, Inhuman or Degrading Treatment or Punishment; among others.[28] Through the conclusion of these treaties, States assumed written and

23 Ibid., Art 42.

24 *See* Robert Kolb, *International Law on the Maintenance of Peace* (Edward Elgar 2018) 133.

25 The collapse of the Soviet Union eliminated the longstanding rivalry between the US and the Soviet Union (as the two world hegemons of the time) that had obstructed UNSC decision-making on several fronts throughout the duration of the Cold War.

26 *See* Kolb (n24) 133–53; Richard B. Lillich, 'The Role of the UN Security Council in Protecting Human Rights in Crisis Situations: UN Humanitarian Intervention in the Post-Cold War Era' (1995) 3 *Tulane Journal of International and Comparative Law* 1.

27 *See* UNSC Res 794 (3 December 1992) UN Doc S/RES/794; UNSC Res 836 (4 June 1993) UN Doc S/RES/836; UNSC Res 929 (22 June 1994) UN Doc S/RES/929.

28 *See* Chinkin (n21) 78 for a list of some of these multilateral treaties. *See also* Convention on the Prevention and Punishment of the Crime of Genocide (adopted 9 December 1948, entered into force 12 January 1951) 78 UNTS 277; International Covenant on Civil and Political Rights (adopted 16 December 1966, entered into force 23 March 1976) 999 UNTS 171 [hereinafter ICCPR]; International Covenant on Economic, Social and Cultural Rights (adopted 16 December 1966, entered into force 3 January 1976) 993 UNTS 3; Convention against Torture and other Cruel, Inhuman or Degrading Treatment or Punishment (adopted 10 December 1984, entered into force 26 June 1987) 1465 UNTS 85 [hereinafter CAT]; European Convention on Human

binding obligations regarding the protection of human rights within their borders, thus voluntarily relinquishing some of their sovereignty in furtherance of this community interest.[29] Most States also became signatories to at least one of these major multilateral human rights treaties, indicating that they were met with widespread acceptance. With that said, however, it should also be cautioned that each treaty was binding only upon States that specifically acceded to it (barring the attainment of its provisions into custom as discussed below). Indeed, stemming from the *Lotus* principle that 'the rules of law binding upon States … emanate from their own free will',[30] States that did not willingly assume such treaty obligations remained unbound by them, in theory leaving their domestic affairs immune from foreign interference.[31]

It was through the development of customary international human rights norms that human rights obligations came to apply to all States irrespective of their specific treaty commitments. In the International Court of Justice's (ICJ) 1986 *Nicaragua* case, for example, the Court noted that 'the absence of such a commitment' by Nicaragua towards the Organization of American States 'would not mean that Nicaragua could with impunity violate human rights',[32] thus affirming that States can be bound to observe core human rights principles without becoming signatories to particular human rights treaties. Presumably stemming from the *Lotus* principle, however, customary international norms could still be opted out of by persistent objectors, namely, States that expressly and consistently oppose their emergence.[33] Therefore, although States could become bound, through custom, to human rights principles to which they had not expressly consented, the possibility remained that they could persistently object to the emergence of such norms and as such remain unbound by them. Further work was thus required on the international front to achieve more universal human rights observance.

As the next stage of human rights development on the international legal scene, obligations *erga omnes* were identified by the ICJ in the 1970 *Barcelona Traction* case as 'obligations of a State towards the international community as a whole … [for which] all States can be held to have a legal interest in their protection.'[34] Obligations *erga omnes* represent norms that all

Rights (adopted 4 November 1950, entered into force 3 September 1953) 213 UNTS 221; American Convention on Human Rights (adopted 22 November 1969, entered into force 18 July 1978) 1144 UNTS 123; African Charter on Human and Peoples' Rights (adopted 27 June 1981, entered into force 21 October 1986) 1520 UNTS 217.

29 *See* Sohn (n13) 18–21; Chris O'Meara, 'Should International Law Recognize a Right of Humanitarian Intervention?' (2017) 66 *International and Comparative Law Quarterly* 441, 447.

30 *See* Chinkin (n21) 79. *See also Lotus* case (n7) 18.

31 CAT (n28) Part II; ICCPR (n28) Part IV.

32 *Case Concerning Military and Paramilitary Activities in and against Nicaragua (Nicaragua v. United States of America)* (Merits) [1986] ICJ Rep 14 Para 267.

33 *See* Andrew T. Guzman, 'Saving Customary International Law' (2005–2006) 27 *Michigan Journal of International Law* 115 at 142–43, 164–71.

34 *Case Concerning the Barcelona Traction, Light and Power Company, Limited (Belgium v. Spain)* (Judgment) [1970] ICJ Rep 3 Para 33 [hereinafter *Barcelona Traction* case].

States have an interest in securing compliance for even if the obligations are not owed to them individually or if they do not suffer direct injury as a result of their breach.[35] They can perhaps be characterised as the very embodiment of community interests as they require the cooperation of all States in order to be fully achieved and furthermore reflect norms that serve the interests of the international community as a whole rather than of individual States. Examples of obligations *erga omnes* include, as per the ICJ's *Barcelona Traction* case, genocide as well as 'principles and rules concerning the basic rights of the human person, including protection from slavery and racial discrimination'.[36]

With the adoption of the International Law Commission's (ILC) Articles on State Responsibility (ASR) upon second reading in 2001, States, in addition to being bound by obligations *erga omnes*, furthermore acquired a standing to call for the observance of these norms in the event of their violation by another State, even if the circumstances of this violation do not affect them directly.[37] To comment briefly on ASR, which codify some of the existing norms on State responsibility and indicate how others may or perhaps should evolve, it should be noted that they have not been formally ratified or adopted in treaty form, meaning that they do not, at face value, represent 'hard law'. Nevertheless, their significance is that they manifest States' general acceptance of the laws of State responsibility and are therefore reflective of *opinio juris.* [38] Their provisions have been largely accepted as authoritative on the international legal scene, as demonstrated through their invocation in 163 cases by international courts, tribunals, and other bodies between their adoption by the ILC in 2001 and 31 January 2016.[39]

With respect to obligations *erga omnes*, Article 48 ASR stipulates that a non-injured (i.e. third-party) State can invoke the responsibility of a State acting in breach of an obligation 'owed to the international community as a whole' (i.e. obligations *erga omnes*) by calling for cessation, non-repetition, and reparation 'in the interest of the injured State or of the beneficiaries of the obligation breached'.[40] Article 54 furthermore allows non-injured States to take 'lawful measures' (i.e. in a manner that does not breach their international legal obligations) to ensure cessation and reparation by a State with respect to

35 *See* Katselli Proukaki (n15) 82; Villalpando (n15) 399–01.

36 *Barcelona Traction* case (n34) Para 34.

37 *See* Annie Bird, 'Third State Responsibility for Human Rights Violations' (2011) 21 *European Journal of International Law* 883, 891–94.

38 *See* Katselli Proukaki (n15) 77–78; James Crawford, *The International Law Commission's Articles on State Responsibility: Introduction, Text, and Commentaries* (Cambridge University Press 2002) 875.

39 Report of the Secretary-General, 'Responsibility of States for Internationally Wrongful Acts: Compilation of Decisions of International Courts, Tribunals and Other Bodies' (2017) UN Doc A/71/80/Add.1 Para 5.

40 ILC, 'Draft Articles on Responsibility of States for Internationally Wrongful Acts, with Commentaries' (2001) II *Yearbook of the International Law Commission* 26 Art 48 (emphasis added) [hereinafter ASR].

obligations owed to the international community as a whole.[41] Together, Articles 48 and 54 ASR impart a standing for third-party States to undertake limited responses to violations of obligations *erga omnes* that occur outside their borders and in contexts that do not directly affect them. They thus shifted the discourse to advocate not only an obligation of States to ensure minimum human rights protections within their own jurisdictions, but also a right to respond through lawful means to such breaches that are committed by any State anywhere in the world.

This development, however, was conditional on two major fronts. The first lies in the means that States are permitted to invoke while responding to *erga omnes* violations by other States. Article 48 ASR, for example, only allows third-party States to *call for* cessation, non-repetition, and reparation, which is seemingly confined to verbal or diplomatic protests of such violations. Similarly, Article 54 permits States to employ only 'lawful' measures to seek cessation and reparation for *erga omnes* violations, or, in other words, measures that are compatible with international law. The unauthorised use of force, for example, would not represent a manner through which States can respond to violations of obligations *erga omnes* – even, for example, the commission of genocide – given that this would contradict Article 2(4) of the UN Charter. Therefore, while Articles 48 and 54 ASR impart a standing upon third-party States to respond to violations of obligations *erga omnes*, they do not confer any new rights upon them to do so.

One potential development in this respect lies in the emergence of third-State countermeasures. Article 49 ASR defines countermeasures as the non-performance of legal obligations towards a State that commits an internationally wrongful act in order to induce it to rectify its behaviour,[42] subject to certain restrictions including the prohibition against the unlawful use of force or the violation of fundamental human rights or peremptory norms.[43] Article 49 permits an injured State to employ countermeasures against the State that causes it injury.[44] No similar provision of ASR, however, specifically articulates a similar right for third-party States to invoke countermeasures (also 'third-State countermeasures') to respond to *erga omnes* violations committed by other States, even though such violations represent particularly serious breaches of international law affecting the international community as a whole.[45]

With that said, however, a number of international legal scholars point out that while ASR do not specifically permit States to engage in third-party countermeasures, they also do not prohibit them from doing so.[46] Instead,

41 Ibid., Art 54.
42 Ibid., Art 49.
43 Ibid., Arts 49–51 and Commentary.
44 Ibid., Art 49.
45 On third-State countermeasures, *see* Elena Katselli, 'Countermeasures by Non-Injured States in the Law on State Responsibility' (*European Society of International Law*, 2005) <http://www.esil-sedi.eu/sites/default/files/Katselli_0.PDF> [hereinafter Katselli Countermeasures]; Bird (n37) 896–99.
46 *See* Christian Tams, *Enforcing Obligations Erga Omnes in International Law* (Cambridge University Press 2005) 200; Katselli Proukaki (n15) 87; Bird (n37) 896.

the official commentary to ASR characterises the legal status of third-party countermeasures as 'uncertain', and thus 'leaves the resolution of the matter to the further development of international law'.[47] In this respect, the official commentary highlights extensive practice whereby third-State countermeasures have been invoked to respond to breaches of *erga omnes* obligations,[48] which Katselli rightly describes as revealing 'a certain *opinio juris* that is moving in the direction of gradually formulating a customary rule of international law' regarding their lawfulness.[49] The recognition of a legal entitlement to employ third-State countermeasures under international law, which is receiving increased support of international legal scholars, could serve to broaden and make more robust the means available to States in responding to violations of international law that impact the international community as a whole, including, as relevant to R2P, the commission of mass atrocity crimes. As detailed in Chapter 5 of this book, this represents an area in which R2P can help promote greater legal clarity.

In addition to limiting the means allowed to States in responding to *erga omnes* violations, another restriction with respect to Articles 48 and 54 ASR is that States' responses to such breaches remain a discretionary right that States can choose to exercise rather than an obligation that they are compelled to observe. This, of course, introduces an obstacle to securing universal compliance with these norms given the inherent selectivity that is inevitable within States' reactions to their breach, as evidenced, for example, in the UNSC's initial reluctance to respond to the 1994 genocide in Rwanda, as well as its failure to mobilise – due to the threat of the Russian veto – to address ethnic cleansing that was perpetrated in Kosovo in the late 1990s. Such perceived failures by the international community spurred the realisation that the emergence of third-State obligations (and not merely rights) to respond to the gross abuse of human rights norms is perhaps equally important to the existence of host State obligations to uphold these norms in the first place.

Overall, the post-Charter era witnessed a fundamental shift from a bilateralist international legal system premised upon States as the sole and primary international legal actors, to a multilateral one that values and promotes community interests including human rights. As such, various human rights norms were codified into multilateral treaties, became binding as custom, and became recognised as obligations *erga omnes*. All States (with the exception of persistent objects) thus became required to observe these norms, and in the case of obligations *erga omnes*, they could even call for their adherence by other States. Nevertheless, despite these critical advancements, there remained pressing gaps in

47 ASR (n40) Commentary to Art 54 Para 6.

48 Ibid., Commentary to Article 54 Paras 3–4. *See also* Tams (n46) 210–28, 231; Katselli Proukaki (n15) 93–201; Martin Dawidowicz, 'Public Law Enforcement without Public Law Safeguards? An Analysis of State Practice on Third-Party Countermeasures and their Relationship to the UN Security Council' (2006) 77 *British Yearbook of International Law* 333; Bird (n37) 896–98.

49 Katselli Countermeasures (n45) 5. *See also* Bird (n37) 898–99.

securing universal compliance with human rights norms and in the prevention of mass atrocities more specifically (as relevant to R2P). The most important of these gaps revolved around enforceability. Namely, States' reactions to human rights breaches remained discretionary and therefore subject to their political whims. Moreover, the measures available at their disposal to call for the observance of obligations *erga omnes* in particular were confined to lawful measures, with only an emerging potential for the employment of third-State countermeasures. The development of a legal framework surrounding *jus cogens* norms, including through a potential obligation to respond to their gross breach as per Article 41 ASR, thus represented the next stage of human rights' normative development.

2.2.2 From discretion to obligation

Jus cogens norms (also 'peremptory norms') are defined in Article 53 of the 1969 Vienna Convention on the Law of Treaties (VCLT) as norms 'accepted and recognized by the international community of States as a whole ... from which no derogation is permitted and which can be modified only by a subsequent norm of general international law having the same character'.[50] They are, in essence, a special category of obligations *erga omnes*, with the distinguishing feature that they cannot be derogated from under any circumstance.[51] *Jus cogens* norms are furthermore recognised to represent the most superior international norms and thus, as noted in the 2012 *Jurisdictional Immunities* judgment, 'always prevail over any inconsistent rule of international law, whether contained in a treaty or in customary international law'.[52] Similar to obligations *erga omnes*, *jus cogens* norms are also highly relevant to the advancement of human rights. The official commentary to Article 40 ASR specifies, for example, that their violation has 'come to be seen as intolerable because of the threat [that they present] to the survival of States and their peoples *and the most basic human values*'.[53] The commentary identifies a number of human rights norms as peremptory, including the prohibition against slavery, genocide, torture, racial discrimination, and apartheid.[54]

Of the various layers of human rights norms discussed within the previous section (e.g. treaty norms, customary international norms and obligations *erga*

50 Vienna Convention on the Law of Treaties (adopted 23 May 1969, entered into force 27 January 1980) 111 UNTS 331 Art 53 [hereinafter VCLT].

51 *See* Margo Kaplan, 'Using Collective Interests to Ensure Human Rights: An Analysis of the Articles on State Responsibility' (2004) 79 *New York University Law Review* 1902, 1909–10.

52 *Jurisdictional Immunities of the State (Germany v. Italy: Greece Intervening)* (Judgment) [2012] ICJ Rep 99 Para 92 [hereinafter *Jurisdictional Immunities* case]. *See also* Article 53 VCLT, which recognises that '[a] treaty is void if, at the time of its conclusion, it conflicts with a peremptory norm of general international law'. VCLT (n50) Art 53.

53 ASR (n40) Commentary to Article 40 Para 3 (emphasis added).

54 Ibid., Commentary to Article 40 Para 4.

omnes), jus cogens norms pose the greatest challenge to the *Lotus* declaration that the obligations of States 'emanate from their free will'.[55] For example, while Article 53 VCLT specifies that *jus cogens* norms are 'recognized [as such] by the international community of States as a whole',[56] the reality is that it is highly unlikely that every State acknowledges their status as peremptory.[57] Moreover, when peremptory norms do arise, it is doubtful that States can opt out of them by persistently objecting to their formation, as they can do with customary international norms. Although Verhoeven maintains that 'there can be no *jus cogens* where States are not in agreement',[58] it is more accurate to say that once a peremptory norm emerges through its recognition as such by the 'international community of States as a whole' (however vague this may be), all States, including persistent objectors, become bound by it.[59] This is because, as identified by Orakhelashvili, 'strict adherence to the consensual approach runs counter to the essence of *jus cogens* and makes it difficult to see how it would perform its function if States can avoid its peremptory status in specific cases'.[60] In this manner, therefore, the emergence of *jus cogens* human rights norms presented a unique challenge to the traditional supremacy of State sovereignty.

In addition to the above, the ramifications of a norm being labelled as peremptory expanded significantly through Article 41 ASR, which imparts a positive obligation upon States 'to cooperate to bring to an end through lawful means any serious breach' of a *jus cogens* norm and to refrain from recognising the situation as lawful or from '[rendering] aid or assistance in maintaining that situation'.[61] In essence, Article 41 requires States to cooperate and react to serious breaches of *jus cogens* norms that occur outside their borders, which is more in line with the ideals aspired to by R2P in that it removes the element of discretion in States' responses to some of the worst human rights violations. Through the emergence of Article 41 ASR, therefore, not only are States bound to observe and uphold human rights norms within their own borders as per the aforementioned treaty, customary, and *erga omnes* obligations, but they must also respond to any fundamental breaches that occur in this respect by other States. Despite these ambitious aims, however,

55 *Lotus* case (n7) 18. *See also* Bruno Simma and Andreas S. Paulus, 'The "International Community": Facing the Challenge of Globalization' (1998) 9 *European Journal of International Law* 266, 276–77.
56 Ibid.
57 Maurizio Ragazzi, *The Concept of International Obligations Erga Omnes* (Clarendon Press 1997) 55–56.
58 Joe Verhoeven, 'Jus Cogens and Reservations or <<Counter-Reservations>> to the Jurisdiction of the International Court of Justice' in Karel Wellens (ed.), *International Law: Theory and Practice* (Martinus Nijhoff Publishers 1998) 196.
59 *See* Katselli Proukaki (n15) 22; Jure Vidmar, 'Norm Conflicts and Hierarchy in International Law: Towards Vertical International Legal System?' in Erika de Wet and Jure Vidmar (eds), *Hierarchy in International Law: The Place of Human Rights* (Oxford University Press 2012) 26–27.
60 Alexander Orakhelashvili, *Peremptory Norms in International Law* (Oxford University Press 2006) 106–08.
61 ASR (n40) Art 41.

the legal remit of Article 41 ASR is subject to key constraints which made the emergence of R2P all the more compelling.

First, although ASR are generally accepted as authoritative in delineating the laws of State responsibility as already discussed,[62] the legal status of Article 41 in particular is inconclusive. The official commentary to this Article, for example, admits that '[i]t may be open to question whether general international law at present prescribes a positive duty of cooperation'.[63] Furthermore, while Article 41 ASR has been invoked in international case law which itself serves as a subsidiary source of international law,[64] such invocations have fallen short of affirming an obligation of States to cooperate through lawful means to respond to serious *jus cogens* breaches as per this Article. In the ICJ's 2012 *Jurisdictional Immunities* case, for example, the Court specifically referenced Article 41 ASR when it distinguished between State immunity (which holds customary status) and *jus cogens* norms. The Court maintained that:

> [R]ecognizing the immunity of a foreign State in accordance with customary international law does not amount to recognizing as lawful a situation created by the breach of a *jus cogens* rule, or rendering aid and assistance in maintaining that situation, and so cannot contravene the principle in Article 41 of the International Law Commission's Articles on State Responsibility.[65]

Upon close reading of this passage, it can be appreciated that the ICJ in this case only specifically affirmed the provisions of Article 41(2) ASR which stipulate that '[n]o State shall recognize as lawful a situation created by a serious breach … nor render aid or assistance in maintaining that situation'.[66] It did not, however, assert an Article 41(1) obligation for States to cooperate through lawful means to respond to serious peremptory breaches.

A stronger stance from the ICJ in this respect presented in the 2004 *Construction of a Wall* case. Here, the Court determined that Israel's construction of a wall in Palestinian territory violated Palestinians' collective right to self-determination[67] (a commonly recognised *jus cogens* norm[68]) and asserted that 'States are under an

62 *See supra* notes 38–39.
63 ASR (n40) Commentary to Art 41 Para 3.
64 On the sources of international law, *see* Statute of the International Court of Justice (adopted 26 June 1945, entered into force 24 October 1945) 1 UNTS XVI Art 38.
65 *Jurisdictional Immunities* case (n52) Para 93.
66 ASR (n40) Art 41(2).
67 *Legal Consequences of the Construction of a Wall in the Occupied Palestinian Territory* (Advisory Opinion) [2004] ICJ Rep 136 Paras 122, 163 [hereinafter *Construction of a Wall* case].
68 *See* ASR (n40) Commentary to Art 40 Para 5; Ian Brownlie, *Principles of Public International Law* (7th edn, Oxford University Press 2008) 512 [hereinafter Brownlie Principles of PIL]; James Crawford, 'The Rights of Peoples: "Peoples" or "Governments"?' in James Crawford (ed.), *The Rights of Peoples* (Clarendon Press 1988) 166; Yasmine Nahlawi, 'Self-Determination and the Right to Revolution: Syria' (2014) 8

obligation not to recognize the illegal situation … [and] not to render aid or assistance in maintaining [it]',[69] thus very closely mirroring the language of Article 41(2) ASR.[70] The ICJ furthermore stated that '[i]t is also for all States, while respecting the United Nations Charter and international law, to see to it that any impediment, resulting from the construction of the wall, to the exercise by the Palestinian people of its right to self-determination is brought to an end',[71] and called upon the UN (the UNGA and UNSC in particular) to 'consider what further action is required to bring to an end the illegal situation resulting from the construction of the wall and the associated regime'.[72] Superficially, this can be seen as a very direct application of Article 41(1) ASR. However, it should be pointed out that the ICJ in this case discussed the concept of self-determination as an obligation *erga omnes* rather than as a *jus cogens* norm, and, although it drew upon particular wordings of Article 41(1) ASR, it failed to specifically cite this Article as the basis for its judgment in this respect (it instead justified its stance by making a vague reference to 'the character and the importance of the rights and obligations involved').[73] Therefore, despite the relevance of the ICJ's stance to Article 41(1) ASR, its findings do not directly support the emergence of an Article 41(1) ASR obligation for States to cooperate through lawful means to bring an end to serious *jus cogens* breaches.

The second limitation to Article 41 ASR mirrors one articulated within the previous section with respect to Articles 48 and 54 ASR (on the legal regime applicable to obligations *erga omnes*), namely, that it does not specify the means that States can or must undertake to respond to serious *jus cogens* violations. Article 41 stipulates that States should cooperate through 'lawful means', which excludes from its remit any measures contrary to international law (for example, the unauthorised use of force). It furthermore, however, calls into question whether third-State countermeasures can be employed by States in this respect, which would represent an expansion of the means explicitly recognised within Article 41. Arguably, without allowing States more robust means of reacting to serious peremptory violations of international law (e.g. through third-State countermeasures), the obligation to respond in itself becomes quite meaningless.

The third and final major shortcoming of Article 41 ASR is that it fails to specify which entities must cooperate to bring an end to serious *jus cogens* breaches. The commentary to this Article merely states that '[c]ooperation could be organized in the framework of a competent international organization, in particular the United

Human Rights and International Legal Discourse 84, 87. The scope of this right, however, is highly contested. For an overview of the debate, *see* Helen Quane, 'The United Nations and the Evolving Right to Self-Determination' (1998) 47 *International and Comparative Law Quarterly* 537.

69 *Construction of a Wall* case (n67) Para 159.

70 *See* ASR (n40) Art 41(2).

71 *Construction of a Wall* case (n67) Para 159.

72 Ibid., Para 160.

73 For discussion on this point, *see* Andrea Bianchi, 'Human Rights and the Magic of Jus Cogens' (2008) 19 *European Journal of International Law* 491, 502.

Nations', or that it could occur through 'non-institutionalized cooperation',[74] which is ambiguous at best. The ICJ in the *Construction of a Wall* case suggested that '[i]t is also for all States ... to see to it that any impediment ... to the exercise by the Palestinian people of its right to self-determination is brought to an end',[75] thus implying that this obligation lies upon each and every State. It remains unclear, however, how international legal responsibility can be asserted on behalf of individual States or entities for a failure to fulfil this obligation, and if so, which ones.

Overall, Article 41 ASR seeks to revolutionise the enforcement of fundamental human rights norms so that the commission of serious peremptory breaches is met with an obligation, rather than a prerogative, of States to respond and bring the resulting situation to an end. Nevertheless, it retains limitations which hinder its effectiveness. Some of these inherent uncertainties pertain to its mechanism of enforcement, including questions over who precisely is obligated to respond to serious *jus cogens* breaches and through what means. Additionally, and arguably more fundamentally, is that the very existence of this obligation remains under dispute; the official commentary to Article 41 ASR concedes that this matter is inconclusive, and the limited invocation of the Article's provisions under international case law has fallen short of affirming the existence of such an obligation. R2P, discussed in the next section, thus emerged as a vehicle through which to address some of these existing gaps and to achieve greater certainty in the identification and implementation of host and third-State obligations to uphold fundamental human rights-related norms (although whether it has succeeded in doing so is evaluated in subsequent chapters).

2.3 Emergence of R2P

R2P made its debut in a 2001 report authored by the Canadian-established International Commission on Intervention and State Sovereignty (ICISS), an independent body of 12 expert commissioners from diverse jurisdictions that grappled with the question posed by then-UN Secretary-General Kofi Annan to States in 2000 regarding how to reconcile State sovereignty with 'gross and systematic violations of human rights that offend every precept of our common humanity'.[76] The 2001 ICISS report defined R2P as being composed of the responsibilities to prevent 'situations of compelling human need', to react to their emergence should prevention efforts fail, and to rebuild the affected country in the aftermath of such a reaction.[77] Although it aspired to 'break new ground in a way that helps generate a new international consensus' regarding the balance between

74 ASR (n40) Commentary to Art 41 Para 2.
75 *Construction of a Wall* case (n67) Para 159.
76 *See* 2001 ICISS Report (n1); Report of the Secretary-General, 'We the Peoples: The Role of the United Nations in the Twenty-first Century' (2000) UN Doc A/54/2000 Para 217;
77 2001 ICISS Report (n1) xi.

State sovereignty and human rights,[78] the report did not advance R2P as a legally binding norm. Instead, it stressed that there was 'not yet a sufficiently strong basis to claim the emergence of a new principle of customary international law' (i.e. of R2P).[79] Similarly, the ICISS, as a panel of experts, was not a legal body and did not enjoy any legal powers *per se.* [80] As such, R2P, as presented in the 2001 ICISS report, represented an ideal, or perhaps a proposal, rather than embodying hard law.

R2P remained the subject of further discussion and debate over the coming years. In 2005, it was reformulated in Paragraphs 138 and 139 of the World Summit Outcome document, which was adopted unanimously by States through UNGA Resolution 60/1.[81] The respective paragraphs defined R2P as such:

> 138 Each individual State has the responsibility to protect its populations from genocide, war crimes, ethnic cleansing and crimes against humanity. This responsibility entails the prevention of such crimes, including their incitement, through appropriate and necessary means. We accept that responsibility and will act in accordance with it. The international community should, as appropriate, encourage and help States to exercise this responsibility and support the United Nations in establishing an early warning capability.
>
> 139 The international community, through the United Nations, also has the responsibility to use appropriate diplomatic, humanitarian and other peaceful means, in accordance with Chapters VI and VIII of the Charter, to help to protect populations from genocide, war crimes, ethnic cleansing and crimes against humanity. In this context, we are prepared to take collective action, in a timely and decisive manner, through the Security Council, in accordance with the Charter, including Chapter VII, on a case-by-case basis and in cooperation with relevant regional organizations as appropriate, should peaceful means be inadequate and national authorities are manifestly failing to protect their populations from genocide, war crimes, ethnic cleansing and crimes against humanity. We stress the need for the General Assembly to continue consideration of the responsibility to protect populations from genocide, war crimes, ethnic cleansing and crimes against humanity and its implications, bearing in mind the principles of the Charter and international law. We also intend to commit ourselves, as necessary and appropriate, to helping States build capacity to protect their populations from genocide, war crimes, ethnic cleansing and crimes against humanity and to assisting those which are under stress before crises and conflicts break out.[82]

78 Ibid., vii.
79 Ibid., Para 2.24.
80 Ibid., Appendix B.
81 2005 World Summit Outcome (n1).
82 2005 World Summit Outcome (n1) Paras 138–39.

Although UNGA Resolution 60/1 received the unanimous endorsement of States, R2P, as presented within the 2005 World Summit Outcome document (which the Resolution adopted), still did not represent a legally binding norm. Importantly, UNGA resolutions do not serve as binding sources of international law.[83] The ICJ in its *Nuclear Weapons* case observed that they may nevertheless 'sometimes have normative value' and outlined several factors that could be indicative of this, namely:

> [I]t is necessary to look at its content and the conditions of [the Resolution's] adoption; it is also necessary to see whether an *opinio juris* exists as to its normative character. Or a series of resolutions may show the gradual evolution of the *opinio juris* required for the establishment of a new rule.[84]

However, analogising these criteria to UNGA Resolution 60/1 fails to build a convincing case that R2P as advanced in the 2005 World Summit Outcome document represented a source of binding international law. First, with reference to the ICJ's mention in the *Nuclear Weapons* case of the 'content' of UNGA resolutions, it should be noted that the relevant paragraphs of the Outcome document do not purport to establish R2P as a legally binding norm. Instead, they 'stress the need for the General Assembly to continue consideration of the responsibility to protect',[85] which highlights States' perceptions that additional discussions were required in order to further develop the doctrine. Other phrases within these paragraphs (for example, 'should, as appropriate', 'we are prepared to take collective action … on a case-by-case basis', and '[w]e also intend to commit ourselves, as necessary and appropriate') further illustrate that R2P was not asserted as legally binding.[86]

Second, with respect to the ICJ's determination that 'it is also necessary to see whether an *opinio juris* exists as to [a UNGA resolution's] normative character', there is insufficient evidence of *opinio juris* regarding the legally binding nature of R2P as defined within the 2005 World Summit Outcome. Some States, for example, vocalised misgivings regarding R2P's anticipated implementation, noting its potential to serve as an interventionist tool.[87] Among these States, China asserted that 'further consultations' were required in order to obtain consensus on the doctrine.[88] Egypt maintained that R2P 'has no legal or practical basis within the international community'.[89] Russia

83 *See* Malcolm Shaw, *International Law* (6th edn, Cambridge University Press 2008) 1212.
84 *Legality of the Threat or Use of Nuclear Weapons* (Advisory Opinion) [1996] ICJ Rep 22 Para 70. *See also Legal Consequences of the Separation of the Chagos Archipelago from Mauritius in 1965* (Advisory Opinion) 2019 <https://www.icj-cij.org/files/case-related/169/169-20190225-01-00-EN.pdf> Paras 152–53, 155.
85 2005 World Summit Outcome (n1) Para 139.
86 Ibid., Paras 138–39.
87 For an overview of State dissent to R2P, *see* Patrick Quinton-Brown, 'Mapping Dissent: The Responsibility to Protect and its State Critics' (2013) 5 *Global Responsibility to Protect* 260.
88 UNGA, '85th Plenary Meeting' (6 April 2005) UN Doc A/59/PV.85, 24.
89 UNGA, '86th Plenary Meeting' (6 April 2005) UN Doc A/59/PV.86, 13.

argued that '[s]trictly speaking, the establishment of an international norm presupposes that there is wide support within the international community for such a norm. However, that is not the case here.'[90] Algeria, Colombia, Iran, and Vietnam delivered statements to the same effect.[91]

Even States that expressed support for R2P as a concept conceded that it was not yet a legally binding norm. For example, while the US agreed that 'the international community has a particular interest and role to play' in addressing mass atrocity situations, it rejected that international law stipulated an obligation for third-party States to intervene in this respect.[92] Canada and Chile both mentioned that they look forward to further discussions to shape the doctrine,[93] thus implying that the doctrine's legal status was inconclusive. Poland and Australia referred to R2P as an 'emerging norm',[94] and Japan maintained that 'the time is now upon us to *look into* the issue of "responsibility to protect"'.[95] The UK, South Korea, Uganda, Norway, Liechtenstein, Iceland and Bulgaria made similar statements.[96]

Therefore, it can be concluded that neither the relevant contents of the 2005 World Summit Outcome document (adopted through UNGA Resolution 60/1) nor indications of *opinio juris* surrounding its adoption asserted R2P as an international legal norm. Instead, the contribution of the 2005 document lies in that it presented a commonly agreed upon framework for R2P which set the basis for the doctrine's future development. This can be seen, for example, in the fact that subsequent UN resolutions[97] and discussions[98] on R2P have been premised upon its formulation. For these reasons, this book adopts the definition of R2P advanced within the 2005 World Summit Outcome document.

90 UNGA, '87th Plenary Meeting' (7 April 2005) UN Doc A/59/PV.87, 6.
91 Ibid., 18; UN Doc A/59/PV.86 (n89) 9, 14; UNGA, '89th Plenary Meeting' (8 April 2005) UN Doc A/59/PV.89, 22.
92 John Bolton, 'Ambassador Bolton's letter on the Responsibility to Protect' (*Human Rights Voices*, 30 August 2005) <http://www.humanrightsvoices.org/assets/attachments/documents/bolton_responsibility_to_protect.pdf>.
93 UN Doc A/59/PV.89 (n91) 27; UN Doc A/59/PV.86 (n89) 20.
94 UN Doc A/59/PV.89 (n91) 4; UNGA, '88th Plenary Meeting' (7 April 2005) UN Doc A/59/PV.88, 8.
95 UN Doc A/59/PV.87 (n90) 29 (emphasis added).
96 UN Doc A/59/PV.85 (n88) 26; UN Doc A/59/PV.87 (n90) 13; UN Doc A/59/PV.88 (n94) 4, 8, 13, 19, 20; UN Doc A/59/PV.89 (n91) 10.
97 *See*, for example, UNSC Res 1674 (28 April 2006) UN Doc S/RES/1674 Para 4; UNSC Res 1706 (31 August 2006) UN Doc S/RES/1706 Preamble; UNSC Res 1894 (11 November 2009) UN Doc S/RES/1894 Preamble; UNSC Res 2117 (26 September 2013) UN Doc S/RES/2117 Preamble; UNSC Res 2150 (16 April 2014) UN Doc S/RES/2150 Para 1; UNSC Res 2171 (21 August 2014) UN Doc S/RES/2171 Para 16; UNSC Res 2220 (22 May 2015) UN Doc S/RES/2220 Preamble; UNGA Res 63/308 (7 October 2009) UN Doc A/RES/63/308 Preamble.
98 *See*, for example, UNSC 5519th Meeting (31 August 2006) UN Doc S/PV.5519 (*see*, especially, comments of United Kingdom); UNSC 6216th Meeting (11 November 2009) UN Doc S/PV.6216 (*see*, especially, comments of Croatia and Italy); UNSC 7155th Meeting (16 April 2014) UN Doc S/PV.7155 (*see*, especially, comments of Chile, Chad, and Nigeria); UNGA '105th Plenary Meeting' (14 September 2009) UN Doc A/63/PV.105.

The next major development for R2P came in 2009 upon the release of a report by then-UN Secretary-General Ban Ki-moon titled 'Implementing the Responsibility to Protect' (Implementing R2P).[99] Using the formulation of R2P presented in the 2005 World Summit Outcome document, this report restructured R2P into three basic 'pillars': Pillar 1 constitutes the protection responsibility of each State towards its population from the four mass atrocity crimes and derives from the first three sentences of Paragraph 138 of the 2005 World Summit Outcome document.[100] Pillar 2 addresses the responsibility of the international community to assume a supportive role and to 'assist states in meeting those [Pillar 1] obligations' and stems from the final sentences of each Paragraphs 138 and 139 of the 2005 document.[101] Finally, Pillar 3 speaks to the responsibility of the international community to 'respond collectively in a timely and decisive manner when a State is manifestly failing to provide such protection' and derives from the first two sentences of Paragraph 139 of the 2005 document.[102] In this manner, the 2009 report restructured R2P in a manner that clearly identifies host and third-State obligations, although importantly, without altering the basic consensus surrounding R2P achieved within the 2005 World Summit Outcome document.

Like the 2001 ICISS report and the 2005 World Summit Outcome document, the 2009 Implementing R2P report is also non-binding. As stated in its introductory section, its role is merely to '[offer] initial thoughts' on how the 2005 document can be enforced 'in a fully faithful and consistent manner', and to 'contribute to a continuing dialogue among Member States' on R2P.[103] It thus serves to facilitate discussion on R2P rather than to create any legal obligations. The report's proposed structure for R2P as being comprised of three distinct Pillars has been largely accepted by both States and academics and has proven useful for contextualising the 2005 World Summit Outcome document.

Overall, therefore, the analysis of both the contents and acceptance (by States) of the major documents that have advanced and shaped R2P confirms that the doctrine does not in itself represent a legally binding norm. With that said, however, this book contends that R2P is not devoid of legal value, and that its significance lies in its articulation of a clear framework for the prevention of and reaction to mass atrocity crimes as well as in its potential to spearhead the development of international law in this respect. As such, this book casts R2P as an emerging umbrella norm of various sub-norms pertaining to the prevention of and the reaction to mass atrocity crimes.[104] Its role as such is to pull together,

99 Report of the Secretary-General, 'Implementing the Responsibility to Protect' (12 January 2009) UN Doc A/63/677, 2.
100 Ibid., Para 11(a). Pillar 1 receives further discussion in Chapter 3 of this book.
101 Ibid., Para 11(b). Pillar 2 receives further discussion in Chapter 4.
102 Ibid., Para 11(c). Pillar 3 receives further discussion in Chapter 5.
103 Ibid., Para 2.
104 *See* Elena Katselli, 'Commentary: R2P as a Transforming and Transformative Concept in the Context of Responsibility as Liability' in Richard Barnes and Vassilis Tzevelekos (eds), *Beyond Responsibility to Protect: Generating Change in International Law* (Intersentia 2016) 415–16; Carsten Stahn, 'Marital Stress or Grounds for Divorce?

repackage, and build upon these sub-norms in order to create one cohesive doctrine that outlines the responsibilities of host and third-party States to prevent and react to the commission of mass atrocity crimes.

In terms of *pulling together* existing norms, this book reveals that many of R2P's provisions derive from existing and emerging treaty and customary norms specifying host and third-State obligations to protect populations from mass atrocity crimes. Such norms draw from diverse legal regimes including the laws of the UN, laws of international organisations, international human rights law, international humanitarian law, international criminal law, international environmental law, and laws of State responsibility, thus highlighting R2P's breadth and ambition. Primarily, these norms help to ascribe legal character to R2P as well as to define the various obligations that the doctrine seeks to establish. The various international legal norms underpinning each of the R2P's three pillars are discussed throughout Chapters 3–5.

R2P's second role is to *repackage* these existing norms with view to arriving at a central and comprehensive framework that stipulates host and third-State obligations to protect populations from mass atrocity crimes. The significance of this function is that existing norms pertaining to human protection are highly fragmented and stem from the diverse and overlapping frameworks mentioned above. This can create confusion with regards to the particular norms and obligations that are applicable in any given scenario, the bearers of these obligations, and the consequences of their breach. In consolidating these norms under one framework, R2P seeks to add clarity and certainty in these respects, although whether it has successfully done so receives consideration throughout this book.

R2P's final role is to *build upon* existing norms, namely, to propel the development of international law where gaps remain in the human protection framework. In this sense, R2P can be seen to represent the international community's aspiration and perhaps even statement of intent as to how international law will or should develop to eradicate mass atrocity crimes. It is worth re-emphasising, for example, that while R2P may not (yet) be normative in itself, it emerged as a natural progression of developments on the international legal scene pertaining to host-State obligations and third-State rights to prevent and respond to breaches of human rights norms.[105] R2P represents an even more ambitious push to this trend, as it suggests that third-party States and the international community as a whole should possess a positive obligation, and not merely a right, to respond to the commission of mass atrocity crimes in the event that they should be perpetrated.[106] As such, R2P is grounded in the progressive evolution of the international legal system and arguably presents the next step of this evolution to which the international community seeks or should aspire to attain. Again, however, the

Re-Thinking the Relationship between R2P and International Criminal Justice' (2015) 26 *Criminal Law Forum* 13, 19–20.

105 For a comprehensive account of this trend in international law, *see* O'Meara (n29).

106 *See* Richard Barnes and Vassilis Tzevelekos, 'Beyond Responsibility to Protect: Ceci n'est pas une Pipe' in Richard Barnes and Vassilis Tzevelekos (eds), *Beyond Responsibility to Protect: Generating Change in International Law* (Intersentia 2016) 11–13.

remaining chapters will critically assess where R2P has fallen short of achieving this objective, and moreover, how it must continue to develop in order to fully accomplish the goals which it set out.

2.4 Conclusion

R2P emerged as a product of ongoing trends within the international legal system that mandated increased obligations for host States to provide minimum protections to their people and furthermore sought to impart a residual obligation upon third-party States to react if and when host States fail to secure such protections. R2P seeks to defragment and to build upon these longstanding developments with view to overcoming gaps that remain within their respective frameworks. As such, it solidifies host State obligations to protect their populations from mass atrocity crimes and furthermore calls for greater third-State responsibility in this respect. It also seeks to remove the element of discretion so that all mass atrocity crimes are met with a response from the international community. As highlighted throughout this book, R2P has not performed any of these functions perfectly. The next three chapters unpack the subtleties within R2P's contributions and gaps and engage constructively with how the doctrine can or should further develop in order to achieve the purpose for which it was created.

3 R2P's Pillar 1

3.1 Introduction

When R2P was first formulated in the 2001 report by the International Commission on Intervention and State Sovereignty, it was suggested that the doctrine would apply to 'situations of compelling human need'.[1] The problem with this construction, however, was easy to predict, namely, that R2P's scope would be ambiguous and its interpretation (and implementation) consequently subject to the whims of States. This, in turn, would fail to attract the support of a significant segment of States that were already wary of powerful States' perceived interventionist ambitions. As such, and recognising the need for greater certainty in delineating R2P's remit, the 2005 World Summit Outcome document restricted the doctrine's scope to 'mass atrocity crimes', defined as genocide, war crimes, crimes against humanity, and ethnic cleansing.[2] In this document, States 'accepted' the responsibility to protect their populations from the mass atrocity crimes and committed to 'act in accordance with' this responsibility.[3] In the UN Secretary-General's 2009 'Implementing the Responsibility to Protect' (Implementing R2P) report, this responsibility of host States to protect their populations from mass atrocity crimes was identified as R2P's first pillar (Pillar 1).[4]

Importantly, the restriction of R2P's Pillar 1 to the four mass atrocity crimes goes well beyond their grave and widely destructive nature (as implied by the term 'mass atrocity crime'). Indeed, these four crimes were selected as a result of State consensus regarding their superior status under international law.[5] With the

1 'The Responsibility to Protect: The Report of the International Commission on Intervention and State Sovereignty' (*International Commission on Intervention and State Sovereignty*, December 2001) at xi <http://responsibilitytoprotect.org/ICISS%20Report.pdf> [hereinafter 2001 ICISS Report].

2 2005 World Summit Outcome, UNGA Res 60/1 (24 October 2005) UN Doc A/RES/60/1 Para 138.

3 Ibid.

4 Report of the Secretary-General, 'Implementing the Responsibility to Protect' (12 January 2009) UN Doc A/63/677 Para 11 [hereinafter Implementing R2P].

5 *See* Auriane Botte, 'Redefining the Responsibility to Protect Concept as a Response to International Crimes' (2015) 19 *The International Journal of Human Rights* 1029, 1030–31.

possible exception of ethnic cleansing (as discussed within this chapter), these crimes are conclusively prohibited under international law as highlighted through extensive treaty, customary, and international case law and are furthermore anchored within *jus cogens*. In this respect, R2P's Pillar 1 does not necessarily represent new law, as obligations for States to protect their populations from mass atrocity crimes already exist irrespective of the doctrine. Instead, the contribution of Pillar 1 is that it groups these crimes into a single category so that they not only require observance from host States, but also more innovatively, their violation triggers a response from the international community as a whole as per Pillar 3.

Despite the strong foundational basis of R2P's Pillar 1, however, this is not to say that it does not contain any structural gaps. Of the four mass atrocity crimes, for example, it is only genocide that holds a conclusive definition under international law. The definitions that exist for the other three mass atrocity crimes (for example, in international criminal statutes) are contested and differ across various jurisdictions.[6] This is not to mention that ethnic cleansing is not defined under any major international criminal statute.

With this in mind, this chapter seeks to pick apart R2P's Pillar 1 in order to shed light on its dimensions which are anchored within existing law as well as others which require further normative development. As such, this chapter engages in an analysis of each one of the four mass atrocity crimes with a view to arriving at their most authoritative definitions and prohibited status under international law. This helps to clarify the nature of the host State responsibility articulated under Pillar 1 and emphasises that even if R2P as a doctrine is not legally binding, this Pillar already largely reflects existing international legal norms. Following this analysis, Pillar 1 is evaluated as a legal concept in itself with its own unique set of obligations, including whether and how it must develop alongside the other two pillars in order to achieve an effective mechanism of preventing and reacting to mass atrocity situations.

3.2 Defining the mass atrocity crimes

R2P's Pillar 1 calls upon States to protect their populations from genocide, war crimes, crimes against humanity, and ethnic cleansing. However, it fails to offer precise definitions of these crimes, which is problematic in that with the exception of genocide, none of the other three mass atrocity crimes are conclusively defined under international law. A 2013 report by the UN Secretary-General suggests that the definitions for genocide, war crimes, and crimes against humanity advanced within the Rome Statute of the International Criminal Court (ICC Statute) can serve as the terms of reference with respect to R2P,[7] and the 2009 Implementing R2P report similarly cites the ICC Statute as 'one of the key instruments relating to the responsibility to protect'.[8] While the ICC Statute's definitions are perhaps

6 Ibid., 1031.
7 Report of the Secretary General, 'Responsibility to Protect: State Responsibility and Prevention' (9 July 2013) UN Doc A/67/929-S/2013/399 Paras 14, 25.
8 Implementing R2P (n4) Para 19.

most reflective of State consensus as discussed below, there remain two issues with respect to adopting them as a basis for R2P's Pillar 1. The first is that States that are not parties to the ICC Statute (including the US, Russia, and China as three of the five UNSC permanent members – P5) and which have historically manifested critical positions towards the ICC could prove resistant to using its definitions as the most authoritative ones for fear of conferring legitimacy upon the Court.[9] This, combined with the fact that there exists no central authority to make determinations regarding when a mass atrocity crime has actually been committed, could result in contestations by States of a situation's factual characterisation as one of mass atrocity, which in turn breeds disagreement over whether R2P should even be triggered.[10] Second, ethnic cleansing is not defined within the ICC Statute nor is it, incidentally, defined within any treaty as such.

With these concerns in mind, this section aims to uncover the most authoritative definitions of each of the four mass atrocity crimes and to examine the existing legal prohibitions against them under international law, with view to situating R2P's Pillar 1 within international legal norms. Any gaps that remain in this respect are pinpointed with view to further developing the doctrine.

3.2.1 Genocide

The most widely recognised definition of genocide, although not without criticism,[11] stems from the Genocide Convention (with 152 State parties). Article 2 of this Convention defines genocide as encompassing a number of acts (for example, murder and causing 'serious bodily or mental harm') that are 'committed with intent to destroy, in whole or in part, a national, ethnical, racial or religious group'.[12] This definition is reproduced in the International Criminal Tribunal for Rwanda (ICTR), International Criminal Tribunal for the Former Yugoslavia (ICTY), and ICC Statutes and has become accepted as binding upon all States regardless of whether they have specifically ratified the Genocide Convention.[13] In the 1951 *Reservations* case, for example, the International Court of Justice (ICJ) confirmed that 'the principles

9 *See*, in general, Jamie Mayerfield, 'Who Shall be Judge?: The United States, the International Criminal Court, and the Global Enforcer of Human Rights' (2003) 25 *Human Rights Quarterly* 93, 95–96.

10 *See* Botte (n5) 1031.

11 *See* William Schabas, *Genocide in International Law: The Crime of Crimes* (2nd edn, Cambridge University Press 2009) 8, 117–18 (highlighting the view, advocated by some authors, that the definition of genocide advanced within the Genocide Convention is overly restrictive).

12 Convention on the Prevention and Punishment of the Crime of Genocide (adopted 9 December 1948, entered into force 12 January 1951) 78 UNTS 277 Art 2.

13 UNSC Res 955 (8 November 1994) UN Doc S/RES/955 Art 2 [hereinafter ICTR Statute]; 'Updated Statute of the International Criminal Tribunal for the Former Yugoslavia' (*ICTY*, September 2009) Art 4 <http://www.icty.org/x/file/Legal%20Library/Statute/statute_sept09_en.pdf> [hereinafter ICTY Statute]; Rome Statute of the International Criminal Court (adopted 17 July 1998, entered into force 1 July 2002) 2187 UNTS 3 Art 6 [hereinafter ICC Statute].

underlying the [Genocide Convention] are principles which are recognized by civilized nations as binding on States, even without any conventional obligation'.[14] In the 2006 *Armed Activities* case, the ICJ went further to affirm that the prohibition against genocide constitutes a *jus cogens* norm,[15] a conclusion widely accepted by scholars of international law.[16] Irrespective of R2P, therefore, the prohibition against genocide cannot be derogated from by any State or under any circumstances. Its classification as a *jus cogens* norm furthermore carries implications with respect to the role of third-party States in reacting to its breach, discussed further in Section 5.2 of this book.

3.2.2 War crimes

The second mass atrocity crime identified within the R2P doctrine is war crimes, generally defined as grave or serious breaches of the laws or customs of war (also, international humanitarian law or IHL).[17] As with genocide, war crimes are prohibited under international law independently of R2P, further illustrating that R2P is not new law, but rather derives from existing international norms. Unlike genocide, however, which is clearly defined through the Genocide Convention, war crimes are not defined through a specialised treaty. Instead, they find their basis within a number of legal instruments that regulate the laws of war, including the four Geneva Conventions and their two Additional Protocols, the Fourth Hague Convention, and customary international law.[18]

14 *Reservations to the Convention on the Prevention and Punishment of the Crime of Genocide* (Advisory Opinion) [1951] ICJ Rep 15, 23.

15 *Case Concerning Armed Activities on the Territory of the Congo (Democratic Republic of the Congo v. Rwanda)* (Judgment) [2006] ICJ Rep 6 Para 64.

16 Jordan Paust et al., *International Criminal Law: Cases and Materials* (Carolina Academic Press 1996) 5; Theodor Meron, *War Crimes Law Comes of Age: Essays* (Oxford University Press 1998) 233; Jan Wouters and Sten Verhoeven, 'The Prohibition of Genocide as a Norm of Ius Cogens and Its Implications for the Enforcement of the Law of Genocide' (2005) 5 *International Criminal Law Review* 401, 415; M. Cherif Bassiouni, 'International Crimes: Jus Cogens and Obligations Erga Omnes' (1996) 59 *Law and Contemporary Problems* 63, 68 [hereinafter Bassiouni International Crimes]; Ekkehard Strauss, 'A Bird in the Hand is Worth Two in the Bush – On the Assumed Legal Nature of the Responsibility to Protect' (2009) 1 *Global Responsibility to Protect* 291, 316–17.

17 *See* Daniel Thürer, *International Humanitarian Law Theory, Practice, Context* (Brill 2011) 42; Gary D. Solis, *The Law of Armed Conflict* (Cambridge University Press 2010) 302.

18 Geneva Convention for the Amelioration of the Condition of the Wounded and Sick in Armed Forces in the Field (adopted 12 August 1949, entered into force 21 October 1950) 75 UNTS 31 [hereinafter Geneva Convention I]; Geneva Convention for the Amelioration of the Condition of Wounded, Sick and Shipwrecked Members of Armed Forces at Sea (adopted 12 August 1949, entered into force 21 October 1950) 75 UNTS 85 [hereinafter Geneva Convention II]; Geneva Convention Relative to the Treatment of Prisoners of War (adopted 12 August 1949, entered into force 21 October 1950) 75 UNTS 135 Art 3 [hereinafter Geneva Convention III]; Geneva Convention Relative to the Protection of Civilian Persons in Time of War (adopted 12 August 1949, entered into force 21 October 1950) 75 UNTS 287 Art 1 [hereinafter Geneva Convention IV]; Protocol Additional to the Geneva Conventions of 12 August 1949, and Relating to the Protection of Victims of International Armed

This admittedly creates ambiguity in the identification of war crimes, given that not every violation of the aforementioned bodies of law constitutes a war crime. Rather, only the most grave and serious violations are considered as such,[19] consistent with R2P's purpose of human protection from crimes that 'shock the conscience of mankind' (i.e. mass atrocity crimes).[20]

Formal definitions of war crimes have been advanced within the major international criminal statutes (i.e. the ICC, ICTR, and ICTY Statutes), although these definitions differ in some respects. The ICTR Statute, for example, defines war crimes in the context of non-international armed conflicts (NIACs),[21] whereas the ICTY Statute is more oriented towards international armed conflicts (IACs).[22] Both of these Statutes were given effect through UNSC Chapter VII resolutions in the context of specific mass atrocity situations (i.e. the Rwanda and Srebrenica genocides, respectively). On the other hand, the ICC Statute is a treaty with 122 State parties detailing war crimes in both IACs and NIACs.[23] Its provisions, which emerged as a result of negotiations between 160 States, are largely premised upon existing international norms as contained within the Geneva Conventions and their Additional Protocols, the Fourth Hague Convention, and customary international law (as further examined below). Although the definition of war crimes contained within the ICC Statute is not uncontested,[24] it is met with the general

Conflicts (adopted 8 June 1977, entered into force 7 December 1978) 993 UNTS 3 [hereinafter API]; Protocol Additional to the Geneva Conventions of 12 August 1949, and Relating to the Protection of Victims of Non-International Armed Conflicts (adopted 8 June 1977, entered into force 7 December 1978) 1125 UNTS 609 [hereinafter APII]; Hague Convention (IV) Respecting the Laws and Customs of War on Land and its Annex: Regulation concerning the Laws and Customs of War on Land (adopted 18 October 1907, entered into force 26 January 1910) 187 CTS 227 [hereinafter Fourth Hague Convention].

19 *See* Andreas Zimmermann, 'Crimes within the Jurisdiction of the Court' in Otto Triffterer (ed.), *Commentary on the Rome Statute of the International Criminal Court* (Nomos Verlagsgesellschaft 1999) 100.

20 *See* 2001 ICISS Report (n1) Para 4.13.

21 The ICTR confines its jurisdiction on war crimes to 'serious violations of Article 3 common to the Geneva Conventions … and of Additional Protocol II', both of which deal exclusively with NIACs. ICTR Statute (n13) Art 4; APII (n18) Art 1; Geneva Convention III (n18) Art 3.

22 The ICTY does not mention war crimes specifically, although it holds jurisdiction over '[g]rave breaches of the Geneva Conventions of 1949' as well as '[v]iolations of the laws or customs of war' of the four Geneva Conventions. ICTY Statute (n13) Arts 2–3.

23 ICC Statute (n13) Arts 8(2)(a–b) (listing war crimes in IACs) and Arts 8(2)(c) and 8(2)(e) (listing war crimes in NIACs).

24 Controversy arose during the drafting of Article 8 ICC Statute regarding the extension of war crimes to NIACs, as well as regarding the inclusion of a prohibition against chemical and nuclear weapons use. *See* Phillippe Kirsch and John Holmes, 'The Rome Conference on an International Criminal Court: The Negotiating Process' (1999) 93 *American Journal of International Law* 2, 6–8; Mahnoush Arsanjani, 'The Rome Statute of the International Criminal Court' (1999) 93 *American Journal of International Law* 22, 32–35; William Schabas, *An Introduction to the International Criminal Court* (2nd edn, Cambridge University Press 2004) 28 [hereinafter Schabas Introduction to the ICC].

acceptance of States and is generally regarded by scholars of international law to be the most authoritative.[25] For these reasons, and given the absence of a more definitive identification of war crimes or of attempts at clarification by the R2P doctrine itself, this book employs, as a baseline, the definition of war crimes contained within the ICC Statute, while acknowledging the potential for this definition to be challenged in practice.[26]

The ICC Statute recognises four different categories of war crimes, two which derive from the Geneva Conventions and two which derive from 'other serious violations of the laws and customs' of war. The first Geneva-related category of war crimes (Article 8(2)(a) of the ICC Statute) consists of 'grave breaches' of the four Geneva Conventions. These grave breaches are specifically identified as such within each of the four Conventions and include acts such as wilful killing and torture.[27] They are applicable to IACs and are commonly accepted as custom.[28] The other category of war crimes that stems from the Geneva Conventions (Article 8(2)(c) of the ICC Statute) encompasses 'serious violations' of Common Article 3, including acts such as 'violence to life and person' and '[c]omitting outrages upon personal dignity'. These war crimes apply to NIACs[29] and are also commonly recognised as custom.[30]

The other two categories of war crimes contained within the ICC Statute (Articles 8(2)(b) and 8(2)(e)) encompass 'other serious violations of the laws and customs' of war within IACs and NIACs, respectively, that emerge from 'within the established framework of international law' (i.e. they purportedly reflect existing treaty or customary norms). Many of these crimes derive from the Fourth

25 *See* Schabas Introduction to the ICC (n24) 28; Zimmerman (n19) 102; Arsanjani (n24) 22, 25 (on the definitions contained within the ICC Statute more generally).

26 *See*, for example, Section 7.2.5 of this book, in which evidence is presented for the inclusion of starvation (as a weapon of war) as a war crime within NIACs although such a provision is not included within the ICC Statute.

27 Geneva Convention I (n18) Art 50; Geneva Convention II (n18) Art 51; Geneva Convention III (n18) Art 130; Geneva Convention IV (n18) Art 147.

28 *See* Meron (n16) 192; Paust et al. (n16) 969, 986; 'Convention (I) for the Amelioration of the Condition of the Wounded and Sick in Armed Forces in the Field. Geneva, 12 August 1949. COMMENTARY OF 2016, ARTICLE 50: GRAVE BREACHES' (*ICRC*, 2016) <https://www.icrc.org/applic/ihl/ihl.nsf/Comment.xsp?action=openDocument&documentId=21B052420B219A72C1257F7D00587FC3#34>.

29 *Note*, however, that the ICJ in the *Nicaragua* case accepted Common Article 3 as binding in both IACs and NIACs. *Case Concerning Military and Paramilitary Activities in and against Nicaragua (Nicaragua v. United States of America)* (Merits) [1986] ICJ Rep 14 Para 218.

30 The ICTY in *Prosecutor v. Delalic* characterised Common Article 3 as '[reflecting] the most universally recognised humanitarian principles'. *Prosecutor v. Delalic* (Judgement) IT-96–21-A (20 February 2001) Para 143. *See also* Meron (n16) 166, 216; 'Convention (I) for the Amelioration of the Condition of the Wounded and Sick in Armed Forces in the Field. Geneva, 12 August 1949. COMMENTARY OF 2016 ARTICLE 3: CONFLICTS NOT OF AN INTERNATIONAL CHARACTER' (*ICRC*, 2016) <https://www.icrc.org/applic/ihl/ihl.nsf/Comment.xsp?action=openDocument&documentId=59F6CDFA490736C1C1257F7D004BA0EC>.

Hague Convention[31] – including '[employing] poison or poisoned weapons'[32] – as well as from Additional Protocols I and II to the Geneva Conventions (API and APII, respectively)[33] – including '[c]ommitting outrages upon personal dignity',[34] '[i]ntentionally using starvation of civilians as a method of warfare',[35] and intentionally directing attacks against civilians or protected objects.[36] The remaining war crimes contained within Articles 8(2)(b) and 8(2)(e) of the ICC Statute either derive from customary international law or were codified for the first time as war crimes.[37] The latter include, for example, some of the gender-related crimes as well as the ban on conscripting or enlisting child soldiers under the age of 15.[38] While the designation of these acts as war crimes could be contested, their inclusion as such into the ICC Statute can perhaps be seen to represent the progressive development of the law of war crimes.[39] In this sense, it should be recalled that the ICC Statute's formulation of war crimes, although imperfect, is the most reflective of State consensus and is regarded by many to be the most authoritative.

Having thus defined war crimes in a general sense, it is next important to examine in greater detail their prohibited status under international law, as this holds implications upon the legally binding nature of R2P's Pillar 1. Similar to genocide, the prohibition against war crimes has a strong basis in *jus cogens*, as evident in the *Nuclear Weapons* case in which the ICJ resolved that the 'fundamental rules [of international humanitarian law] are to be observed by all States whether or not they have ratified the [Hague and Geneva] conventions that contain them, because they constitute intransgressible principles of international customary law'.[40] This passage is directly applicable to Articles 8(2)(a) and 8(2)(c) of the ICC Statute which contain Geneva-derived war crimes, as well as to the

31 A report by the UN Secretary-General in 1993 characterised the Fourth Hague Convention as 'part of conventional international humanitarian law which has beyond doubt become part of international customary law'. UNSC, 'Report of the Secretary-General Pursuant to Paragraph 2 of Security Council Resolution 808 (1993)' (3 May 1993) UN Doc S/25704 Para 35.
32 *See*, in particular, Fourth Hague Convention (n18) Art 23. Although this Convention applies strictly to IACs, some of its provisions are replicated within Article 8(2)(e) ICC Statute which applies to NIACs.
33 The ICTY declared in the *Tadić* case that '[m]any provisions of [APII] can now be regarded as declaratory of existing rules or as having crystallised emerging rules of customary law'. API is also largely considered to be premised upon existing customary law. *See Prosecutor v. Tadić* (Decision on the Defence Motion of Interlocutory Appeal on Jurisdiction) ICTY-94–1 (2 October 1995) Para 117; Meron (n16) 212, 235, 273–74; Paust et al. (n16) 969; Fausto Pocar, 'To What Extent Is Protocol I Customary International Law?' (2002) 78 *International Law Studies* 337 (undertaking detailed analysis of the provisions of API and the extent to which they reflect custom).
34 *See* API (n18) Art 75.
35 *See* ibid., Art 54.
36 *See* APII (n18) Arts 13, 16.
37 *See* Schabas Introduction to the ICC (n24) 60, 64–65.
38 Ibid.; ICC Statute (n13) Arts 8(2)(b)(xxii), 8(2)(b)(xxvi), 8(2)(e)(vi–vii).
39 Schabas Introduction to the ICC (n24) 60.
40 *Legality of the Threat or Use of Nuclear Weapons* (Advisory Opinion) [1996] ICJ Rep 226 Para 79.

Hague-derived war crimes contained within Article 8(2)(b). In characterising these violations as 'intransgressible', the Court implied that there can be no derogation from them. While it declined to comment specifically on whether such violations are prohibited as *jus cogens*, [41] the International Law Commission (ILC) in its commentary to the Articles on State Responsibility maintained that '[i]n the light of the description by ICJ of the basic rules of international humanitarian law applicable in armed conflict as "intransgressible" in character, it would also seem justified to treat these as peremptory'.[42]

While the *Nuclear Weapons* opinion affirms the *jus cogens* status of the two Geneva-derived categories of war crimes (contained in Articles 8(2)(a) and 8(2)(c) of the ICC Statute) as well as the Hague-derived war crimes (at least part of Article 8(2)(b)), the other war crimes that exist with respect to both IACs and NIACs (which derive from API, APII, custom, or which were newly included within the ICC Statute) were not specifically recognised as peremptory in this case. Here, it is worth noting the ICTY's decision in the *Kupreškić* case that 'most norms of international humanitarian law, in particular those prohibiting war crimes, crimes against humanity and genocide, are also peremptory norms of international law or *jus cogens*'.[43] The Tribunal here spoke of a *jus cogens* status of war crimes in general, without differentiating between the various acts entailed under this crime. While a minority of international legal scholars disagree with this approach and argue instead that each war crime should be evaluated independently for *jus cogens* status,[44] the majority support it and thus assert a peremptory status upon all war crimes.[45] This in turn holds implications regarding the role of third-party States in addressing the commission of war crimes (discussed further in Section 5.2 of this book), and is furthermore significant for the purposes of the Libyan and Syrian case studies discussed in Chapters 6 and 7, given that war crimes were perpetrated in the context of both conflicts.

3.2.3 Crimes against humanity

The third mass atrocity crime encompassed under the R2P doctrine, namely crimes against humanity, can be broadly identified as a number of specified acts that are 'committed as part of a widespread or systematic attack directed against

41 Ibid., Para 83.

42 ILC, 'Draft Articles on Responsibility of States for Internationally Wrongful Acts, with Commentaries' (2001) II *Yearbook of the International Law Commission* 26 Commentary to Art 40 Para 5.

43 *Prosecutor v. Kupreškić et al.* (Judgement) IT-95–16-T (14 January 2000) Para 520 [hereinafter *Kupreškić* case].

44 *See* Rafael Nieto-Navia, 'International Peremptory Norms (Jus Cogens) and International Humanitarian Law' (*Coalition for the International Criminal Court*, 2001) at 26 <http://www.iccnow.org/documents/WritingColombiaEng.pdf>.

45 *See* Paust et al. (n16) 12; Christian Tams, *Enforcing Obligations Erga Omnes in International Law* (Cambridge University Press 2005) 145; Faustin Ntoubandi, *Amnesty for Crimes against Humanity under International Law* (Martinus Nijhoff Publishers 2007) 220.

any civilian population, with knowledge of the attack'.[46] The high threshold for such attacks to be 'widespread' or 'systematic' reflects the focus of the R2P doctrine, namely, to prevent and respond to mass atrocity crimes that 'shock the conscience of mankind'.[47] Unlike genocide and war crimes which derive totally or in part from pre-existing bodies of law (i.e. the Genocide, Geneva, and Hague Conventions as well as the two Additional Protocols to the Geneva Conventions), crimes against humanity have been defined through the successive development of customary international law,[48] and were codified through a series of international criminal statutes including the ICTR, ICTY, and ICC Statutes.[49] More recently, this has culminated in the adoption by the ILC upon second reading of a Draft Convention on Crimes against Humanity (ILC Draft Convention) in May 2019 which, although non-binding, bears the fruits of collaborative efforts by both States and international legal experts and enjoys significant State support.[50]

The specific acts of crimes against humanity listed within the ICTR, ICTY, and ICC Statutes as well as the ILC Draft Convention are fundamentally similar, including murder; extermination; enslavement; deportation; imprisonment; torture; rape; persecution on political, racial, and religious grounds; and other inhumane acts. The ICC Statute and the ILC Draft Convention add to these the crimes of enforced disappearance and apartheid. However, the definition of the term 'crime against humanity' takes on a different form within these various documents.[51] For example, the ICTY Statute links the definition of crimes against humanity to the presence of an IAC or NIAC, a stipulation which is not found within the other documents. On the other hand, the ICTR Statute details that crimes against humanity must be premised upon political, ethnic, religious, national, or ethnic grounds, although the other documents contain no such specification.

As with the ICC Statute's definition of war crimes, its definition (in Article 7) of crimes against humanity is not perfect.[52] However, its drafting history remains the most reflective of international consensus and its provisions arguably most closely

46 ICC Statute (n13) Art 7.

47 On the definitions of the terms 'widespread' and 'systematic', *see Prosecutor v. Akayesu* (Judgement) ICTR-96-4-T (2 September 1998) Paras 578–80 [hereinafter *Akayesu* case].

48 *See* William Schabas, *The International Criminal Court: A Commentary on the Rome Statute* (Oxford University Press 2010) 141.

49 ICTR Statute (n13) Art 3; ICTY Statute (n13) Art 5; ICC Statute (n13) Art 7.

50 UNGA, 'Report of the International Law Commission: Seventy-first Session' (29 Apr–7 June and 8 July–9 Aug 2019) UN Doc A/74/10 Ch IV. *See also* on the Draft Convention, Sean D. Murphy, 'Crimes against Humanity and Other Topics: The Sixty-Ninth Session of the International Law Commission' (2017) 111 *American Journal of International Law* 970; Leila Nadya Sadat, 'A Contextual and Historical Analysis of the International Law Commission's 2017 Draft Articles for a New Global Treaty on Crimes against Humanity' (2018) *Journal of International Criminal Justice* 683.

51 For further discussion, *see* Leila Nadya Sadat, 'Crimes against Humanity in the Modern Age' (2013) 107 *American Journal of International Law* 334.

52 Some of the issues that arose during the drafting of Article 8 of the ICC Statute, for example, include whether crimes against humanity should be confined to situations of armed conflict and whether they should be widespread *and* systematic or widespread *or* systematic. *See* Arsanjani (n24) 30–32.

mirror customary international law.[53] This is not to mention the status of the ICC Statute as a binding treaty with 122 State parties, as well as its characterisation in the UN Secretary-General's 2009 Implementing R2P report as 'one of the key instruments relating to the responsibility to protect'.[54] Additionally, it is important to note that with the exception of three changes,[55] the definition of crimes against humanity advanced within the ICC Statute mirrors that of the ILC Draft Convention word for word.[56] For these reasons, this book employs the definition of crimes against humanity contained within the ICC Statute (and, by default, that within the ILC Draft Convention).

Like genocide and war crimes, the prohibition against crimes against humanity is also recognised to be binding upon States regardless of whether or not they have specifically accepted this prohibition (for example, by signing the ICC Statute). At a minimum, it is recognised to be binding as custom.[57] Furthermore, with the exception of a minority of international legal scholars such as Bassiouni, who assumes a more cautious approach,[58] most international legal scholars agree that crimes against humanity are prohibited as *jus cogens*, [59] a conclusion that is also articulated in the *Kupreškić* case as well as in the Preamble to the ILC Draft Convention.[60] In support of this, and recalling the definition of peremptory norms as norms 'from which no derogation is permitted',[61] it should be pointed out that crimes against humanity are generally not accepted as lawful derogations from major human rights treaties, even in exceptional situations. General Comment 29 to the International Covenant on Civil and Political Rights, for instance, reveals that

53 *See supra* notes 25 and accompanying text. *See also* Geoffrey Robertson, *Crimes against Humanity: The Struggle for Global Justice* (New Press 1999) 357; Rodney Dixon, 'Crimes against Humanity: "Chapeau"' in Otto Triffterer (ed.), *Commentary on the Rome Statute of the International Criminal Court* (Nomos Verlagsgesellschaft 1999) 124–25.

54 *See supra* notes 7–8 and accompanying texts.

55 On the differences between the two documents, see UN Doc A/74/10 (n50) 30.

56 Ibid., Para 44 (Article 2).

57 *See* Darryl Robinson, 'Defining "Crimes against Humanity" at the Rome Conference' (1999) 93 *American Journal of International Law* 43, 44.

58 Bassiouni argues that each crime against humanity should be evaluated independently for peremptory status. Bassiouni International Crimes (n16) 69–70; M. Cherif Bassiouni, 'Crimes against Humanity: The Case for a Specialized Convention' (2010) 9 *Washington University Global Studies Law Review* 575, 582 [hereinafter Bassiouni Crimes against Humanity].

59 *See* Brian D. Lepard, *Customary International Law: A New Theory with Practical Applications* (Cambridge University Press 2010) 7–8; Ntoubandi (n45) 220; Paust et al. (n16) 12, 1079; Strauss (n16) 315; Lauri Hannikainen, *Peremptory Norms (Jus Cogens) in International Law: Historical Development, Criteria, Present Status* (Finnish Lawyers' Pub. Co. 1988) 596–600; Meron (n16) 233; Ruti Teitel, *Humanity's Law* (Oxford University Press 2011) 108.

60 *See supra* note 43 and accompanying text. *See also* UN Doc A/74/10 (n50) Para 44 (Preamble).

61 Vienna Convention on the Law of Treaties (adopted 23 May 1969, entered into force 27 January 1980) 111 UNTS 331 Art 53.

'article 4 of the Covenant cannot be used as justification that a state of emergency exempted the State in question from its responsibility in relation to [crimes against humanity]'.[62] The European Convention on Human Rights and American Convention on Human Rights also prohibit derogations in the form of acts that constitute crimes against humanity, including murder, torture, slavery, and unlawful imprisonment.[63] When crimes against humanity are committed, perpetrating States offer alternative legal justifications to defend their actions, indicating that they do not view crimes against humanity as acceptable under any circumstances. This was evident in Syria, for example, in which the State rejected allegations that its actions constituted crimes against humanity, arguing instead that it was combating terrorism.[64] These trends together are indicative of solidifying consensus regarding the peremptory character of crimes against humanity. Again, this carries implications for the involvement of third-party States in the event of their breach, discussed in Section 5.2 of this book.

3.2.4 Ethnic cleansing

Like war crimes and crimes against humanity, the final mass atrocity crime under R2P, ethnic cleansing, is not codified within any specialised treaty. Unlike them, however, ethnic cleansing is not incorporated into the ICTR, ICTY, or ICC Statutes, nor does it hold a precise legal definition or a clear status under international law.[65] Even when it is invoked in international case law, the term is largely dropped without explanation of what it entails or of the criteria for determining its commission.[66] This was apparent in the ICTY's *Kupreškić* case, for example, in which the Trial Chamber maintained that a number of specified acts are 'in non-legal terms … *commonly referred to* as "ethnic cleansing"',[67] as well as in its *Krstić*

62 Human Rights Committee, 'General Comment 29, States of Emergency' (2001) UN Doc CCPR/C/21/Rev.1/Add.11 Para 12.
63 European Convention on Human Rights (adopted 4 November 1950, entered into force 3 September 1953) 213 UNTS 221 Art 15; American Convention on Human Rights (adopted 22 November 1969, entered into force 18 July 1978) 1144 UNTS 123 Art 27.
64 *See*, for example, Bashar al-Assad, 'Bashar al-Assad Interview: The Fight against Terrorists in Syria' (*Global Research*, 21 January 2014) <http://www.globalresearch.ca/bashar-al-assad-interview-the-fight-against-terrorists-in-syria/5365613>. The Syrian conflict is discussed in further detail in Chapter 7 of this book.
65 *See* Strauss (n16) 315–16.
66 *See*, for example, *Prosecutor v. Tadić* (Opinion and Judgment) ICTY-94–1-T (7 May 1997) Paras 84, 178, 188, 373, 574; *Kupreškić* case (n43) Paras 338, 606, 705, 760; *Prosecutor v. Krstić* (Judgement) ICTY-98–33T (2 August 2001) Paras 562, 588, 612, 619, 622 [hereinafter *Krstić* case]; *Case Concerning Application of the Convention on the Prevention and Punishment of the Crime of Genocide (Bosnia & Herzegovina v. Serbia & Montenegro)* (Separate Opinion of Judge ad hoc Lauterpacht) [1997] ICJ Rep 243 Para 69 [hereinafter *Bosnia* case Separate Opinion of Judge ad hoc Lauterpacht].
67 *Kupreškić* case (n43) Para 705 (emphasis added).

case, in which it stated that 'there are obvious similarities between a genocidal policy and the policy ***commonly known as*** "ethnic cleansing"'.[68] Similarly, Judge ad hoc Lauterpacht, in his Separate Opinion to the ICJ's *Bosnia* case, made reference to a 'forced migration of civilians, ***more commonly known as*** "ethnic cleansing"'.[69]

Perhaps the most authoritative definition of ethnic cleansing was advanced in a 1993 report of a Commission of Experts established by then-UN Secretary-General Boutros Boutros-Ghali following the adoption of UNSC Resolution 780. This Commission defined ethnic cleansing as 'rendering an area ethnically homogeneous by using force or intimidation to remove persons of given groups from the area'.[70] Although not legally binding,[71] this definition was replicated in the ICJ's *Bosnia* case and is fundamentally similar to the definitions advanced by scholars of international law.[72] It is this definition of ethnic cleansing, therefore, that is adopted for the purposes of this book.

Ethnic cleansing stands in stark contrast to the other mass atrocity crimes of genocide, war crimes, and crimes against humanity, all of which have been recognised as international crimes (for example, through the ICTR, ICTY, and ICC Statutes) and which also have a strong basis in *jus cogens* norms. This makes the inclusion of ethnic cleansing into the R2P doctrine somewhat puzzling. Strauss suggests that it was incorporated into the doctrine in order to allow for 'a more factual than legal assessment of events on the ground'.[73] In this sense, whereas establishing the perpetration of other mass atrocity crimes requires a high evidentiary threshold (genocide requires intent to destroy, war crimes require the existence of an armed conflict, and crimes against humanity must be widespread or systematic), ethnic cleansing could serve to lower the bar for international action in the face of mass atrocities.

Although ethnic cleansing does not enjoy a distinct legal definition or legal status, it should be noted that many of the acts that constitute ethnic cleansing have been recognised to fall under the categories of genocide, war crimes, and crimes against humanity.[74] The same Commission of Experts established pursuant

68 *Krstić* case (n66) Para 562 (emphasis added).
69 *Bosnia* case Separate Opinion of Judge ad hoc Lauterpacht (n66) Para 69 (emphasis added).
70 UNGA, 'Interim Report of the Commission of Experts Established Pursuant to Security Council Resolution 780 (1992)' (10 February 1993) UN Doc S/25274 Para 55.
71 The Commission was called upon to draw conclusions regarding breaches of Geneva law and IHL rather than to make authoritative determinations of the law. UNSC Res 780 (6 October 1992) UN Doc S/RES/780 Para 2.
72 *See Case Concerning Application of the Convention on the Prevention and Punishment of the Crime of Genocide (Bosnia & Herzegovina v. Serbia & Montenegro)* (Judgment) [2007] ICJ Rep 43 Para 190; Thomas H. Lee, 'The Law of War and the Responsibility to Protect Civilians: A Reinterpretation' (2014) 55 *Harvard International Law Journal* 251, 309; Gareth Evans, *The Responsibility to Protect: Ending Mass Atrocity Crimes Once and for All* (Brookings Institution Press 2008) 13.
73 Strauss Legal Nature of R2P (n16) 315–16. *See also* Evans (n72) 12–13.
74 *See* John Quigley, 'State Responsibility for Ethnic Cleansing' (1999) 32 *University of California Davis Law Review* 341, 345–46; Teitel (n59) 79.

to UNSC Resolution 780, for example, stated that '[t]hose practices [of ethnic cleansing] constitute crimes against humanity and can be assimilated to specific war crimes. Furthermore, such acts could also fall within the meaning of the Genocide Convention.'[75] More specifically, UN bodies have affirmed that ethnic cleansing can include the commission of following acts, many of which fall under one or more of the three other mass atrocity crimes:

> [M]urder, torture, arbitrary arrest and detention, extra-judicial executions, rape and sexual assaults, confinement of civilian population in ghetto areas, forcible removal, displacement and deportation of civilian population, deliberate military attacks or threats of attacks on civilians and civilian areas, and wanton destruction of property.[76]

Therefore, even if ethnic cleansing does not enjoy a legal status of its own, a strong argument can be made that acts constituting ethnic cleansing are prohibited under customary international law, and even *jus cogens*, if they reflect one or more of the other mass atrocity crimes.[77] This is significant for the purpose of the R2P doctrine, particularly in ascribing third-State responsibility to react to the commission of ethnic cleansing as discussed in Section 5.2 of this book.

3.3 Conclusion

This chapter highlighted that the obligations called for under R2P's Pillar 1 reflect existing international legal prohibitions against genocide, war crimes, crimes against humanity, and ethnic cleansing, all of which (with the potential exception of ethnic cleansing) are anchored within custom and furthermore have a strong basis in *jus cogens*. The role of R2P, however, extends beyond the mere regurgitation of these norms. Rather, as discussed in Chapter 2 of this book, the doctrine serves as an instrument that pulls together, repackages, and builds upon these norms. As such, Pillar 1 first serves to consolidate existing norms that prohibit each one of the four mass atrocity crimes. The choice of these crimes helps to delineate R2P's contours and furthermore emphasises that the doctrine applies to only the most egregious crimes for which there is widespread support under international law regarding their conclusively prohibited status.

Second, Pillar 1 repackages these various fragmented norms into one central framework of 'mass atrocity crimes'. This is significant not so much for establishing host State responsibilities for preventing these crimes given that such obligations already exist under international law, but rather for the development of a third-State responsibility to react to their commission as per Pillar 3. In this sense,

75 UN Doc S/25274 (n70) Para 56. *See also Krstić* case (n66) Paras 562, 578.
76 UN Doc S/25274 (n70) Para 56. *See also* UNGA, 'Report of the Committee on the Elimination of Racial Discrimination' (15 September 1993) UN Doc A/48/18 Para 467.
77 *See* Quigley (n74) 341, 344–46; Strauss Legal Nature of R2P (n16) 315–16.

Pillar 1 can represent a warning or trigger mechanism that gives rise to a collective expectation or obligation under Pillar 3 that the international community will react to the crimes encompassed under its scope, including through the use of coercive measures if and as necessary.

Finally, Pillar 1 must build upon these existing norms in order to contribute to the emergence of a cohesive and effective R2P doctrine. This is perhaps where further work is required. One shortcoming of Pillar 1, for example, is that it does not ascribe definitions to the four mass atrocity crimes, which is significant in that of these crimes, only genocide is conclusively defined under international law. As this chapter highlighted, the ICC Statute contains definitions of war crimes and crimes against humanity that reflect the general acceptance of States. In the interest of R2P's maximum operationalisation, however, these (or other) definitions should be formally agreed to by States as part of the doctrine so as to prevent a scenario whereby the mere existence of a mass atrocity situation becomes contested, let alone achieving a response to this situation. Furthermore, clarity must be obtained regarding the crime of ethnic cleansing which, as of yet, does not enjoy a legal definition.

In this respect, the designation of a central and independent authority that can make determinations with respect to the existence of a mass atrocity situation could represent part of the solution. Relevant here is the post of the UN Special Adviser on the Responsibility to Protect who 'leads the [doctrine's] conceptual, political, institutional and operational development'.[78] Such a central authority can facilitate a standardised procedure by which to monitor potential mass atrocity situations, gauge when such a situation has materialised, and similarly establish when the international community's responsibility is triggered with respect to supporting host States as per Pillar 2 or reacting to the commission of mass atrocity crimes as per Pillar 3. As the next two chapters highlight, while the roles of third-party States in preventing and reacting to mass atrocity crimes do exist to an extent under international law, they are not as developed as those specifying host-State responsibilities. This is where R2P's potential contributions are the most profound.

78 'Mandate' (*United Nations Office on Genocide Prevention and the Responsibility to Protect*) <http://www.un.org/en/genocideprevention/office-mandate.shtml>.

4 R2P's Pillar 2

4.1 Introduction

The UN Secretary-General's 2009 'Implementing the Responsibility to Protect' report identifies R2P's Pillar 2 as 'the commitment of the international community to assist States in meeting [their Pillar 1 obligations]'.[1] This Pillar calls for the provision of support to States, for example in the forms of capacity-building or assistance-giving, to enable them to uphold their Pillar 1 responsibilities. The inclusion of this Pillar within R2P serves two fundamental purposes. First, it underscores R2P's focus upon mass atrocity prevention rather than reaction, and thus seeks to placate concerns that the doctrine embodies an interventionist agenda. Second, through soliciting the commitment of all States (and other international actors) to prevent mass atrocity crimes, Pillar 2 affirms that the ideals espoused by R2P represent community interests and as such reflect a shared international concern.

However, while a 2014 report by the UN Secretary-General on R2P's Pillar 2 insists that this pillar holds a 'central place' in R2P's implementation,[2] Pillar 2 is arguably not as established under international law as is Pillar 1. Indeed, it is doubtful whether an international legal obligation can be extracted for the international community (for example, States and international organisations) to provide assistance to States to help them in meeting their Pillar 1 obligations. Nevertheless, as thoroughly dissected within this chapter, some emerging norms as well as parallel legal frameworks (for example, in the realm of international environmental law) may foretell of the future development of international law in line with the ideals espoused by Pillar 2. With this in mind, this chapter offers an overview of this Pillar's scope and legal underpinnings, identifying relevant supporting legal frameworks that strengthen the case for an emerging Pillar 2 obligation as well as remaining gaps that R2P must evolve to fill.

1 Report of the Secretary-General, 'Implementing the Responsibility to Protect' (12 January 2009) UN Doc A/63/677 Para 11(b).

2 Report of the Secretary-General, 'Fulfilling our Collective Responsibility: International Assistance and the Responsibility to Protect' (2014) UN Doc A/68/947-S/2014/449 Para 5.

4.2 Pillar 2 under international law

4.2.1 Responsibility or obligation?

The precise undertakings entailed within R2P's Pillar 2 can be extracted from the 2005 World Summit Outcome document, whereby States declared that the 'international community should, as appropriate, encourage and help States to exercise this responsibility [of protecting their populations from mass atrocity crimes]'.[3] States also affirmed in this document that:

> We also intend to commit ourselves, as necessary and appropriate, to helping States build capacity to protect their populations from genocide, war crimes, ethnic cleansing and crimes against humanity and to assisting those which are under stress before crises and conflicts break out.[4]

In contrast to States' commitment in the 2005 World Summit Outcome document to discharge their (Pillar 1) host-State obligations to protect their populations from mass atrocity crimes ('We accept that responsibility and will act in accordance with it'),[5] the wordings of the above passages do not indicate that the Pillar 2 responsibility was assumed by States as a legal obligation. Rather, the phrases 'should, as appropriate', 'intend', and 'as necessary and appropriate', indicate that this Pillar represents a non-binding commitment at most. The above passages furthermore fail to identify key contours pertaining to Pillar 2, such as how the international community should take action to encourage, help, or assist host States in fulfilling their Pillar 1 responsibility,[6] whether or how international legal responsibility can be asserted following a failure to uphold Pillar 2, or which actor(s) should bear such a responsibility.[7]

States' reactions to the ideals embedded within R2P's Pillar 2 confirm that they did not accept this Pillar as a legally binding obligation. Austria, for example, maintained that the 'international community's role in assisting States to live up to their responsibility is of a supplementary nature'.[8] Japan claimed that the 'measures listed under pillar two ... seem to be wide-ranging and somewhat overstretched'.[9] Pakistan characterised Pillar 2 as a 'commitment' rather than an obligation,[10] and Singapore merely suggested that the 'international community should ... be *prepared* to support national efforts with resources and

3 2005 World Summit Outcome, UNGA Res 60/1 (24 October 2005) UN Doc A/RES/60/1 Para 138.
4 Ibid., Para 139.
5 Ibid., Para 138.
6 *See*, on this point, UN Doc A/68/947-S/2014/449 (n2) Paras 28–69. *See also* Adrian Gallagher, 'The Promise of Pillar II: Analysing International Assistance under the Responsibility to Protect' (2015) 91 *International Affairs* 1259, 1263–1264.
7 *See*, on this point, UN Doc A/68/947-S/2014/449 (n2) Paras 20–27.
8 UNGA, '98th Plenary Meeting' (24 July 2009) UN Doc A/63/PV.98, 1.
9 Ibid., 22.
10 Ibid., 3.

assistance'.[11] China indicated that the 'international community *can* provide assistance' to States in upholding their Pillar 1 responsibility.[12] None of these articulations of the Pillar 2 responsibility reveal *opinio juris* that States perceived or internalised it as a legal obligation. Rather, it seems that Pillar 2 was simply asserted as a morally recommended course of action.

4.2.2 Relevant (emerging) international legal norms

Although States were reluctant to accept R2P's Pillar 2 as legally binding, and while fundamental ambiguities pertaining to this Pillar's operationalisation persist (for example, with respect to the specific bearers of a Pillar 2 responsibility and how such a responsibility can be asserted in practice), international legal norms from parallel legal frameworks can serve as reference points to establish a basis for a nascent R2P Pillar 2 obligation. The first such norm is the international legal duty to cooperate,[13] which can be extracted from both the UN Charter (with obligations superseding those of any other treaty for its member-States)[14] as well as the Declaration on Friendly Relations (which is widely accepted as representing customary international law).[15] Article 1(3) of the UN Charter lists one of the purposes of the UN as '[achieving] international cooperation in solving international problems of an economic, social, cultural, or humanitarian character'.[16] The Declaration on Friendly Relations similarly imparts a 'duty' upon States 'to co-operate with one another … in order to maintain international peace and security and to promote international economic stability and progress'.[17] It includes, as

11 Ibid., 7 (emphasis added).
12 Ibid., 23 (emphasis added).
13 *See* Vaughan Lowe, *International Law* (Oxford University Press 2007) 110–12; Annie Bird, 'Third State Responsibility for Human Rights Violations' (2011) 21 *European Journal of International Law* 883, 886–87 (highlighting several human rights treaties that assert a duty to cooperate); Christina Leb, 'One Step at a Time: International Law and the Duty to Cooperate in the Management of Shared Water Resources' (2015) 40 *Water International* 21 at 23 and 27.
14 Article 103 of the UN Charter states that '[i]n the event of a conflict between obligations of the Members of the United Nations under the present Charter and their obligations under any other international agreement, their obligations under the present Charter shall prevail'. Charter of the United Nations (adopted 24 October 1945) 1 UNTS XVI Art 103 [hereinafter UN Charter].
15 *See* Robert Rosenstock, 'The Declaration of Principles of International Law Concerning Friendly Relations: A Survey' (1971) 65 *American Journal of International Law* 713, 714–15 (arguing that the Declaration most likely represents an elaboration upon some of the obligations contained within the UN Charter). *See also Case Concerning Military and Paramilitary Activities in and against Nicaragua (Nicaragua v. United States of America)* (Merits) [1986] ICJ Rep 14 Paras 188 and 191 (claiming that 'consent to the text of such resolutions … may be understood as an acceptance of the validity of the rule or set of rules declared by the resolution by themselves').
16 UN Charter (n14) Art 1(3).
17 Declaration on Principles of International Law Concerning Friendly Relations and Co-operation Among States in Accordance with the Charter of the United Nations,

part of this, a duty to cooperate in the 'promotion of universal respect for, and observance of, human rights and fundamental freedoms for all'.[18]

A general international legal duty to cooperate can help to justify the premise of R2P's Pillar 2 which calls for 'international assistance and capacity building' to help host States in upholding their Pillar 1 obligations to protect their populations from mass atrocity crimes. However, it should be cautioned that the duty to cooperate pertains to the coordination and pooling of resources,[19] whereas the Pillar 2 responsibility entails a positive provision of assistance. In other words, the duty to cooperate is premised upon relationships of sharing (whether of resources, information, or efforts), whereas Pillar 2 seemingly calls for relationships of giving (whether financially or otherwise). Of course, it would be expected that international cooperation in pursuit of the ideals advanced by the UN Charter and the Declaration on Friendly Relations (for example, on social, cultural, and humanitarian issues) would entail by default at least some relationships of assistance-giving between States. Nevertheless, it would arguably be stretching the obligation to cooperate too far to assert it as a basis for an existing Pillar 2 obligation under international law.

In this respect, limited obligations for the positive provision of assistance can be observed within the field of international environmental law. For example, Article 4 of the 1994 United Nations Framework Convention on Climate Change calls upon 'developed country Parties' to 'assist the developing country Parties that are particularly vulnerable to the adverse effects of climate change in meeting costs of adaptation to those adverse effects'.[20] Similarly, Article 25 of the 1995 Agreement for the Implementation of the Provisions of the United Nations Convention on the Law of the Sea relating to the Conservation and Management of Straddling Fish Stocks and Highly Migratory Fish Stocks calls upon States to provide 'financial assistance, assistance relating to human resources development, technical assistance, transfer of technology, including through joint venture arrangements, and advisory and consultative services' to developing States to help them meet their treaty obligations.[21] Admittedly, these treaties, which call for assistance-giving in the domain of international environmental law, are fundamentally different to the R2P Pillar 2 responsibility to provide assistance to States to

UNGA Res 2625 (1970) GAOR 25th Session at 123 [hereinafter Declaration on Friendly Relations]. *See also* Lowe (n13) 110.

18 Declaration on Friendly Relations (n17) 123.

19 *See*, for example, Margaret Young and Sebastian Sullivan, 'Evolution through the Duty to Cooperate: Implications of the Whaling Case at the International Court of Justice' (2015) 16 *Melbourne Journal of International* Law 311, 333.

20 United Nations Framework Convention on Climate Change (adopted 9 May 1992, entered into force 21 March 1994) 1771 UNTS 107 Art 4.

21 Agreement for the Implementation of the Provisions of the United Nations Convention on the Law of the Sea relating to the Conservation and Management of Straddling Fish Stocks and Highly Migratory Fish Stocks (adopted 4 August 1995, entered into force 11 December 2001) 2167 UNTS 3 Art 25. *See also* Elise Anne Clark, 'Strengthening Regional Fisheries Management – An Analysis of the Duty to Cooperate' (2011) 9 *New Zealand Journal of Public and International Law* 223, 232.

strengthen their capacities to protect their populations from mass atrocity crimes. At a minimum, however, they could perhaps serve as templates to outline what an obligation to provide positive assistance should actually entail.

Outside the field of international environmental law and more relevant to R2P's Pillar 2, a call for international assistance can be found within Article 2(1) of the International Covenant on Economic, Social and Cultural Rights (ICESCR), which stipulates that:

> Each State Party to the present Covenant undertakes to take steps, individually and through international assistance and co-operation ... to the maximum of its available resources, with a view to achieving progressively the full realization of the rights recognized in the present Covenant by all appropriate means.[22]

In its commentary to this Article, the Committee on Economic, Social and Cultural Rights specified that 'international cooperation for development and thus for the realization of economic, social and cultural rights is an obligation of all States' and that it 'is particularly incumbent upon those States which are in a position to assist others in this regard'.[23] The Committee's interpretation of Article 2(1) ICESCR therefore effectively calls upon States that possess the relevant capacity to provide assistance to other States to help them meet the economic, social, and cultural rights specified within the treaty.[24]

While a nexus can undoubtedly be established between an obligation under Article 2(1) ICESCR to provide assistance for the achievement of economic, social, and cultural rights as well as R2P's Pillar 2 responsibility to provide assistance to prevent the outbreak of mass atrocity crimes,[25] a few clarifications must be made regarding the extent to which the former can justify the existence of a Pillar 2 obligation. Importantly, Article 2(1) ICESCR represents a treaty obligation that is binding only upon State parties to the ICESCR,[26] so it can have only a limited

22 International Covenant on Economic, Social and Cultural Rights (adopted 16 December 1966, entered into force 3 January 1976) 993 UNTS 3 Art 2(1) [hereinafter ICESCR]
23 Committee on Economic, Social and Cultural Rights, 'General Comment 3, The Nature of States Parties' Obligations' (1 January 1991) UN Doc E/1991/23 Para 14.
24 *See* Matthew Craven, *The International Covenant on Economic, Social and Cultural Rights: A Perspective on its Development* (Oxford University Press 1995) 144–45.
25 For example, Article 55 of the UN Charter pledges UN support for 'higher standards of living, full employment, and conditions of economic and social progress and development' as well as 'solutions of international economic, social, health, and related problems; and international cultural and educational cooperation' as a means of '[creating] conditions of stability and well-being which are necessary for peaceful and friendly relations among nations'. UN Charter (n14) Art 55. *See also* 'The Responsibility to Protect: The Report of the International Commission on Intervention and State Sovereignty' (International Commission on Intervention and State Sovereignty, December 2001) Paras 3.18–19 <http://responsibilitytoprotect.org/ICISS%20Report.pdf>.
26 *See* Philip Alston and Gerard Quinn, 'The Nature and Scope of States Parties' Obligations under the International Covenant on Economic, Social and Cultural Rights' (1987) 9 *Human Rights Quarterly* 156, 160.

impact in establishing a universal duty of assistance-giving as per R2P's Pillar 2. Furthermore, this Article calls upon States to provide assistance 'to the maximum of [their] available resources',[27] which makes it difficult to identify concrete obligations for States in this respect.[28] Finally, it does not seem that States share the interpretation of the Committee on Economic, Social and Cultural Rights regarding the existence of an Article 2(1) ICESCR duty to provide assistance.[29] During the drafting of the Covenant, only Chile agreed that such a duty exists,[30] while Tunisia, the Soviet Union, Greece, New Zealand, Mexico, Saudi Arabia, and France voiced disagreement on this point, contending that international assistance should be offered and received through the full consent of States.[31] Together, these factors serve as significant constraints to generalising the Article 2(1) ICESCR commitment to offer support and assistance to an R2P Pillar 2 obligation.

In addition to Article 2(1) ICESCR, UNGA Resolution 2626 (adopted without vote) specifies that '[e]ach economically advanced country will progressively increase its official development assistance to the developing countries and will exert its best efforts to reach a minimum net amount of 0.7 per cent of its gross national product'.[32] Similar to R2P's Pillar 2, this provision calls upon States to offer positive assistance to other States to help with development and capacity building. Where it stops short of supporting a Pillar 2 obligation, however, can be identified in three primary respects. First, Resolution 2626 – as a UNGA resolution – represents a non-binding source of international law. Second, the objective of assistance-giving as per Resolution 2626 is presumably tied to the Resolution's central theme of international development and not, as per R2P's Pillar 2, the prevention of the outbreak of mass atrocity crimes (although a link can undoubtedly be established between the respective goals). Third and finally, the nature of development assistance called for within Resolution 2626 lacks certainty. The relevant provision indicates, for example, that economically advanced States 'will progressively increase' their development assistance, although there are no specified benchmarks in this respect. The Resolution only maintains that States 'will exert [their] best efforts' to reach the 0.7 per cent target, which represents a commitment that is difficult to translate into a distinct legal obligation. Tellingly, this 0.7 per cent development assistance target has since been reaffirmed in the context of the UN, although only as an aspiration but not an obligation.[33] As

27 ICESCR (n22) Art 2(1).
28 *See* Craven (n24) 133, 147.
29 *See* ibid., 148; Alston and Quinn (n26) 189–91.
30 UNGA, 'Third Committee, 1203rd Meeting' (5 December 1962) UN Doc A/C.3/SR.1203, 342.
31 Ibid., 342–43; UNGA, 'Third Committee, 1204th Meeting' (6 December 1962) UN Doc A/C.3/SR.1204 at 346–47, 349; UNGA, 'Third Committee, 1205th Meeting' (7 December 1962) UN Doc A/C.3/SR.1205, 352.
32 International Development Strategy for the Second United Nations Development Decade, UNGA Res 2626 (1970) GAOR 25th Session Para 43.
33 *See*, for example, Report of the Secretary-General's High-Level Panel on Threats, Challenges and Change, 'A More Secure World: Our Shared Responsibility' (2004) UN Doc A/59/565 at Annex I Para 2.

such, while UNGA Resolution 2626 reveals the more elevated role allocated to international assistance and cooperation under international law, it continues to fall short of supporting the emergence of an R2P Pillar 2 obligation.

4.3 Conclusion

Neither the language of the 2005 World Summit Outcome document nor the positions of States subsequent to its adoption indicate that R2P's Pillar 2 represents a legally binding obligation upon States and/or other international actors to support host States in upholding their Pillar 1 responsibilities. Nevertheless, this chapter highlighted that similar obligations or commitments can be extracted from parallel international legal frameworks, including the general international legal duty to cooperate contained within the UN Charter and the Declaration on Friendly Relations, specific duties to cooperate under international environmental law, and calls for international cooperation under the ICESCR and UNGA Resolution 2626. These frameworks highlight increased inter-State dependence under international law, although they fall short of justifying the emergence of an R2P Pillar 2 obligation. However, given that R2P serves pressing community interests of tackling mass atrocity crimes, it is not unreasonable to predict that its Pillar 2 may acquire legal standing through the further development of international law, although this conclusion cannot be made at present. By far the most controversial aspect of R2P, however, is its Pillar 3, which is discussed in the next chapter.

5 R2P's Pillar 3

5.1 Introduction

R2P's Pillar 3 pertains to the 'responsibility of Member States to respond collectively in a timely and decisive manner when a State is manifestly failing' to protect its population from mass atrocity crimes.[1] On this aspect of R2P, the 2001 report by the International Commission on Intervention and State Sovereignty (2001 ICISS report, which first introduced the doctrine) spoke of a 'responsibility to react,' namely, a responsibility of third-party States to intervene (although not necessarily militarily) when mass atrocities break out.[2] Essentially, the responsibility to react sought to further propel decades of human rights advancements detailed in Chapter 2 of this book: whereas developments in the post-Charter era required States to uphold minimum rights to individuals within their own jurisdictions and granted increased standing to third-party States to respond to breaches of obligations owed to the international community as a whole (e.g. human rights), the responsibility to react sought to eliminate the need or the expectation for any nexus to be established (whether territory- or nationality-based) in order for a State to be legally obligated to take action in response to the commission of a mass atrocity crime anywhere in the world.[3] It thus sought to shift the terms of the debate from speaking of a legal right to react to a mass atrocity situation (e.g. through the UNSC or through other institutional or non-institutional means) to establishing a positive duty upon third-party States to do so.

However, this ambitious formulation of R2P was scaled back in the 2005 World Summit Outcome document. Here, States merely affirmed that they are 'prepared' to take 'collective action' when host States fail to protect their populations, and

1 Report of the Secretary-General, 'Implementing the Responsibility to Protect' (12 January 2009) UN Doc A/63/677 Para 11(c).
2 'The Responsibility to Protect: The Report of the International Commission on Intervention and State Sovereignty' (*International Commission on Intervention and State Sovereignty*, December 2001) Paras 4.1–4.3 <http://responsibilitytoprotect.org/ICISS%20Report.pdf> [hereinafter 2001 ICISS Report].
3 *See* Ruti Teitel, *Humanity's Law* (Oxford University Press 2011) 159; Richard Barnes and Vassilis Tzevelekos, 'Beyond Responsibility to Protect: Ceci n'est pas une Pipe' in Richard Barnes and Vassilis Tzevelekos (eds), *Beyond Responsibility to Protect: Generating Change in International Law* (Intersentia 2016) 12–13.

thus fell short of assuming any concrete legal obligations to respond to the outbreak of mass atrocity situations.[4] States furthermore maintained through this document that they will take such action 'on a case-by-case basis', a commitment that would inevitably yield varying degrees of action or inaction for each R2P case.[5]

An examination of State practice and *opinio juris* reinforces the notion that States do not view R2P's Pillar 3 as a legally binding obligation.[6] In UNGA discussions on the UN Secretary-General's 2009 'Implementing the Responsibility to Protect' report, for example, the United States declared that '[w]here prevention fails and a State is manifestly failing to meet its obligations, we also need to be prepared *to consider* a wider range of collective measures'.[7] Russia called for 'further in-depth work on [the] main elements' of R2P's implementation and iterated that this 'work is far from complete'.[8] Mali maintained that 'discussion on the third pillar must continue in the General Assembly'.[9] Other States hinted that Pillar 3 could be abused and employed as an interventionist tool by powerful States. Singapore, for example, noted that 'it is clear that there are some concerns over pillar three, and those will have to be discussed further'.[10] Vietnam stated that 'the qualifier "timely and decisive" collective action, described as pillar three in the Secretary-General's report, requires a clear and rational definition to prevent its possible confinement to coercive military force as the only alternative'.[11] A number of States – including Pakistan, Ecuador, Morocco, China, Venezuela, Cuba, Sudan, Iran, and Nicaragua – delivered similar statements, implying that Pillar 3 could serve to legitimise interventionist agendas and should thus be considered with a high degree of caution.[12]

The backtracking of the 2005 World Summit Outcome document from the 2001 ICISS report effectively means that R2P's Pillar 3, in its current form, does not seek to establish an obligation upon third-party States to react to mass atrocity crimes that are perpetrated outside their jurisdictions. This chapter, however, argues that the notion of third-State obligations to react to mass atrocity crimes can nevertheless be extracted in various (albeit limited) ways from existing and overlapping legal frameworks, including the Article 1 Genocide Convention obligation to prevent genocide, the Common Article 1 Geneva Conventions obligation to ensure respect for the Conventions, and the Article 41 obligation in the

4 2005 World Summit Outcome, UNGA Res 60/1 (24 October 2005) UN Doc A/RES/60/1 Para 139 [hereinafter 2005 World Summit Outcome].
5 Ibid.
6 *See* Patrick Quinton-Brown, 'Mapping Dissent: The Responsibility to Protect and Its State Critics' (2013) 5 *Global Responsibility to Protect* 260 (mapping State dissent against R2P, which the author discovered to centre around means of implementation i.e. Pillar 3).
7 UNGA, '97th Plenary Meeting' (23 July 2009) UN Doc A/63/PV.97, 17–18.
8 UNGA, '100th Plenary Meeting' (28 July 2009) UN Doc A/63/PV.100, 12.
9 UNGA, '98th Plenary Meeting' (24 July 2009) UN Doc A/63/PV.98, 25.
10 Ibid., 8.
11 Ibid., 28.
12 Ibid., 4, 9, 13, 24; UNGA, '105th Plenary Meeting' (14 September 2009) UN Doc A/63/PV.105, 3–7.

International Law Commission's Articles on State Responsibility (ILC's ASR) for States to 'cooperate to bring to an end through lawful means any serious [breaches]' of peremptory norms. This chapter dissects the precise stipulations entailed within each of these rules with view to determining whether and to what degree they support the emergence of an R2P Pillar 3 obligation. This is accompanied with a thorough analysis of the shortcomings that these frameworks retain in fully achieving the ideals of Pillar 3, including how these gaps must be addressed in order to give rise to a binding and enforceable Pillar 3 obligation for third-party States to react to the commission of mass atrocity crimes. Furthermore, recognising that the UNSC's fulfilment of its responsibility to maintain international peace and security is essential to the consistent and effective discharge of R2P's Pillar 3 (as the only body that can impose binding obligations upon all UN member-States as well as authorise the use of force absent self-defence), this chapter devotes special attention to scrutinising the legal entitlement enjoyed by the UNSC's five permanent members (P5) to the veto with view to determining what, if any, constraints operate upon its exercise. It concludes with an examination of two potential alternatives to UNSC action in the event that the body is paralysed from responding to a mass atrocity situation, namely, 'Uniting for Peace' (UforP) as well as regional authorisation.

5.2 Existing and emerging obligations to react to mass atrocity crimes

5.2.1 Genocide

In the context of the Srebrenica genocide, Bosnia filed an application with the International Court of Justice (ICJ) against Serbia for committing, conspiring, inciting, attempting to commit, and failing to prevent and punish genocide.[13] The Court evaluated these claims with reference to the Genocide Convention as well as customary international rules of State responsibility (as reflected in the ILC's ASR and the ICJ's *Nicaragua* case[14]). In its 2007 judgment, the Court concluded that the Srebrenica genocide was not attributable to Serbia,[15] stating that it was not 'committed by [Serbia's] organs or by persons or entities wholly dependent upon it'[16] nor upon Serbia's 'instructions or under the direction [of its] organs'.[17] The Court also found that Serbia did not '[exercise] effective control over the

13 Among other acts. *Case Concerning Application of the Convention on the Prevention and Punishment of the Crime of Genocide (Bosnia & Herzegovina v. Serbia & Montenegro)* (Judgment) [2007] ICJ Rep 43 Para 64.
14 Ibid., Paras 385–401, 408–15. *See also* ILC, 'Draft Articles on Responsibility of States for Internationally Wrongful Acts, with Commentaries' (2001) II *Yearbook of the International Law Commission* 26 Arts 4–11 [hereinafter ASR]; *Case Concerning Military and Paramilitary Activities in and against Nicaragua (Nicaragua v. United States of America)* (Merits) [1986] ICJ Rep 14 Paras 110, 115.
15 *Bosnia* case (n13) Para 415.
16 Ibid., Para 395.
17 Ibid., Para 413.

operations in the course of which those massacres … were perpetrated',[18] nor did it find Serbia complicit in the act of genocide.[19] Ultimately, however, the Court did find Serbia legally responsible for failing to take action to discharge its obligation to prevent genocide as per Article 1 of the Genocide Convention, meaning that Serbia's international legal responsibility was incurred not for positive actions that it undertook with respect to the Srebrenica genocide, but rather for its omissions (i.e. for failing to take action to prevent it).[20]

In reaching this conclusion, the ICJ emphasised that Article 1 Genocide Convention imparts a specific obligation of prevention upon 'each contracting State'[21] that 'places States under positive obligations, to do their best to ensure that [genocide and other acts listed under Article 3 of the Genocide Convention] do not occur'.[22] It further specified that the 'obligation in question is one of conduct and not one of result', meaning that a State would not incur legal responsibility if genocide is perpetrated despite its prevention efforts, but rather only if it 'manifestly failed to take all measures to prevent genocide which were within its power, and which might have contributed to preventing the genocide'.[23] In this manner, the duty under Article 1 Genocide Convention to prevent genocide was asserted (not without criticism[24]) as an obligation upon all State parties to take positive action to prevent (and, as argued later in this section, to react to) genocide even in situations to which they are not a party or do not have any direct or indirect links of any kind.[25] In other words, this obligation to prevent genocide, the Court emphasised, exists irrespective of any jurisdictional or other nexus that a State may or may not hold to a particular situation of actual or impending genocide.

Importantly, the ICJ did not make any express reference to R2P in the *Bosnia* judgment despite the doctrine's clear relevance in this case (namely, genocide constitutes one of the four mass atrocity crimes encompassed under the doctrine). This means that strictly speaking, the Court's determinations in this case failed to set a precedent with respect to how the doctrine can or should be implemented. Nevertheless, the Court's decision presents a useful contribution in building the case for an emerging Pillar 3 obligation, namely, through advancing the notion that States should be lawfully required (and not merely invited) to react to the

18 Ibid., Para 413.
19 Ibid., Para 424.
20 Ibid., Para 438.
21 Ibid., Para 427.
22 Ibid., Para 432.
23 Ibid., Para 430.
24 *See*, for example, *Case Concerning Application of the Convention on the Prevention and Punishment of the Crime of Genocide (Bosnia & Herzegovina v. Serbia & Montenegro)* (Separate Opinion of Judge Tomka) [2007] ICJ Rep 310 Paras 66–67; *Case Concerning Application of the Convention on the Prevention and Punishment of the Crime of Genocide (Bosnia & Herzegovina v. Serbia & Montenegro)* (Declaration of Judge Skotnikov) [2007] ICJ Rep 366, 379.
25 *See* Marco Longobardo, 'Genocide, Obligations Erga Omnes, and the Responsibility to Protect: Remarks on a Complex Convergence' (2015) 19 *International Journal of Human Rights* 1199, 1200–01.

commission of certain acts outside their jurisdictions. The *Bosnia* decision is, however, subject to certain constraints in this regard.

The first limitation of the *Bosnia* case as pertains to building a case for an R2P Pillar 3 obligation is that the ICJ confined its judgment to 'the specific scope of the duty to prevent in the Genocide Convention'.[26] Although the Court noted that a duty to prevent can be found within other international instruments,[27] it stressed that the 'content of [such a] duty varies from one instrument to another, according to the wording of the relevant provisions, and depending on the nature of the acts to be prevented'.[28] The Court therefore emphasised that it did not 'purport to establish a general jurisprudence applicable to all cases where a treaty instrument, or other binding legal norm, includes an obligation for States to prevent certain acts'.[29]

These passages suggest that the ICJ's findings with respect to the Article 1 Genocide Convention obligation to prevent genocide are confined to the Convention's State parties, and also, by default, only to prevention obligations for genocide but not for the other mass atrocity crimes of war crimes, crimes against humanity, and ethnic cleansing. In response to the former point, however, scholars of international law are in general agreement that the obligation to prevent genocide exists as a matter of custom, and is therefore binding even upon non-parties to the Genocide Convention.[30] As for the latter point, it should be pointed out that while the ICJ restricted itself to examining the duty to prevent in the context of Article 1 of the Genocide Convention, it did not reject that this interpretation could theoretically extend to other crimes with prevention obligations. In line with this, Gibney highlights that the Court's approach to defining the duty to prevent in the *Bosnia* case very likely represents 'the only sensible way of reading human rights law',[31] a notion that is met with support from other authors.[32] Strauss furthermore suggests that the *Bosnia* decision can be used as a starting

26 *Bosnia* case (n13) Para 429.
27 Including, for example, Convention against Torture and other Cruel, Inhuman or Degrading Treatment or Punishment (adopted 10 December 1984, entered into force 26 June 1987) 1465 UNTS 85 Art 2; Convention on the Prevention and Punishment of Crimes against Internationally Protected Persons, Including Diplomatic Agents (adopted 14 December 1973, entered into force 20 February 1977) 1035 UNTS 168 Art 4; International Convention for the Suppression of Terrorist Bombings (adopted 15 December 1997, entered into force 23 May 2001) 2149 UNTS 256 Art 15.
28 *Bosnia* case (n13) Para 429.
29 Ibid.
30 Heieck even maintains that this obligation is binding as *jus cogens*. *See* John Heieck, *A Duty to Prevent Genocide: Due Diligence Obligations among the P5* (Edward Elgar Publishing 2018).
31 Mark Gibney, 'Genocide and State Responsibility' (2007) 7 *Human Rights Law Review* 760, 769.
32 *See*, for example, Emma McClean, 'The Responsibility to Protect: The Role of International Human Rights Law' (2008) 13 *Journal of Conflict and Security Law* 123, 145–46. *See also* Andrea Gattini, 'Breach of the Obligation to Prevent and Reparation Thereof in the ICJ's Genocide Judgment' (2007) 18 *European Journal of International Law* 695 at 699–700, 698.

point to define prevention obligations for all mass atrocity crimes under R2P's Pillar 3.[33] In this manner, the ICJ's *Bosnia* decision can at least serve as a basis for the development of an obligation to prevent mass atrocity crimes more generally.

The second limitation of the ICJ's *Bosnia* case is that it examines the responsibility to *prevent* genocide under the Genocide Convention, whereas R2P's Pillar 3 pertains to a responsibility to *react* to mass atrocity crimes. The 2005 World Summit Outcome document elaborates that the latter arises when States are 'manifestly failing to protect their populations' from mass atrocity crimes,[34] meaning that it comes into effect after mass atrocity crimes are underway. In contrast, the ICJ specified that the obligation to prevent genocide arises 'at the instant that the State learns of, or should normally have learned of, the existence of a serious risk that genocide will be committed'.[35] In other words, obligation to prevent is triggered before genocide is even committed, and requires State parties to the Genocide Convention to make use of available means that are 'likely to have a deterrent effect on those suspected of preparing genocide'.[36]

On this point, Mayroz suggests that the obligation to prevent genocide can encompass an obligation to react, arguing that 'the duty to prevent [genocide] covers not only an impending but also an already ongoing genocide'.[37] While acknowledging that this does not constitute 'prevention' in the strictest sense, he illustrates that reactions to genocide simultaneously constitute prevention measures to hinder the continued perpetration of this crime. Support for Mayroz's argument can be gleaned from the *Bosnia* judgment, whereby the ICJ identified one of the parameters for assessing State responsibility for failing to prevent genocide as 'the [State's] capacity to influence effectively the action of persons likely to commit, *or already committing*, genocide'.[38] Similarly, the Court determined that 'a State's capacity to influence may vary depending on its particular legal position vis-à-vis the situations and persons facing the danger, *or the reality*, of genocide'.[39] In both passages, the Court clearly communicated that the obligation to prevent genocide can extend temporally beyond the actual commission of genocide, and thus encompasses acts that, under the R2P doctrine, would be labelled as reactions. The logic of the Court can be appreciated, for surely it would not make sense for the Genocide Convention's obligation to prevent genocide to exist only until genocide is perpetrated, after which States are absolved of their responsibility to take action to cease the commission of this act.

33 Ekkehard Strauss, 'A Bird in the Hand is Worth Two in the Bush – On the Assumed Legal Nature of the Responsibility to Protect' (2009) 1 *Global Responsibility to Protect* 291, 317.
34 2005 World Summit Outcome (n4) Para 138.
35 *Bosnia* case (n13) Para 431.
36 Ibid.
37 Eyal Mayroz, 'The Legal Duty to "Prevent": After the Onset of "Genocide"' (2012) 14 *Journal of Genocide Research* 79, 84–85.
38 *Bosnia* case (n13) Para 430 (emphasis added).
39 Ibid. (emphasis added).

The third major limitation of the *Bosnia* decision is that short of establishing equal responsibility among all States to prevent genocide, it introduced a two-pronged 'due diligence' test for attributing State responsibility for failure to discharge this obligation.[40] Due diligence can be defined as a 'standard of care' that States must exercise in order to uphold specified duties under international law.[41] It is an obligation of conduct and not of result,[42] requiring States to employ 'all appropriate, necessary, and proportional measures at [their] disposal' to prevent, investigate, and punish the violation of certain norms.[43] In delineating the due diligence standard for the duty to prevent genocide, the ICJ first maintained that 'the obligation to prevent ... [arises] at the instant that the State learns of, or should normally have learned of, the existence of a serious risk that genocide will be committed'.[44] This threshold is quite low: although it could be difficult to prove that a State held actual knowledge of an impending genocide, the Court also included a less stringent requirement ('should normally have learned of') which could be fulfilled through a State's close links to a particular situation or through the situation's general prominence on the international scene.[45] Indeed, the Court found that this element of the due diligence test was satisfied in the *Bosnia* case not through solid proof that demonstrated Serbia's awareness of the impending Srebrenica genocide, but rather because it determined that Serbia 'could hardly have been unaware of' such a serious risk.[46]

The second component of the ICJ's due diligence test with respect to the Article 1 Genocide Convention obligation to prevent genocide is the existence of a 'capacity to influence effectively' the party that is planning or perpetrating genocide.[47] This implies that although the obligation to prevent genocide rests with all State parties to the Genocide Convention, the attribution of State responsibility for a failure to uphold this obligation requires a particularly strong nexus between the State in question and the party planning or executing genocide, namely, in the form of the capacity to effectively influence. The Court elaborated that this capacity can be assessed by 'geographical distance ... and on the strength of the

40 On the Court's due diligence test, *see*, in general John Heieck, 'The Responsibility Not to Veto Revisited: How the Duty to Prevent Genocide as a Jus Cogens Norm Imposes a Legal Duty Not to Veto on the Five Permanent Members of the Security Council' in R. Barnes and V. Tzevelekos (eds), *Beyond Responsibility to Protect: Generating Change in International Law* (Intersentia 2016) 116–17 [hereinafter Heieck RN2V Revisited]. *See*, however, Gattini (n32) 702–05, 713 (contending that 'most arguments of the Court leave the impression that they were rather conveniently tailored to the case at hand').

41 Heieck RN2V Revisited (n40) 112. *See also* Barnes and Tzevelekos (n3) 16–17.

42 *See* Nigel D. White, 'Due Diligence Obligations of Conduct: Developing a Responsibility Regime for PMSCs' (2012) 31 *Criminal Justice Ethics* 233, 243.

43 Heieck RN2V Revisited (n40) 113. *See also Osman v UK* (App no 23452/94) ECtHR 28 October 1998 Paras 115–16; *Velásquez Rodríguez v Honduras*, Judgment of July 29, 1988, Inter-Am.Ct.H.R. (Ser. C) No. 4 (1988) Para 172.

44 *Bosnia* case (n13) Para 431.

45 *See* Heieck RN2V Revisited (n40) 117.

46 *Bosnia* case (n13) Para 436–37.

47 Ibid., Para 430.

political links, as well as links of all other kinds' between the two States.[48] In determining Serbia's responsibility for failing to prevent genocide, the Court noted that Serbia's 'position of influence … [was] unlike that of the other States parties to the Genocide Convention owing to the strength of the political, military and financial links' that it held with the groups that perpetrated the genocide.[49]

It has been argued by scholars of international law that the due diligence standard articulated within the *Bosnia* case is overly restrictive, to the point where it becomes difficult to assert a breach of the obligation to prevent genocide in practice.[50] While this point represents a topic for further discussion elsewhere, it can at least be appreciated that some sort of limiting factor must be delineated in order to render the obligation to prevent genocide operational and enforceable. Rosenberg eloquently describes why this is so, observing that '[i]f all states are always under some vague obligation to prevent genocide wherever it occurs, then no one state is ever under any specific obligation to prevent genocide in a particular instance'.[51] This holds true to the potential establishment of an R2P Pillar 3 obligation: should such an obligation emerge, it will be presumably subject to some sort of due diligence standard, as it is extremely unlikely that States will ever come to endorse a Pillar 3 obligation that is not only highly controversial in itself (e.g. due to its association with Western interventionism), but that will also indefinitely expand their accountability for actions over which, in essence, they have no immediate control. In this manner, although the due diligence standard articulated within the ICJ's *Bosnia* judgment need not necessarily be assumed for the development of similar due diligence criteria regarding a Pillar 3 responsibility to react to all mass atrocity crimes, it can perhaps be employed as a starting point in this regard.

The final limitation of the *Bosnia* judgment as pertains to building a case for an R2P Pillar 3 obligation is the ICJ's statement that States 'may only act within the limits permitted by international law' in discharging their duty to prevent genocide.[52] This statement holds the greatest significance when it comes to the use of force. If unauthorised humanitarian intervention is not recognised as a lawful exception to the UN Charter's Article 2(4) prohibition against the use of force (as agreed by the majority of States as well as international legal scholars),[53] then the *Bosnia* judgment does not advance a right of third-party States to engage in such an intervention to prevent or alleviate a mass atrocity situation of genocide.[54] This,

48 Ibid.

49 Ibid., Para 434.

50 *See*, for example, Gibney (n25) 768–69.

51 Sheri P. Rosenberg, 'Responsibility to Protect: A Framework for Prevention' (2009) 1 *Global Responsibility to Protect* 442, 467.

52 *Bosnia* case (n13) Para 430.

53 *See*, for example, Ian Brownlie, 'International Law and the Use of Force by States Revisited' (2000) 21 *Australian Yearbook of International Law* 21; Christine Gray, 'The Use of Force for Humanitarian Purposes' in Nigel D. White and Christian Henderson (eds), *Research Handbook on International Conflict and Security Law* (Edward Elgar Publishing Limited 2013). *See*, however, Harold Koh, 'The War Powers and Humanitarian Intervention' (2016) 53 *Houston Law Review* 971.

54 *See* Longobardo (n25) 1203.

in turn, underpins a central dilemma within the R2P doctrine, namely, how to address R2P situations when the UNSC – as the only body that can legally authorise force – is unable to respond effectively.[55]

The requirement for States to remain within the limits of international law when taking action to prevent genocide furthermore raises questions regarding the lawfulness of third-State countermeasures which, as discussed in Chapter 2 of this book, have been neither conclusively permitted nor prohibited under the ILC's ASR.[56] Rather, their legal status has been left to the further development of the law, although there exists extensive State practice regarding their invocation in order to respond to *erga omnes* and *jus cogens* breaches. Given States' flat rejection of humanitarian intervention, the formal recognition of a legal entitlement to third-State countermeasures can arguably strengthen the enforceability of a potential R2P Pillar 3 obligation as it would, at the very least, allow States to undertake non-military responses to mass atrocity crimes (for example, through imposing sanctions or through failing to fulfil specific treaty obligations such as those pertaining to weapons or other deals), in violation of their international legal obligations and independently of the UNSC, when the body is paralysed due to the permanent veto.[57] Furthermore, because third-State countermeasures are inherently non-forceful, such an entitlement would reinforce that R2P's Pillar 3 can be implemented through a diverse range of measures rather than being centred upon the use of military force as is often mistakenly assumed.

Overall, the ICJ's attribution of legal responsibility to Serbia in the *Bosnia* case for failing to prevent genocide as per Article 1 Genocide Convention offers a framework that can help guide the development of an R2P Pillar 3 obligation. Namely, this case interpreted Article 1 Genocide Convention as imparting an obligation upon State parties to take positive action to prevent the commission of genocide even if it is not committed within their jurisdiction or by organs or actors attributable to them or under their control. While it is true that the decision, in the strictest sense, was confined to the crime of genocide and within the framework of the Genocide Convention, this section demonstrated that its findings can serve as a tool, among others to be discussed in the subsequent sections, to build an argument in favour of an emerging Pillar 3 obligation. The next section examines similar duties of prevention and reaction that exist with respect to war crimes.

5.2.2 War crimes

Similar to genocide, a third-State obligation to react to war crimes can be extracted to some extent from existing international legal norms which help to build the case for an emerging R2P Pillar 3 obligation and to define its potential legal scope

55 The UNSC, and particularly its permanent five members' right to the veto, receives further discussion in Section 5.3 of this book.

56 *See* Section 2.2.2 of this book.

57 *See* Longobardo (n25) 1204–05; Elena Katselli Proukaki, *The Problem of Enforcement in International Law: Countermeasures, the Non-Injured State and the Idea of International Community* (Routledge 2009) 88.

and applicability. Common Article 1 to the Geneva Conventions is the most significant in this regard, stating that '[t]he High Contracting Parties undertake to respect and to *ensure respect for* the present Convention in all circumstances'.[58] The relevance of this Article to an obligation to react to war crimes is that, as detailed in Chapter 3 of this book, two of the four categories of war crimes identified within the ICC Statute (specifically, Articles 8(2)(a) and 8(2)(c) of the ICC Statute) derive from the Geneva Conventions.[59] However, the precise definitions of the terms 'respect' and 'ensure respect' under Common Article 1 require further clarification.

Focarelli points out that comparable obligations to the Common Article 1 duty to respect and ensure respect contained within other multilateral human rights instruments are interpreted quite restrictively.[60] The 'respect' component in such treaties, he notes, is understood to impart an obligation upon contracting States and their organs to comply with treaty provisions wherever they may act (i.e. even extraterritorially).[61] In turn, he identifies that the 'ensure respect' component is seen as requiring States to secure compliance of all actors within their territory to the respective treaty provisions, including non-State entities and individuals.[62] He concludes, therefore, that the obligations to respect and ensure respect (or similar) contained within such multilateral human rights instruments call upon States to ensure that the conventions in question are adhered to by all State and non-State actors that operate within their borders, as well as by their own agents when they act extraterritorially. They do not, importantly, require States to secure the compliance of other contracting States to the respective treaty obligations.

In the context of Common Article 1, however, the International Committee of the Red Cross's (ICRC) official commentary to the Geneva Conventions has been influential in asserting a more expansive interpretation of the terms 'respect' and 'ensure respect'. Namely, the commentary argues that the obligation to 'ensure respect' for the Conventions means that 'in the event of a Power failing to fulfil its obligations, the other Contracting Parties (neutral, allied or enemy) may, and

58 *See* Geneva Convention Relative to the Treatment of Prisoners of War (adopted 12 August 1949, entered into force 21 October 1950) 75 UNTS 135 Art 1 (emphasis added) [hereinafter Geneva Convention III].

59 Rome Statute of the International Criminal Court (adopted 17 July 1998, entered into force 1 July 2002) 2187 UNTS 3 Arts 8(2)(a) and 8(2)(c) (describing Geneva violations in IACS and NIACs, respectively) [hereinafter ICC Statute]. *See also* Section 3.2.2 of this book.

60 *See*, for example, International Covenant on Civil and Political Rights (adopted 16 December 1966, entered into force 23 March 1976) 999 UNTS 171 Art 2(1); European Convention on Human Rights (adopted 4 November 1950, entered into force 3 September 1953) 213 UNTS 221 Art 1; American Convention on Human Rights (adopted 22 November 1969, entered into force 18 July 1978) 1144 UNTS 123 Art 1(1).

61 *See* Carlo Focarelli, 'Common Article 1 of the 1949 Geneva Conventions: A Soap Bubble?' (2010) 21 *European Journal of International Law* 125, 138–42.

62 Ibid.

should, endeavour to bring it back to an attitude of respect for the Convention'.[63] This interpretation effectively calls for an obligation to react to violations of the Geneva Conventions, including, by default, to war crimes that derive from these Conventions (which is important for the purposes of R2P's Pillar 3). The obligation is furthermore asserted irrespective of a State's direct or indirect involvement within a particular armed conflict.

Pushing the ICRC's interpretation even further, de Chazournes and Condorelli maintain that Common Article 1 imparts an obligation upon State parties to the Geneva Conventions 'to take active part in ensuring compliance with rules of international humanitarian law by all concerned, but also to react against violations of that law'.[64] Importantly, their use of the phrase 'by all concerned' rather than 'by all States' denotes their view that contracting States must ensure respect for the Conventions by both State as well as non-State parties to armed conflicts. In other words, they suggest that contracting States to the Geneva Conventions must react to violations of the Conventions that are perpetrated by both State and non-State parties within armed conflicts that occur anywhere in the world. This interpretation is reflected in the ICRC's more recent commentary to Common Article 1 – which calls for 'ensuring respect for the Conventions by *others that are Party* to a conflict'[65] – and becomes relevant for the purposes of examining R2P's applicability to mass atrocity crimes committed by non-State actors (discussed in Section 7.5 of this book).

The view that the Common Article 1 obligation to 'ensure respect' extends beyond a State's own territory and to armed conflicts which it is not itself a party is supported by State practice and case law. In the *Construction of a Wall* case, for example, the ICJ, commenting on Common Article 1, maintained that 'every State party to [the Fourth Geneva Convention], *whether or not it is a party to a specific conflict*, is under an obligation to ensure that the requirements of the instruments in question are complied with'.[66] It furthermore declared that 'all States parties to the [Fourth Geneva Convention] have in addition the obligation, while respecting the United Nations Charter and international law, to ensure compliance by Israel with international humanitarian law as embodied in that

63 Jean Pictet et al., *Commentary: Geneva Convention for the Amelioration of the Condition of the Wounded and Sick in Armed Forces in the Field*, vol. I (ICRC 1952) 26; Oscar M. Uhler et al., *Commentary: Geneva Convention Relative to the Protection of Civilian Persons in Time of War*, vol. IV (ICRC 1958) 16.

64 *See* Laurence Boisson de Chazournes and Luigi Condorelli, 'Common Article 1of the Geneva Conventions Revisited: Protecting Collective Interests' (2000) 82 *International Review of the Red Cross* 67, 70. *See also* Andrea Breslin, 'A Reflection on the Legal Obligation for Third States to Ensure Respect for IHL' (2017) 22 *Journal of Conflict and Security Law* 5, 12–13.

65 'Commentary of 2016, Article 1: Respect for the Convention' (*ICRC*, 2016) at Paras 153–56 <https://www.icrc.org/applic/ihl/ihl.nsf/Comment.xsp?action=openDocument&documentId=72239588AFA66200C1257F7D00367DBD> (emphasis added).

66 *Legal Consequences of the Construction of a Wall in the Occupied Palestinian Territory* (Advisory Opinion) [2004] ICJ Rep 136 Para 158 (emphasis added) [hereinafter *Construction of a Wall* case].

Convention'.[67] The ICJ thus called upon all State parties to the Fourth Geneva Convention – rather than only States that retained direct or indirect involvement with Israel's construction of a wall through occupied Palestinian territory – to ensure Israel's compliance with the Convention.

The UNGA and UNSC assumed a similar approach within several resolutions adopted by the respective bodies on the Palestinian issue, including UNGA Resolution 45/69 (adopted 141 votes to 2 with 3 abstentions); UNSC Resolution 681 (adopted unanimously); UNGA Resolution 58/97 (adopted 164 votes to 6 with 4 abstentions); UNGA Resolution 59/122 (adopted 160 votes to 7 with 11 abstentions); and UNGA Resolution 64/92 (adopted 168 votes to 6 with 4 abstentions).[68] Each of these resolutions calls upon '[all] High Contracting Parties' to the Fourth Geneva Convention to 'ensure respect' for its provisions by Israel, thus affirming that the Common Article 1 obligation exists independently of any particular nexus that a State may or may not have to an armed conflict. Although none of these Resolutions are legally binding,[69] their recurring nature, combined with States' widespread acceptance of their provisions as evidenced through the overwhelming voting pattern in their favour, allows for the extraction of State practice and *opinio juris* regarding the authoritativeness of this interpretation of Common Article 1.

Common Article 1 thus offers a compelling legal basis from which to establish a Pillar 3 obligation for States to react to war crimes. However, several aspects of this obligation need to be clarified. First, Common Article 1 represents a treaty provision, and as such, could be argued to be binding only upon State parties to the Geneva Conventions. On this point, the ICJ in the *Nicaragua* case stressed that the Common Article 1 obligations '[do not] derive only from the Conventions themselves, but from the general principles of humanitarian law to which the Conventions merely give specific expression'.[70] The Court therefore held that Common Article 1 is binding upon all States regardless of their specific accession to the Geneva Conventions, a notion that is generally accepted within legal scholarship.[71] As such, it can be safely maintained that Common Article 1 establishes a universal obligation upon States to ensure respect for the rules prohibiting the commission of war crimes that derive from the Geneva Conventions.

67 Ibid., Para 163.

68 UNGA Res 45/69 (6 December 1990) UN Doc A/RES/45/69 Para 3; UNSC Res 681 (20 December 1990) UN Doc S/RES/681 Para 5; UNGA Res 58/97 (17 December 2003) UN Doc A/RES/58/97 Para 3; UNGA Res 59/122 (25 January 2005) UN Doc A/RES/59/122 Para 3; UNGA Res 64/92 (19 January 2010) UN Doc A/RES/64/92 Para 3. *See also* Report of the United Nations High Commissioner for Human Rights, 'Ensuring Accountability and Justice for all Violations of International Law in the Occupied Palestinian Territory, Including East Jerusalem' (19 March 2018) UN Doc A/HRC/37/41 Paras 40–41.

69 UNSC Resolution 681 was adopted under Chapter VI of the UN Charter and is thus recommendatory in nature. UNGA resolutions are inherently non-binding.

70 *Nicaragua* case (n14) Para 220.

71 *See* Focarelli (n61) 126–27; de Chazournes and Condorelli (n64) 70.

Following on from this point, another clarification that needs to be made with respect to the scope of Common Article 1 is that strictly speaking, it applies only to the war crimes that derive from the Geneva Conventions, namely, those contained within Articles 8(2)(a) and 8(2)(c) of the ICC Statute which identify grave and serious Geneva breaches within IACs and NIACs, respectively.[72] As such, the responsibility to 'ensure respect' may not apply to the war crimes contained within Articles 8(2)(b) and 8(2)(e) of the ICC Statute which derive from non-Geneva sources such as the Fourth Hague Convention, the two Additional Protocols to the Geneva Conventions, or customary international law.

Some arguments, however, could be made to broaden the application of Common Article 1 to all war crimes. Importantly, those war crimes that do not derive from the Geneva Conventions are defined within the ICC Statute as '[o]ther *serious* violations of the laws and customs' of war,[73] which reflects the grave nature of their breach. Additionally, as detailed in Chapter 3 of this book, many international legal scholars attribute a peremptory status to all war crimes without differentiating between their specific legal basis (i.e. Geneva or non-Geneva derived).[74] Along these lines, it would perhaps not make sense to argue that States possess an obligation to ensure respect for some of the less serious laws of war contained within the Geneva Conventions (for example, the obligation to allow people within a conflict area to give and receive news from members of their family[75]), but not for the more serious ones that have arguably attained peremptory status (for example, Hague-derived war crimes including 'attacking or bombarding' undefended towns, villages, or buildings that do not constitute military targets, as well as 'employing poison or poisoned weapons').[76] In this manner, the ICRC contends that the Common Article 1 'obligation to respect and ensure respect is not limited to the Geneva Conventions but to the entire body of international humanitarian law binding upon a particular State'.[77]

The above arguments admittedly stretch the provisions of Common Article 1 to the Geneva Conventions well beyond their literal meaning. They are also not based upon any official pronouncements that have been made through primary sources of international law. However, it is not unreasonable to predict that the scope of the Common Article 1 obligation, given the continued progression of international law in line with community interests, could expand to apply to all war crimes (for example, through the development of a customary rule to this

72 *See supra* note 59 and accompanying text. *See also* Section 3.2.2 of this book (on the categories of war crimes more generally).
73 ICC Statute (n59) Arts 8(2)(b) and 8(2)(e) (emphasis added).
74 *See* Section 3.2.2 of this book.
75 Geneva Convention III (n58) Art 25.
76 Hague Convention (IV) Respecting the Laws and Customs of War on Land and its Annex: Regulation concerning the Laws and Customs of War on Land (adopted 18 October 1907, entered into force 26 January 1910) 187 CTS 227 Arts 23 and 25; ICC Statute (n59) Arts 8(2)(b)(v) and 8(2)(b)(xvii). *Recall* from Chapter 3 of this book that the Hague-derived war crimes were described in the *Nuclear Weapons* case to constitute peremptory norms of international law.
77 'Commentary of 2016, Article 1: Respect for the Convention' (n65) Para 9.

effect). In the meantime, however, this existing gap, whereby the Common Article 1 obligation to 'ensure respect' applies to only some but not all prohibitions against war crimes, underscores the need for the development of an R2P Pillar 3 obligation. Namely, while the duty to react to mass atrocity crimes can be found in a piecemeal fashion among existing international legal norms, Pillar 3 offers the potential to establish a single umbrella obligation of reacting to all mass atrocity crimes.

Other limitations to employing Common Article 1 of the Geneva Conventions as a basis from which to work towards establishing an R2P Pillar 3 obligation are similar to those discussed in the previous section on genocide (5.2.1). First, while the obligation to ensure respect under Common Article 1 is, similar to the obligation to prevent genocide, one of conduct and not of result,[78] there are no specified means that States are expected or allowed to employ to react to violations of the Geneva Conventions.[79] The only parameter that the ICJ established in the *Construction of a Wall* case is that contracting States must ensure respect for the Geneva Conventions 'while respecting the United Nations Charter and international law'.[80] As identified in the similar analysis above regarding the ICJ's findings in the *Bosnia* case, this means that unauthorised humanitarian intervention, because it contradicts the prohibition against the use of force contained within Article 2(4) of the UN Charter, is not a valid means for ensuring respect as per Common Article 1.[81] It also, however, raises questions regarding the lawfulness of third-State countermeasures which, although not specifically permitted through the ILC's ASR, have also been argued above to constitute a means by which R2P's Pillar 3 can acquire greater enforceability.[82]

Another limitation of Common Article 1 which also came up in the discussion on genocide pertains to the need for the development of a due diligence standard that can help with attributing State responsibility for failing to ensure respect for the Geneva Conventions. As argued by Focarelli, it is highly unrealistic to assert an obligation upon every State to react to every breach of the Geneva Conventions, as this would give rise to the legal responsibility of all States for each violation of the Conventions that is not met with an international reaction.[83] In other words, if the duty to ensure respect for the provisions of the Geneva Conventions is not subject to a limiting principle, then the obligation becomes highly impractical in its enforcement. There is, however, only limited precedent on this issue: whereas

78 Ibid., Para 48. *See also* Sophie Rondeau, 'The Responsibility to Protect Doctrine, and the Duty of the International Community to Reinforce International Humanitarian Law and its Protective Value for Civilian Populations' in Richard Barnes and Vassilis Tzevelekos (eds), *Beyond Responsibility to Protect: Generating Change in International Law* (Intersentia 2016) 263.
79 *See* Marco Sassòli, 'State Responsibility for Violations of International Humanitarian Law' (2002) 84 *International Review of the Red Cross* 401, 422.
80 *Construction of a Wall* case (n66) Para 163.
81 *See also* 'Commentary of 2016, Article 1: Respect for the Convention' (n65) Para 57.
82 *See* ibid., Para 64; Sassòli (n79) 427–28.
83 Focarelli (n61) 147.

Common Article 1 has been cited to call upon third-party States to ensure respect for the Geneva Conventions,[84] it has yet to be invoked to establish the legal responsibility of a State for failing to do so.

Some guidance on this matter can perhaps be borrowed from the ICJ's *Bosnia* case, which developed a two-pronged due diligence test for attributing State responsibility for a failure to prevent genocide as per the Genocide Convention, as detailed in the previous section. While this test, as the ICJ stressed, was tailored specifically to Article 1 of the Genocide Convention, it could perhaps be used as a starting point for the development of an equal or similar due diligence standard for the obligation to ensure respect for the Geneva Conventions, and, beyond this, for a general Pillar 3 obligation for States to react to mass atrocity crimes more generally. This is critical because as it currently stands, Pillar 3 only holds legal character to the effect of the legal standing of its sub-rules, which are themselves fragmented and ambiguous. However, in order to progress to become a legal norm in itself, Pillar 3 (and R2P more generally) must acquire a legal character that speaks to the overarching framework of mass atrocity crimes. The ILC's ASR, discussed in the following section, come closer to achieving this goal for Pillar 3.

5.2.3 Article 41 of the Articles on State Responsibility

In contrast to genocide and war crimes, no similar treaty or customary provisions stipulate a responsibility of States to react to the commission of crimes against humanity or ethnic cleansing. Article 41 ASR, which articulates a positive obligation upon States to 'cooperate to bring to an end through lawful means any serious [breaches]' of peremptory norms,[85] is useful in filling at least part of this gap. Recalling from Chapter 3 of this book that the four mass atrocity crimes, although perhaps not peremptory in their entirety, have a strong basis within *jus cogens*, [86] it can be appreciated that the scope of Article 41 is relevant to the commission of mass atrocity crimes in general. This is in contrast to the obligations discussed thus far within the Genocide and Geneva Conventions, each of which address only one specific mass atrocity crime. Additionally, it should be noted that R2P situations entail 'serious' (defined in the official commentary to ASR as 'gross or systematic'[87]) violations of these norms as required to trigger Article 41 ASR. For example, genocide is committed with an 'intent' (indicating a systematic policy) to 'destroy, in whole or in part' (indicating an act which is gross or widespread). War crimes are defined as grave or *serious* breaches of the laws or customs of war. Crimes against humanity are defined as widespread or *systematic* violations against civilian populations. Ethnic cleansing, although without an official legal definition, also entails gross or systematic violations by virtue of it being aimed at changing

84 *See supra* notes 66–68 and accompanying text. *See also* 'Rule 144. Ensuring Respect for International Humanitarian Law Erga Omnes' (*ICRC*, 2016) <https://www.icrc.org/customary-ihl/eng/docs/v1_rul_rule144#refFn_11_9>.

85 ASR (n14) Art 41. *See also* Section 2.2.2 of this book.

86 *See* Section 3.2 of this book.

87 Ibid., Commentary to Art 40 Para 7.

the ethnic composition of a population, and also by virtue of it being reflective of the other three mass atrocity crimes. Taking all of the above into account, the relevance of Article 41 ASR to a potential Pillar 3 obligation to react to all mass atrocity crimes is clear.

There are some limitations, however, to the extent to which Article 41 ASR can be invoked as a basis for the emergence of a binding Pillar 3 obligation. The first pertains to its legal standing. While Chapter 2 of this book highlighted that Article 41 ASR has been invoked international case law, it was stressed that this was not in the context of affirming an obligation of States to 'cooperate to bring to an end through lawful means' serious peremptory breaches.[88] In general, there is no agreement that this Article 41 ASR obligation has attained customary status. Second, Article 41 does not stipulate what measures States can or should take to bring serious peremptory breaches to an end.[89] The provision that States should cooperate through 'lawful means' rules out the unauthorised use of force.[90] It furthermore calls into question whether third-State countermeasures can be employed to address serious *jus cogens* violations, an issue that has been thoroughly discussed in the previous two sections of this book on genocide and war crimes (5.2.1 and 5.2.2).

The final major limitation to Article 41 ASR in serving as a basis for an emerging R2P Pillar 3 obligation is that it contains no means by which to establish State responsibility for a failure to take action to end serious *jus cogens* breaches. The collective nature of the obligation (i.e. States should 'cooperate' to bring serious *jus cogens* breaches to an end) implies that it should be fulfilled through multilateral means, including but not exclusively through international institutions.[91] Article 41 does not, therefore, purport to establish an obligation upon individual States to react to serious *jus cogens* breaches.[92] However, a standard of attribution is arguably required in order to operationalise this obligation. As with the duties to prevent and react to genocide and war crimes, this comes down to the development of a clear due diligence standard by which to establish State responsibility.

5.2.4 Working towards an R2P Pillar 3 obligation

The analysis undertaken thus far on the Article 1 Genocide Convention obligation to prevent genocide, the Common Article 1 obligation to ensure respect for the Geneva Conventions, and the Article 41 ASR (emerging) obligation for States to

88 *See* Section 2.2.2 of this book.
89 ASR (n14) Commentary to Art 41 Paras 2–3. *See also* Monica Hakimi, 'Toward a Legal Theory on the Responsibility to Protect' (2014) 39 *Yale Journal of International Law* 247, 256.
90 ASR (n14) Art 50(1).
91 *See* ibid., Commentary to Art 41 Para 2; Sassòli (n79) 429–30.
92 *See* Elena Katselli, 'Commentary: R2P as a Transforming and Transformative Concept in the Context of Responsibility as Liability' in Richard Barnes and Vassilis Tzevelekos (eds), *Beyond Responsibility to Protect: Generating Change in International Law* (Intersentia 2016) 421.

cooperate to bring serious *jus cogens* breaches to an end demonstrates that although the 2005 World Summit Outcome document refrained from articulating an obligation upon third-party States to react to mass atrocity crimes (as per R2P's Pillar 3), such an obligation can nevertheless be derived in a number of limited respects through existing international legal norms. Bearing in mind international law's continued progression in line with community interests, a Pillar 3 obligation arguably represents the next stage of human rights development to which the international community should aspire. Of course, considerable obstacles exist in this respect, most notably States' rejection of a Pillar 3 obligation which would significantly expand their international legal responsibility in situations outside their immediate control and which would furthermore require them to exert substantial resources in this regard. Nevertheless, it should be recalled that major human rights advancements that emerged in the post-Charter era (in the form of multilateral human rights treaty regimes as well as customary international human rights norms), as detailed in Chapter 2 of this book,[93] were achieved with explicit State consent despite the considerable implications of these moves upon State sovereignty. It is therefore not entirely unreasonable to suggest that a Pillar 3 obligation could transpire through the future development of international law in line with the community interests of preventing and responding to mass atrocity crimes, even if such an obligation is not currently recognised as part of R2P.

Should R2P's Pillar 3 develop to attain normative status, a number of key clarifications regarding its content and scope must be established. First, the Pillar 3 obligation itself must become better defined. For example, Article 1 of the Genocide Convention calls upon States to 'prevent' genocide, while Common Article 1 to the Geneva Conventions calls upon them to 'ensure respect' for Convention provisions, while Article 41 ASR calls upon them to 'cooperate to bring to an end' serious *jus cogens* breaches. While all of these responsibilities, generally speaking, embody third-State obligations to react to some or all of the mass atrocity crimes, they undoubtedly retain differences in their scope and application. In this manner, R2P's Pillar 3 must achieve greater clarity regarding what a 'responsibility to react' actually entails.

The second major clarification that must be sought regarding an emerging Pillar 3 obligation pertains to the methods that States can or should employ to react to mass atrocity situations. Specifically, R2P has failed to propel changes with respect to the international legal framework on the use of force, meaning that non-authorised (humanitarian) intervention remains unlawful even in response to R2P cases for which the UNSC is unable to act. A potential tool for achieving greater enforceability of Pillar 3 lies in the invocation of third-State countermeasures, which would allow third-party States to take non-military action in violation of their legal duties to react to mass atrocity crimes (for example, through imposing sanctions or through failing to fulfil treaty or customary commitments). Given the uncertainty surrounding the lawfulness of third-State countermeasures, R2P's future development should advocate for the crystallisation of this right into law as well as for its official incorporation into the doctrine.

93 *See* Section 2.2 of this book.

The final major clarification that must be achieved in order to delineate the scope of R2P's Pillar 3 is that it must acquire a distinct due diligence standard by which to establish responsibility of third-party States for failing to fulfil their obligations to react. As detailed in Section 5.2.1 of this book, the ICJ developed a due diligence standard for assessing a State's responsibility for failing to discharge its Article 1 Genocide Convention obligation to prevent genocide. However, the Court made it clear in this case that this standard applies only to the obligation to prevent genocide as per the Genocide Convention. Furthermore, this due diligence standard has been criticised by scholars of international law for setting an unrealistically high threshold which makes it difficult in practice to assert the legal responsibility of States for failing to fulfil the obligation. These factors make the emergence of a due diligence standard for a Pillar 3 obligation particularly compelling.

Notwithstanding the above issues that must be addressed as a prerequisite to the development of an effective R2P Pillar 3 obligation, an equally important element in this respect lies in the UNSC's ability and the willingness to respond consistently to mass atrocity situations. The UNSC represents a key player in the implementation of R2P's Pillar 3 as the only international body that can issue binding obligations upon all UN member-States and that can authorise the use of force absent self-defence. The body has, however, at times subverted R2P's effective discharge, most particularly through the right to the veto enjoyed by the body's P5 members. The UNSC's role in the implementation of R2P's Pillar 3 is discussed in the next section, with view to identifying means of limiting or overcoming the right to the veto in mass atrocity situations.

5.3 UN Security Council

5.3.1 The permanent veto

Given the UNSC's pivotal role as the only body that can impose binding obligations upon all UN member-States as well as authorise the use of force absent self-defence, an effective Pillar 3 obligation cannot be fully achieved without addressing and enhancing the body's response mechanism to mass atrocity crimes. Most significant in this respect is the permanent veto enjoyed by the UNSC's P5 – the US, UK, France, Russia, and China[94] – and its potential to entirely obstruct the UNSC's ability to engage with a particular mass atrocity situation. This section undertakes an analysis of some of the legal issues associated with the permanent veto and suggests how they can or should be addressed as a prerequisite to achieving R2P's efficient and consistent application.

The right to the permanent veto is incorporated into Article 27 of the UN Charter, which states that '[d]ecisions of the Security Council [on non-procedural matters] shall be made by an affirmative vote of nine members *including the concurring votes of*

94 Charter of the United Nations (adopted 24 October 1945) 1 UNTS XVI Art 10 [hereinafter UN Charter].

the permanent members'.[95] This means that should any of the P5 vote against (veto) a UNSC draft resolution, then this resolution fails to pass, even if it enjoys the support of all remaining UNSC member-States.[96] This effectively subjects the UNSC's response to mass atrocity situations to the support, or at least the acquiescence, of all P5 members, which is often difficult to attain given the inherently divergent national interests entertained by some of these powers. The Syrian R2P situation, discussed further in Chapter 7 of this book, is a tragic case in point, in which the UNSC's response to the ongoing atrocities was effectively grounded to a halt as a result of Russian, and to a lesser extent Chinese, vetoes.[97] This situation resonates heavily with that of Kosovo in the 1990s, in which the threat of the Russian veto paralysed the UNSC from taking appropriate action in response to the ethnic cleansing that was being perpetrated by Serb forces against Kosovar Albanians.[98] The result was that NATO forces circumvented the UNSC entirely and conducted unauthorised bombing against Yugoslavia, which tilted the balance of power away from the Serbs and ultimately paved the way for the creation of an independent State of Kosovo. R2P emerged as a direct response to the legal dilemma that presented itself in this situation, although, as discussed below, it seems that the doctrine has yet to overcome this very obstacle for which it was created to address.

Importantly, the right to the veto as stipulated under Article 27 of the UN Charter is not subject to any relevant limitations, implying that it can be exercised by the P5 without constraint.[99] Even more, formally amending the Charter to eliminate or limit the veto power ironically requires, as per Article 108, the support of the P5 themselves as part of a two-thirds majority vote within the UNGA.[100] As such, strong opposition by the P5 members (with the exception of France, as discussed below) has been sufficient to obstruct initiatives to formally curtail the right to the veto in mass atrocity situations or to otherwise reform the UNSC to make it more representative and/or democratic (for example, through increasing the body's membership).[101] For

95 Ibid., Art 27 (emphasis added).

96 With the exception of UNSC draft resolutions dealing with procedural issues, as discussed in Section 5.3.2.1 of this book.

97 *See* Section 7.2, and in particular Section 7.2.2 of this book.

98 On the Kosovo example, *see* Bruno Simma, 'NATO, the UN and the Use of Force: Legal Aspects' (1999) 10 *European Journal of International Law* 1; Louis Henkin, 'Kosovo and the Law of "Humanitarian Intervention"' (1999) 93 *American Journal of International Law* 824.

99 Article 27 of the UN Charter only specifies that 'in decisions under Chapter VI, and under paragraph 3 of Article 52, a party to a dispute shall abstain from voting'. This does not, however, apply to decisions taken under Chapter VII of the UN Charter. UN Charter (n94) Art 27. *See also* Andrew J. Carswell, 'Unblocking the UN Security Council: The Uniting for Peace Resolution' (2013) 18 *Journal of Conflict and Security Law* 453, 470.

100 UN Charter (n94) Art 108.

101 For an overview of some of these initiatives, *see* Graham Melling and Anne Dennett, 'The Security Council Veto and Syria: Responding to Mass Atrocities through the "Uniting for Peace" Resolution' (2017) 57 *Indian Journal of International Law* 285, 294–97. On reform of the UNSC, *see* UNGA, 'Follow-up to the Outcome of the Millennium Summit' (2 December 2004) UN Doc A/59/565 Paras 244–57.

example, the 2001 ICISS report recommended a 'code of conduct' whereby permanent members would at least abstain from voting on R2P situations unless their vital national interests were at stake.[102] This proposal was met with disapproval from the P5 and was thus excluded from the 2005 consensus on R2P as embodied in the World Summit Outcome document.[103] Similarly, a draft resolution was put forward in the UNGA in 2012 by a group of five States (Costa Rica, Jordan, Lichtenstein, Singapore, and Switzerland) calling upon the UNSC to consider a number of modifications to its working methods, including those pertaining to the use of the veto in R2P situations.[104] However, this draft resolution was rescinded due to political pressure by the P5.[105] Another attempt was made in 2013 by France (significant in that France is itself a permanent member), which called upon the P5 to 'voluntarily regulate their right to exercise their veto' in R2P situations and thus to modify the working methods of the UNSC through a 'mutual commitment' rather than through a formal amendment to the UN Charter.[106] This measure too, however, failed to gain traction. Therefore, despite several attempts to limit the use of the veto in R2P situations, there remain no formal or informal restrictions to its invocation.

Notwithstanding the above, Judge Alvarez recognised as early as 1950 the potential for the veto power to be abused, and he thus argued in his dissenting opinion to the *Competence* case that 'the exercise of this right of veto must be kept within proper limits'.[107] More recently, and in the context of R2P, an argument has emerged among international legal scholars in favour of a 'responsibility not to veto', namely, a responsibility of the UNSC's P5 to refrain from exercising their veto power in R2P situations unless this conflicts with their vital national interests.[108] Carswell, for example, makes a compelling case that the veto can constitute a breach of the good faith requirement stipulated by Article 2(2) of the UN Charter, in which States must 'fulfil in good faith the obligations assumed by them in accordance with the present Charter'.[109] In this respect, one of the listed purposes of the UN under Article 1 of the Charter is the maintenance of international peace and

102 2001 ICISS Report (n2) Para 6.21.

103 *See* Alicia L. Bannon, 'The Responsibility to Protect: The U.N. World Summit and the Question of Unilateralism' (2005–2006) 115 *Yale Law Journal* 1157, 1160.

104 UNGA Draft Resolution (3 May 2012) UN Doc A/66/L.42/Rev.1, Annex Paras 19–21.

105 *See* Theresa Reinold, 'The "Responsibility Not to Veto", Secondary Rules, and the Rule of Law' (2014) 6 *Global Responsibility to Protect* 269, 285–86.

106 Laurent Fabius, 'A Call for Self-Restraint at the U.N.' (*New York Times*, 4 October 2013) <http://www.nytimes.com/2013/10/04/opinion/a-call-for-self-restraint-at-the-un.html>.

107 *Competence of the General Assembly for the Admission of a State to the United Nations* (Dissenting Opinion of Judge Alvarez) [1950] ICJ Rep 12, 20. *See also* Michael Byers, 'Abuse of Rights: An Old Principle, A New Age' (2002) 47 *McGill Law Journal* 389 (providing an overview of the notion of abuse of rights under international law).

108 On the responsibility not to veto, *see* Ariela Blätter and Paul D. Williams, 'The Responsibility Not to Veto' (2011) 3 *Global Responsibility to Protect* 301; Heieck RN2V Revisited (n40).

109 UN Charter (n94) Art 2(2); Carswell (n99) 470.

security,[110] a responsibility that is primarily entrusted to the UNSC as per Article 24(1).[111] Putting together Articles 1, 2, and 24 of the UN Charter, therefore, Carswell maintains that the P5 are under an obligation to discharge their responsibility to maintain international peace and security in good faith. The relevance of R2P in this scenario is that UNSC resolutions that invoke the doctrine in context-specific situations almost necessarily reference a threat to or breach of international peace and security, as can be seen, for example, in R2P resolutions on Libya,[112] Darfur,[113] Côte d'Ivoire,[114] South Sudan,[115] Mali,[116] and the Central African Republic.[117]

Another potential legal argument in favour of a responsibility not to veto lies in Article 41 ASR (which, as detailed in Section 2.2.2 of this book, has been invoked in international case law although it is not yet recognised to be conclusively binding). Recalling that R2P situations almost necessarily entail serious breaches of *jus cogens* norms,[118] Article 41 in effect calls upon States to take collective action to bring these situations to an end, including, for example, through the UNSC. While cooperation outside the UNSC may be sufficient in bringing an end to R2P situations (and hence, UNSC inaction in such cases would not entail a violation of Article 41 ASR), the UNSC, as the only body that can adopt binding obligations upon all UN member-States as well as authorise the use of force absent self-defence, undoubtedly bears a significant degree of responsibility in this regard.

Peters argues that the exercise of a veto would lie contrary to Article 41 ASR if the UNSC draft resolution in question represents the only means by which an R2P situation can be resolved.[119] While there is value to this suggestion, there are nevertheless significant evidential difficulties with establishing that a certain UNSC draft resolution constitutes, as she writes, the 'only means to bring an end to R2P crimes and violations'.[120] It notably sets a high threshold for invoking the responsibility of P5 member-States which is difficult to assert in practice. Instead, it is proposed that the P5, in order to be in compliance with (the emerging) Article 41 ASR and with their good faith obligations under Articles 1, 2, and 24 of

110 UN Charter (n94) Art 1.
111 Ibid., Art 24(1).
112 *See* UNSC Res 1973 (17 March 2011) UN Doc S/RES/1973 Preamble.
113 *See* UNSC Res 1706 (31 August 2006) UN Doc S/RES/1706 Preamble, Para 12; UNSC Res 1755 (30 April 2007) UN Doc S/RES/1755 Preamble.
114 *See* UNSC Res 1975 (30 March 2011) UN Doc S/RES/1975 Preamble.
115 *See* UNSC Res 2057 (5 July 2012) UN Doc S/RES/2057 Preamble, Para 4; UNSC Res 2155 (27 May 2014) UN Doc S/RES/2155 Preamble.
116 *See* UNSC Res 2085 (20 December 2012) UN Doc S/RES/2085 Preamble, Paras 9 and 17.
117 *See* UNSC Res 2127 (5 December 2013) UN Doc S/RES/2127 Preamble, Para 21; UNSC Res 2134 (28 January 2014) UN Doc S/RES/2134 Preamble; UNSC Res 2149 (10 April 2014) UN Doc S/RES/2149 Preamble, Para 30.
118 *See* Sections 3.2 and 5.2.3 of this book.
119 Anne Peters, 'The Security Council's Responsibility to Protect' (2011) 8 *International Organizations Law Review* 1, 24.
120 Ibid.

the UN Charter, should refrain from vetoing a UNSC draft resolution addressing an R2P situation unless they can offer compelling evidence that they are pursuing alternative means of responding to the situation that are at least as likely to be as effective as the measures proposed by the draft resolution.[121] This can be paired with an after-the-fact assessment of the situation – bearing in mind White's observation that the 'continued commission of core crimes' following the use of a veto is a primary indicator that this veto '[constituted] a dereliction of the duty to protect placed on the UNSC by R2P' – to ascertain legal responsibility, if any, that falls upon vetoing States.[122]

Overall, although the right of the P5 to invoke the permanent veto is not specifically qualified within the UN Charter, and although a formal amendment to restrict its use is nearly impossible to achieve, some arguments in favour of a responsibility not to veto in R2P situations can nevertheless be advanced through existing international legal norms as embodied within Articles 1, 2, and 24 of the UN Charter, as well as through the emerging Article 41 ASR. With that said, however, it must be conceded that there exists no mechanism of accountability that can hold the P5 to account regarding abusive invocations of the veto, nor has such an attempt been made to assert the legal responsibility of one or more of the P5 members for exercising vetoes that obstructed UNSC action in the context of an R2P situation.[123] Nevertheless, overcoming the veto power in R2P situations is crucial if the doctrine is ever to attain full functionality, as it is difficult to see how a Pillar 3 responsibility can be consistently discharged if the UNSC maintains business as usual. One alternative may lie in the identification of means by which States and/or international organisations can circumvent the UNSC (including through the pursuit of force) when the body is paralysed from taking action in response to a mass atrocity situation. The 2001 ICISS report identifies two such potential routes which are discussed in the following section.

5.3.2 Alternatives to the UN Security Council

5.3.2.1 Uniting for Peace mechanism

The first potential means identified within the 2001 ICISS report for circumventing the UNSC when the body is paralysed from responding to R2P situations is the

121 *See* Nigel D. White, 'Commentary: International Institutions and their Role in R2P' in Richard Barnes and Vassilis Tzevelekos (eds), *Beyond Responsibility to Protect: Generating Change in International Law* (Intersentia 2016) 150.

122 Ibid.

123 *See* John Quigley, 'State Responsibility for Ethnic Cleansing' (1999) 32 *University of California Davis Law Review* 341, 377. Bosnia entertained serious thought to instituting proceedings in the ICJ against the UK for failing to prevent genocide (presumably, due to its exercise of the veto against the lifting of the arms embargo), although this was not pursued. *See* 'Letter Dated 24 November 1993 from the Permanent Representative of Bosnia and Herzegovina to the United Nations Addressed to the Secretary-General' (26 November 1993) UN Doc A/48/659; Mark Toufayan, 'The World Court's Distress When Facing Genocide: A Critical Commentary on the *Application of the Genocide Convention Case (Bosnia and Herzegovina v. Yugoslavia (Serbia and Montenegro))*' (2005) 40 *Texas International Law Journal* 233, 241.

Uniting for Peace Resolution (UNGA Resolution 377),[124] which was adopted in 1950 by a vote of 52–5 against the backdrop of continuous Soviet vetoes on the situation in Korea.[125] The purpose of Uniting for Peace (UforP) is to facilitate international action when the UNSC is paralysed – because of the veto – from responding to a situation that threatens or breaches international peace and security.[126] Essentially, it allows for the referral of any matter pertaining to international peace and security (inclusive of R2P situations[127]) from the UNSC to the UNGA if the UNSC is unable to exercise its primary responsibility in this regard due to a 'lack of unanimity of the [UNSC] permanent members' (i.e. one or more permanent members block the adoption of a draft resolution through the exercise of a veto).[128] This is to be distinguished from situations in which a draft resolution fails to be adopted due to insufficient support within the UNSC – namely, that it does not garner the minimum nine required affirmative votes – in which case UforP would not be applicable. The referral of a situation from the UNSC to the UNGA can occur through either a UNSC procedural vote, which requires the support of nine UNSC member-States and for which there is no right to the veto,[129] or through a simple UNGA majority vote. Following such a referral, the UNGA can issue recommendations for collective measures, including for the use of force where there is a 'breach of the peace or act of aggression', through a two-thirds majority vote.[130] Through this mechanism, UforP offers a potential means of overcoming UNSC paralysis (due to the veto) in R2P situations.

Although UforP assumes the form of a UNGA resolution (meaning that it is inherently non-binding), Carswell rightly maintains that it does not confer new powers upon the UNGA, but rather '[reveals] the latent potential of the Assembly already residing within the UN Charter'.[131] In other words, a close examination of the UforP Resolution confirms that its provisions largely derive from the UN Charter and thus do not, in the strictest sense, represent 'new' law. Rather, UforP repackages existing rules within the UN Charter and consolidates them into an identified procedure for facilitating international action in response to situations that threaten or breach international peace and security – including, importantly, R2P situations – when UNSC action is not forthcoming due to the veto. This can be appreciated through a nuanced overview of the UforP Resolution and the UN Charter provisions from which it derives.

The first aspect of UforP, namely, the referral of a situation that threatens international peace and security from the UNSC to the UNGA, derives from

124 2001 ICISS Report (n2) Para 6.29.
125 UNGA Res 377(V) (3 November 1950) UN Doc A/RES/377 Para 1.
126 *See* Carswell (n99) 455.
127 *See supra* notes 112–117 and accompanying text.
128 UN Doc A/RES/377 (n125) Para 1.
129 *See infra* notes 134–135 and accompanying text for more information on the procedural vote.
130 UN Doc A/RES/377 (n125) Para 1.
131 Carswell (n99) 476. *See also* Juraj Andrassy, 'Uniting for Peace' (1956) 50 *American Journal of International Law* 563, 572.

Articles 20, 27, and 18 of the UN Charter. Article 20 states in general terms that '[s]pecial sessions [of the UNGA] can be convoked by the Secretary-General at the request of the Security Council or of a majority of the Members of the United Nations'.[132] The two means identified within this Article through which to convene a UNGA special session – namely, through a UNSC request or UNGA majority vote – reflect the two mechanisms of referring a situation from the UNSC to the UNGA under UforP. As for the former, the UNSC can issue a request for the convocation of a UNGA special session through a procedural vote as per Article 27(2) UN Charter.[133] In contrast to a non-procedural UNSC vote described in Article 27(3), which requires 'the concurring votes of the permanent members'[134] (i.e. in which a negative vote by any one of the P5 member-States would veto and hence defeat the draft resolution in question), a procedural vote simply requires an 'affirmative vote of [nine] members' and hence does not include a right to the veto.[135] It is commonly accepted that the referral of a situation from the UNSC to the UNGA, and more specifically the convocation of a UNGA special session, represents a procedural matter for the UNSC.[136]

The second means of referring a situation to the UNGA as per UforP, namely, a UNGA majority vote, also holds support from the UN Charter. Article 20, as mentioned above, allows for the convening of a UNGA special session 'at the request ... of a majority of the Members of the United Nations'. Given that the UNGA is the only UN body in which all member-States are represented, Article 20 essentially requires a UNGA majority vote in order to convene a UNGA special session, thus mirroring the second means of referring a situation to the UNGA under UforP. Also relevant in this respect is Article 18(3) UN Charter, which states that UNGA decisions on questions that are not deemed 'important' require 'a majority [vote] of the members present and voting'.[137] Neither the referral of a matter from the UNSC to the UNGA nor the calling for a UNGA special session are considered to qualify as 'important questions',[138] and hence the application of this provision.

Following the referral of a situation from the UNSC to the UNGA, UforP stipulates that the UNGA can issue recommendations for member-States to respond, including through the use of force where there is aggression or a breach of the peace, through a two-thirds majority vote.[139] The UNGA's right to issue such recommendations can be gleaned from Article 18(2) of the Charter, which states

132 UN Charter (n94) Art 20.
133 Ibid., Art 27(2).
134 Ibid., Art 27(3).
135 Article 27(2) originally stipulated that a UNSC procedural vote requires an affirmative vote of seven members. However, following the UNSC's expansion in 1965, this was changed to nine votes.
136 *See* Sydney D. Bailey, 'Veto in the Security Council' (1968) 37 *International Conciliation* 1, 16.
137 UN Charter (n94) Art 18(3).
138 Examples of 'important questions' are listed within Article 18(2) UN Charter.
139 UN Doc A/RES/377 (n125) Para 1.

that '[d]ecisions of the General Assembly on important questions shall be made by a two-thirds majority of the members present and voting'.[140] This Article specifies that 'recommendations with respect to the maintenance of international peace and security' represent 'important questions' for the UNGA, hence mirroring UforP's recommendations procedure.

Article 11(2) UN Charter is also instructive in this respect, stipulating that the UNGA 'may make recommendations' on 'questions relating to the maintenance of international peace and security … except as provided in Article 12'.[141] Article 12 states that 'the General Assembly shall not make any recommendation with regard to [a] dispute or situation' if the UNSC is 'exercising in respect of [this] dispute or situation the functions assigned to it in the present Charter … unless the Security Council so requests'.[142] Essentially, these Articles allow the UNGA to make recommendations on issues pertaining to international peace and security if the UNSC is not actively seized of these issues or if the UNSC otherwise requests such a recommendation from the UNGA.

Further clarification regarding the scope of Articles 11(2) and 12 of the UN Charter was offered in the ICJ's *Construction of a Wall* case. Here, the Court noted that Article 12 of the UN Charter was traditionally 'interpreted and applied … to the effect that the Assembly could not make a recommendation on a question concerning the maintenance of international peace and security while the matter remained on the Council's agenda'.[143] This would theoretically prevent the UNGA from issuing recommendations on R2P situations as per UforP if they technically remain on the UNSC agenda. However, the Court went on to clarify that such an interpretation of Article 12 'has evolved' and that 'there has been an increasing tendency … for the General Assembly and the Security Council to deal in parallel with the same matter concerning the maintenance of international peace and security'.[144] Therefore, as highlighted by Simma, the UNGA 'has adopted the practice of making recommendations on issues with which the [UNSC is] itself dealing quite actively',[145] meaning that the UNGA is not necessarily precluded from dealing with issues pertaining to international peace and security – or, similarly, with R2P situations – concurrently with the UNSC.

The analysis conducted thus far affirms the UNGA's general competence to make recommendations on issues pertaining to international peace and security – including, as relevant to this chapter, in R2P situations. However, the nature of such recommendations remains contentious, specifically whether it can include a

140 UN Charter (n94) Art 18(2). Importantly, as per Rule 86 of the UN's rules of procedure, 'the phrase "members present and voting" means members casting an affirmative or negative vote. Members which abstain from voting are considered as not voting.' 'Rules of Procedure' (*General Assembly of the United Nations*) <http://www.un.org/en/ga/about/ropga/plenary.shtml>.

141 UN Charter (n94) Art 11(2).

142 Ibid., Art 12(1).

143 *Construction of a Wall* case (n66) Para 27.

144 Ibid.

145 Bruno Simma, *The Charter of the United Nations: A Commentary*, vol. I (2nd edn, Oxford University Press 2002) 290.

call for the use of force which would seemingly contradict the UN Charter's Article 2(4) prohibition against force save self-defence or UNSC authorisation. On this issue, Article 11(2) of the UN Charter states that any 'question on which action is necessary shall be referred to the Security Council',[146] which some authors interpret as precluding the UNGA from recommending force even in situations (e.g. R2P situations) in which the UNSC is paralysed from taking any appropriate action.[147] Orakhelashvili, for example, argues that '[w]hen the Council fails to act, no other organ can serve as its surrogate'.[148] Dinstein similarly rejects the UNGA's competence to recommend force absent UNSC authorisation, insisting that at most, the UNGA can only affirm an already-existing right of self-defence.[149] Other authors allude to the wording of the UforP Resolution, which allows the UNGA to make only 'recommendations', but not 'authorisations', for the use of force.[150] They argue, therefore, that UNGA recommendations for the use of force fail to impart lawfulness upon such action. Still others point out that while eleven resolutions have been adopted under UforP to recommend a range of non-military measures[151] – including calling upon parties to cease the use of force,[152] condemning acts of intervention,[153] establishing humanitarian efforts,[154] demanding that States abide by UNSC resolutions,[155] calling upon States to impose sanctions,[156] and seeking an advisory opinion from the ICJ[157] – the mechanism has never been invoked to recommend force. This, they maintain, is indicative of the UNGA's lack of authority to do so.

146 UN Charter (n94) Art 11(2).
147 *See* Dominik Zaum, 'The Security Council, the General Assembly, and War: The Uniting for Peace Resolution' in Vaughan Lowe et al. (eds), *The United Nations Security Council and War* (Oxford University Press 2008) 158; Hans Kelsen, *The Law of the United Nations: A Critical Analysis of its Fundamental Problems* (Frederick A. Praeger 2011) 205; Alexander Orakhelashvili, *Collective Security* (Oxford University Press 2011) 48–49; Yoram Dinstein, *War, Aggression and Self-Defence* (4th edn, Cambridge University Press 2005) 317–18.
148 Orakhelashvili (n147) 48–49.
149 Dinstein (n147) 317–18.
150 *See* James E. Hickey Jr, 'Challenges to Security Council Monopoly Power over the Use of Force in Enforcement Actions: The Case of Regional Organizations' (2004) 10 *Ius Gentium* 77, 97–98.
151 *See* 'Emergency Special Sessions' (*General Assembly of the United Nations*) <http://www.un.org/en/ga/sessions/emergency.shtml>; 'Security Council Deadlocks and Uniting for Peace: An Abridged History' (*Security Council Report*, October 2013) <https://www.securitycouncilreport.org/atf/cf/%7B65BFCF9B-6D27-4E9C-8CD3-CF6E4FF96FF9%7D/Security_Council_Deadlocks_and_Uniting_for_Peace.pdf>.
152 UNGA Res 997 (ES-1) (2 November 1956) UN Doc A/RES/997(ES-1).
153 UNGA Res 1004 (ES-II) (4 November 1956) UN Doc A/RES/1004(ES-II).
154 UNGA Res 1006 (ES-II) (9 November 1956) UN Doc A/RES/1006(ES-II); UNGA Res 1474 (ES-IV) (20 September 1960) UN Doc A/RES/1474(ES-IV) Para 4; UNGA Res 2252(ES-V) (4 July 1967) UN Doc A/RES/2252(ES-V).
155 UN Doc A/RES/1474(ES-IV) (n154) Para 5.
156 UNGA Res ES-9/1 (5 February 1982) UN Doc A/RES/ES-9/1.
157 UNGA Res ES-10/14 (12 December 2003) UN Doc A/RES/ES-10/14.

However, further analysis of Article 11(2) of the UN Charter reveals that the UNGA is not precluded from recommending the use of force upon its consideration of a matter pertaining to international peace and security. Importantly, it should be clarified that the term 'action' within this Article refers to binding and mandatory decisions that member-States are obligated to carry out, which lies within the UNSC's exclusive competency.[158] This receives support from the ICJ's *Expenses* case, in which the Court stated that 'only the Security Council … can require enforcement by coercive action' and that the UNSC's right to authorise 'action' means that it can 'impose an explicit obligation of compliance'.[159] On the Article 11(2) provision that any 'question on which action is necessary shall be referred to the Security Council', the ICJ affirmed that '[this provision] has no application where the necessary action is not enforcement action'.[160]

The ICJ's interpretation of the term 'action' in the *Expenses* case resonates with Article 25 of the UN Charter in which member-States 'agree to accept and carry out the decisions of the Security Council', indicating their mandatory and binding nature.[161] It also reflects the original intention of the Charter manifested in Articles 42 and 43 that the UNSC would be able to adopt binding decisions for the use of force under Chapter VII and that it would have a standing army under its control to oversee the implementation of such decisions.[162] Although the UNSC has historically 'authorised' rather than 'decided' the use of force, this interpretation of the two Articles remains sound. The UNSC's exclusive right to authorise 'action' is therefore contrasted with the UNGA's right to issue 'recommendations' on issues pertaining to international peace and security, which are commonly understood to represent mere suggestions that States can voluntarily act upon or ignore.[163] Hence, a UNGA recommendation for the use of force would not constitute a call for 'action' (i.e. a binding and mandatory call upon States to use force), and therefore would not be in violation of Article 11(2) of the Charter.

A final point that must be clarified is how a UNGA recommendation for the use of force under UforP can be reconciled with what many authors agree to be a *jus cogens* prohibition against the use of force.[164] Carswell suggests that the UNSC's power to

158 *See* Harry Reicher, 'The Uniting for Peace Resolution on the Thirtieth Anniversary of its Passage' (1981) 20 *Columbia Journal of Transnational Law* 1, 28–29.

159 *Certain Expenses of the United Nations* (Advisory Opinion) [1962] ICJ Rep 151, 163 [hereinafter *Expenses* case]. *See also* Carswell (n99) 473–74; Nigel D. White, 'The Legality of Bombing in the Name of Humanity' (2000) 5 *Journal of Conflict and Security Law* 27, 39 [hereinafter White Legality of Bombing].

160 *Expenses* case (n159) 165.

161 UN Charter (n94) Art 25.

162 *See Expenses* case (n159) 166–67; Christine Gray, 'The Charter Limitations on the Use of Force: Theory and Practice: The Evolution of Thought and Practice since 1945' in Vaughan Lowe et al. (eds), *The United Nations Security Council and War* (Oxford University Press 2008) 87–88.

163 *See* Reicher (n158) 17, 28; Andrassy (n131) 567–68; Simma (n145) 283.

164 *See*, for example, *Legal Consequences of the Construction of a Wall in the Occupied Palestinian Territory* (Separate Opinion of Judge Elaraby) [2004] ICJ Rep 246, 254; Bruno Simma and Philip Alston, 'The Sources of Human Rights Law: Custom, Jus

authorise force under Chapter VII is not subsumed within Article 2(4) of the Charter, but exists separately to it.[165] He notes that the wording of Article 2(4) prohibits the use of force by 'Members' of the UN, but not the 'Organisation' (as written in Articles 2 (1) and 2(6)). He also points to the wording of Article 42 of the UN Charter which attributes the use force to the UNSC and not to individual member-States. Hence, Carswell argues that a recommendation for the use of force by the UNGA, which is regulated by Articles 10–12 of the Charter and supplemented by UforP, would similarly be attributable to the UN and not to individual member-States, and hence would not violate the Article 2(4) prohibition against the use of force.

The difficulty with the above interpretation, however, is that it could be used to legitimise force authorised by any regional or international organisation under the premise that such force would be attributable to the authorising organisation but not to individual member-States. This, however, is contrary to the spirit of the UN Charter which sought to limit the use of force to a set of highly defined circumstances. Instead, as noted by White, given that the UNSC authorises military force on behalf of the UN as a whole (as per Article 24 of the Charter), then 'the exceptions to the ban on force are those undertaken in legitimate self-defence and those authorized by the *United Nations*'.[166] White therefore clarifies that UNGA authorisation does not require the creation of a third exception to the non-use of force, but is rather subsumed within the UNSC's right to authorise force under its Chapter VII powers.

White's arguments gain support upon closer scrutiny of UN Charter provisions addressing the use of force. To begin, it is worth examining the precise prohibition articulated under Article 2(4):

> All Members shall refrain in their international relations from the threat or use of force against the territorial integrity or political independence of any state, or in any other manner inconsistent with the Purposes of the United Nations.[167]

It is important to note here that Article 2(4) does not specify that the use of force is prohibited with the exceptions of self-defence and UNSC Chapter VII authorisation. It rather presents an all-encompassing prohibition against the use of force, and it is only through a holistic reading of the Charter that the exceptions of self-defence and UNSC authorisation emerge. Even when these exceptions are mentioned in Articles 51 and 42, respectively, they are not directly linked to Article 2(4). For example, Article 51 merely states that '[n]othing in the present Charter shall impair the inherent right of individual or collective self-defence',[168] and Article 42 allows the UNSC to 'take such action by air, sea, or land forces as

Cogens, and General Principles' (1988–1989) 12 *Australian Yearbook of International Law* 82, 103.

165 Carswell (n99) 461. *See also* Michael Ramsden, '"Uniting for Peace" and Humanitarian Intervention: The Authorising Function of the U.N. General Assembly' (2016) 25 *Washington International Law Journal* 267, 284–85.

166 White Legality of Bombing (n159) 39–40.

167 UN Charter (n94) Art 2(4).

168 Ibid., Art 51.

may be necessary to maintain or restore international peace and security'.[169] Therefore, while legal scholarship has routinely maintained that the Article 2(4) prohibition against the use of force has two exceptions of self-defence and UNSC authorisation, the reality is that these rules are not spelled out as such within the UN Charter. Instead, they have been identified through an integrated reading of the Charter, whereby the rules pertaining to the use of force have been interconnected to yield the currently accepted framework. In the process, however, it seems that the supplementary role of the UNGA in maintaining international peace and security has been relegated. Nevertheless, as per the analysis conducted in this section, it becomes clear that the UN Charter does indeed support the UNGA's right to recommend the use of force as per UforP, and that this is fully consistent with Article 2(4).

In addition to being lawful, it is also important to point out that any international mobilisation in R2P situations stemming from UforP would furthermore enjoy a high degree of legitimacy. First, UforP requires a high threshold for invocation, namely, a UNSC procedural vote or a UNGA majority vote to refer a situation to the UNGA, followed by a two-thirds UNGA majority vote in order to issue specific recommendations. Attaining such a level of State consensus can presumably be achieved only in the most compelling situations. Second, it is expected that any use of force undertaken pursuant to UforP would stem from a defined mandate (in the form of a UNGA recommendation) which would likely specify a clear purpose as well as limitations for the use of force. This is in contrast to unauthorised humanitarian intervention – traditionally invoked as the default solution to overcoming UNSC paralysis in R2P cases – which is both unlawful and prone to abuse.[170] Finally, UforP's historically limited use – employed only 11 times since its adoption in 1950[171] – highlights that its invocation has been confined to the most exceptional situations in which the UNSC was paralysed from acting, and that it has not otherwise created a substantial challenge to what may constitute legitimate uses of the veto or to the UNSC's primary responsibility for the maintenance of international peace and security.[172]

UforP thus offers both a lawful and legitimate means of responding to R2P situations in which the UNSC is paralysed due to the veto, all the while preserving the international legal framework pertaining to the use of force. Although the mechanism has yet to be invoked in the context of recommending the use of force, it confers the potential to bring about such a robust response if required. As such, it is argued that UforP presents a compelling tool that should be revived as a means of further developing R2P, most particularly to address R2P situations in which the UNSC is paralysed from acting. This point becomes especially important when considering the Syrian case which is discussed in Chapter 7 of this book.

169 Ibid., Art 42.
170 *See* Ramsden (n165) 277–78. *See also* Carswell (n99) 465.
171 *See supra* notes 151–157.
172 *See* Carswell (n99) 476–77.

5.3.2.2 Regional authorisation

The second means identified within the 2001 ICISS report to circumvent the UNSC when the body is paralysed from responding to an R2P situation is through 'collective intervention ... by a regional or sub-regional organization'.[173] The proximity of regional organisations to mass atrocity situations suggests that they are well-positioned to understand their context and dynamics and to gauge the most effective means of responding to them.[174] Regional players also tend to feel the more immediate effects of such situations (for example, through the spill-over of violence or through the flow of refugees across borders), and thus hold greater incentives to ensure that they are effectively dealt with.[175] For these reasons, regional organisations were deemed in the 2001 ICISS report to represent appropriate and legitimate actors to take action – including forceful action – in R2P cases that witness UNSC paralysis.

However, the prevailing view under international law is that military intervention by regional organisations absent UNSC authorisation is unlawful.[176] This is supported by a plain text reading of Article 53 of the UN Charter which states that 'no enforcement action shall be taken under regional arrangements or by regional agencies without the authorization of the Security Council'.[177] While regional organisations have on several occasions engaged in unauthorised military interventions, including those which received *ex post facto* approval by the UNSC, such interventions were not without legal controversy even if they were deemed morally legitimate.[178] Even the 2001 ICISS report concedes that 'the letter of the

173 2001 ICISS Report (n2) Para 6.31.

174 *See* Jason Dominguez Meyer, 'From Paralysis in Rwanda to Boldness in Libya: Has the International Community Taken "Responsibility to Protect" from Abstract Principle to Concrete Norm under International Law?' (2011–2012) 34 *Houston Journal of International Law* 87, 99.

175 Ibid.

176 *See*, for example, ibid., 99, 107; Hickey (n150) 137; Zsuzsanna Deen-Racsmány, 'A Redistribution of Authority between the UN and Regional Organizations in the Field of the Maintenance of Peace and Security?' (2000) 13 *Leiden Journal of International Law* 297, 304.

177 UN Charter (n94) Art 53. The previous section noted that the UNSC's exclusive right to authorise 'action' refers to binding and mandatory decisions that UN member-States are obligated to carry out. This, it was detailed, does not preclude the UNGA from recommending force through its residual responsibility to maintain international peace and security under the UN Charter. A similar argument, however, cannot be extended to regional organisations given that even a recommendation by a regional organisation for the use of force would contradict the Article 2(4) *jus cogens* prohibition, which, it was noted, precludes the use of force with the exceptions of self-defence and authorisation by the UN as a whole. *See supra* notes 158–163 and 166 and accompanying paragraphs.

178 For example, Cuba in 1962 by the Organization of American States, Lebanon by the League of Arab States in 1976, Grenada in 1983 by the Organization of Eastern Caribbean States, Liberia in 1992 by the Economic Community of West African States (ECOWAS), Kosovo by NATO in 1999, and the Gambia by ECOWAS in 2017. *See* Hickey (n150) 105–19; Monica Hakimi, 'To Condone or Condemn? Regional

Charter requires action by regional organizations always to be subject to prior authorisation from the Security Council',[179] implying the inherent unlawfulness of unauthorised interventions by regional organisations even if employed, for example, to address an R2P situation.

An emerging challenge to this established legal framework lies in Article 4(h) of the African Union's (AU) Constitutive Act (adopted in 2000), which permits the AU to 'intervene in a Member State pursuant to a decision of the Assembly in respect of grave circumstances, namely: war crimes, genocide and crimes against humanity'.[180] Essentially, this Article confers a right upon the AU to intervene militarily in its member-States to respond to R2P situations (with the exception of ethnic cleansing, which is not stipulated under this Article) even if UNSC authorisation is not forthcoming. Unsurprisingly, however, it has elicited significant controversy among international legal scholars.

For example, it is questionable whether Article 4(h) of the Constitutive Act can hold against Articles 2(4) and 53 of the UN Charter, which prohibit the use of force in general and by regional organisations in particular absent UNSC authorisation or self-defence.[181] It is furthermore commonly accepted that Article 2(4) of the Charter embodies a peremptory norm of international law,[182] which could have the effect of voiding Article 4(h) (and even the wider Constitutive Act) as per Article 53 of the Vienna Convention on the Law of Treaties, which states that a treaty is 'void if ... it conflicts with' a *jus cogens* norm.[183] Also relevant is Article 103 of the UN Charter, which stipulates that '[i]n the event of a conflict between the obligations of the Members of the United Nations under the present Charter and their obligations under any other international agreement, their obligations under the present Charter shall prevail'.[184]

Kioko, a former legal advisor to the AU, reveals that '[w]hen questions were raised [within the AU] as to whether the Union could possibly have an inherent right to intervene other than through the Security Council, they were dismissed out of hand'.[185] He details that African States did not seem entirely vested in ensuring compliance with international norms governing the use of force in this

Enforcement Actions in the absence of Security Council Authorization' (2007) 40 *Vanderbilt Journal of Transnational Law* 643.

179 2001 ICISS Report (n2) Para 6.35.

180 The Constitutive Act of the African Union (adopted 11 July 2000, entered into force 26 May 2001) 2158 UNTS 3 Art 4(h) [hereinafter Constitutive Act].

181 UN Charter (n94) Arts 2(4) and 53.

182 *See supra* note 164 and accompanying text.

183 Vienna Convention on the Law of Treaties (adopted 23 May 1969, entered into force 27 January 1980) 111 UNTS 331 Art 53.

184 UN Charter (n94) Art 103. *See also Case Concerning the Military and Paramilitary Activities in and against Nicaragua (Nicaragua v. United States of America)* (Jurisdiction of the Court and Admissibility of the Application) [1984] ICJ Rep 392 Para 107.

185 Ben Kioko, 'The Right of Intervention under the African Union's Constitutive Act: From Non-interference to Non-intervention' (2003) 85 *International Review of the Red Cross* 807, 821.

respect due to frustrations with what they perceived to be a wider de-prioritisation of African problems within the existing international legal order. Despite such reported indifference, however, some international legal scholars nevertheless contend that unauthorised military intervention under Article 4(h) of the Constitutive Act could be deemed lawful through prior treaty-based consent.[186] Their argument holds that the prohibition against the use of force is qualified rather than absolute, meaning that it enjoys a number of exceptions including self-defence and intervention by invitation. In this sense, these authors assert, just as intervention by invitation does not conflict with the prohibition against the use of force, then intervention premised upon prior treaty-based consent similarly does not contradict this norm.[187] Kuwali adds that 'if a state is free to extinguish its sovereignty altogether by merging with another state, equally a state may therefore accept a lesser infringement of its sovereignty in the form of a treaty-based right of intervention'.[188] He takes this argument even further, contending that Article 4(h) of the Constitutive Act should in fact stipulate an obligation, rather than a mere right, of the AU to intervene in mass atrocities, basing his case on the *jus cogens* status of mass atrocity crimes as well as the international legal obligation for States to bring to an end serious *jus cogens* violations (although interestingly, he does not specifically cite Article 41 ASR).[189]

Such arguments, while intriguing, have yet to gain the general acceptance of States and international legal scholars.[190] Even Kuwali, for example, admits that 'any enforcement action without Security Council authorization is undertaken on a presumption of unlawfulness'.[191] The AU itself seems to share this view, as it stated in its 2005 Ezulwini Consensus:

> Since the General Assembly and the Security Council are often far from the scenes of conflicts and may not be in a position to undertake effectively a proper appreciation of the nature and development of conflict situations, it is imperative that Regional Organizations, in areas of proximity to conflicts, are

186 *See*, for example, Dan Kuwali, 'Protect Responsibly: The African Union's Implementation of Article 4(h) Intervention' (2010) 11 *Yearbook of International Humanitarian Law* 51, 87 [hereinafter Kuwali Protect Responsibly]; Ademola Abass and Mashood A. Baderin, 'Towards Effective Collective Security and Human Rights Protection in Africa: An Assessment of the Constitutive Act of the New African Union' (2002) 49 *Netherlands International Law Review* 1, 18–19.

187 *See* Kuwali Protect Responsibly (n186) 87; Abass and Baderin (n186) 17–19; Ademola Abass, 'Consent Precluding State Responsibility: A Critical Analysis' (2004) 53 *International and Comparative Law Quarterly* 211, 223–24.

188 Kuwali Protect Responsibly (n186) 65.

189 Dan Kuwali, 'From Stopping to Preventing Atrocities: Actualisation of Article 4(h)' (2015) *African Security Review* 248, 250–51 [hereinafter Kuwali From Stopping to Preventing Atrocities].

190 *See*, for example, Nabil Hajjami, 'The Institutionalisation of the Responsibility to Protect' in Richard Barnes and Vassilis Tzevelekos (eds), *Beyond Responsibility to Protct: Generating Change in International Law* (Intersentia 2016) 97.

191 Kuwali Protect Responsibly (n186) 94.

> empowered to take actions in this regard. The African Union agrees with the Panel that the intervention of Regional Organizations should be with the approval of the Security Council; although in certain situations, such approval could be granted 'after the fact' in circumstances requiring urgent action.[192]

In essence, the AU acknowledged in this document that by law, it should seek UNSC authorisation prior to any military intervention. It seemed to simultaneously contend, however, that it would be morally justifiable for the body to take action absent such approval, for example in response to exceptional situations in which UNSC action is not forthcoming.[193]

It should be cautioned that the AU has yet to invoke Article 4(h) of the Constitutive Act, so it is uncertain how the international community will react to its exercise and whether it will consider such regional military action to be lawful absent UNSC authorisation.[194] Even should this Article's lawfulness come to be recognised, however, it should be stressed that this would constitute an acceptance of a treaty-based right of intervention rather than being indicative of a wider normative shift under international law that recognises regional intervention as a lawful means of overcoming UNSC deadlock in R2P situations (as originally suggested in the 2001 ICISS report). At present, therefore, treaty-based consent to regional military action may represent an emerging challenge to the UNSC's primacy in authorising the use of force in R2P situations, although this does not extend to a wider allowance for unauthorised regional intervention in such cases.

5.4 Conclusion

This chapter outlined that although States continue to reject that they are carriers of an obligation to react to mass atrocities that occur outside their borders as per R2P's Pillar 3, there are nevertheless indications that such an obligation can be extracted to a limited extent from a series of fragmented yet interconnected international legal norms pertaining to the prevention of and reaction to mass atrocity crimes. As such, this chapter identified several legal frameworks that provide support for an emerging Pillar 3 obligation, including Article 1 of the Genocide Convention, Common Article 1 to the Geneva Conventions, and Article 41 ASR. It furthermore argued that because R2P's Pillar 3 reflects fundamental community interests, it is not unreasonable to suggest that it may come to acquire legal standing through the progressive development of international law, although this comes with significant obstacles, most notably securing States' acceptance of such an obligation.

192 African Union, 'The Common African Position on the Proposed Reform of the United Nations: The Ezulwini Consensus' (2005) Ext/EX.CL/2 (VII), Para B(i).

193 *See* Kuwali From Stopping to Preventing Atrocities (n189) 259.

194 *See* Kwesi Aning and Frank Okyere, 'The African Union' in Alex J. Bellamy and Tim Dunne (eds), *The Oxford Handbook of the Responsibility to Protect* (Oxford University Press 2016) 363–64.

This chapter furthermore detailed the legal developments that Pillar 3 must undergo in order for it to present a robust framework for ensuring consistent and effective international reactions to mass atrocity crimes. Primarily, it was noted that this Pillar must become legally binding rather than discretionary. This should include the establishment of a legal definition of a 'responsibility to react' to ascertain what such an obligation should actually entail, the identification of means that States may or should employ in order to fulfil it, and the specification of a due diligence standard for determining State responsibility for failing to react.

This chapter stressed that equally important for the emergence of an R2P Pillar 3 obligation is to overcome the selective nature of the UNSC's current response mechanism to mass atrocity situations, particularly given the body's pivotal role in spearheading international reactions to such cases. The first means through which this can happen is through imparting clear limitations upon the exercise of the permanent veto in R2P situations. Should such limitations fail to be accepted or implemented in practice, then the doctrine must come to identify alternative means of facilitating international action when the UNSC is paralysed from responding effectively to mass atrocity situations due to the permanent veto, particularly with respect to the use of military force which remains within the body's primary remit absent self-defence. Regional authorisation in the form of prior treaty-based consent represents an emerging option in this regard, particularly with respect to Article 4(h) of the AU's Constitutive Act. A more established option lies in the Uniting for Peace mechanism, which was demonstrated in this chapter to be both lawful and legitimate. In the interest of strengthening R2P's enforceability and ensuring that UNSC paralysis does not retain the potential to obstruct international mobilisation towards R2P situations, greater emphasis should be placed upon reviving this mechanism as part of the doctrine's future development.

6 The application of R2P to the Libya Case

6.1 Introduction

Anti-government protests erupted in Libya on 15 February 2011 against the backdrop of over 40 years of repressive rule by the Gaddafi regime.[1] The regime responded to these protests with force, making it clear that it intended to wipe out any dissent.[2] Most famously, then-Libyan President Gaddafi declared on Libyan National Television on 22 February that he would lead 'millions to purge Libya inch by inch, house by house, ... alley by alley, and individual by individual' to 'purify' the land from protesters ('rats'), who needed to be executed.[3] This statement, in addition to similar ones articulated by himself and his son,[4] drew stark comparison with the incitement to genocide in Rwanda in 1994 through the labelling of ethnic Tutsis as 'inyenzi', or cockroaches,[5] and sure enough, was followed by the commission of crimes against humanity and war crimes against the civilian population. Specifically, an International Commission of Inquiry on Libya established by the UN Human Rights Council (HRC) concluded that the Libyan regime, throughout the uprising, committed crimes against humanity of murder,

1 *See* HRC, 'Report of the International Commission of Inquiry to Investigate all Alleged Violations of International Human Rights Law in the Libyan Arab Jamahiriya' (12 January 2012) UN Doc A/HRC/17/44 Para 27. *See also* 'Truth and Justice Can't Wait: Human Rights Developments in Libya amid Institutional Obstacles' (*Human Rights Watch*, 2009) <https://www.hrw.org/report/2009/12/12/truth-and-justice-cant-wait/human-rights-developments-libya-amid-institutional>.

2 *See* UN Doc A/HRC/17/44 (n1) Paras 27, 30.

3 Ibid., Para 29.

4 On 17 March 2011, Muammar Gaddafi again promised 'no mercy' to those who resisted him. His son Saif al-Islam Gaddafi also vowed publicly on 21 February to fight 'until the last man standing'. Richard Spencer, 'Libya: Protests Gather Pace as Gaddafi's Son Vows to Fight to the End' (*Telegraph*, 21 February 2011) <http://www.telegraph.co.uk/news/worldnews/africaandindianocean/libya/8337546/Libya-protests-gather-pace-as-Gaddafis-son-vows-to-fight-to-the-end.html>; David D. Kirkpatrick and Kareem Fahim, 'Qaddafi Warns of Assault on Benghazi as U.N. Vote Nears' (*New York Times*, 17 March 2011) <http://www.nytimes.com/2011/03/18/world/africa/18libya.html?pagewanted=all&_r=0>.

5 *See Nahimana et al. (Media Case)* (Judgement) ICTR-99–52 (28 November 2007) Section XIII.

torture, persecution, enforced disappearance, and imprisonment and other severe deprivations of physical liberty, as well as the war crimes of murder, outrages upon personal dignity, and intentionally directing attacks against protected persons and targets.[6] These violations made the R2P doctrine directly relevant to the situation in Libya.

Armed anti-government groups quickly emerged on the scene to oppose Gaddafi's rule and the situation morphed into a NIAC towards the end of February 2011.[7] As a regime onslaught against the city of Benghazi became imminent, the UNSC authorised the use of force on 17 March 2011 through Resolution 1973.[8] French, British and American forces began implementing this Resolution two days later through targeted airstrikes and yielded to a North Atlantic Treaty Organization (NATO) operation on 31 March.[9] When NATO officially concluded its military operations in Libya on 31 October, Libyan president Muammar Gaddafi had been killed by Western-backed Libyan rebels and plans were underway for a political transition within the country.[10] Unfortunately, however, the situation in Libya deteriorated thereafter due to insufficient international engagement with the rebuilding of the country. Mass atrocity crimes (most particularly, war crimes) continue to be committed by various armed groups and there are fears that Libya may soon become a failed State, if it has not become one already.[11]

This chapter explores the Libyan uprising in the context of the R2P doctrine. Specifically, it analyses whether and how R2P shaped the international reaction to the Libyan conflict, and furthermore how developments in Libya in turn influenced the interpretation of and support for the doctrine. Importantly, the focus of this chapter lies in R2P's Pillars 1 and 3, as the conflict's rapid escalation and the Libyan regime's manifest failure to protect its population from mass atrocity crimes necessitated the international community's assumption of its Pillar 3 responsibilities at the exclusion of the provision of assistance to the Libyan regime as per Pillar 2.

Through its examination of the Libyan R2P situation, this chapter considers the roles of various actors as well as a range of dimensions that their R2P responses assumed (both military and non-military). In order to make the analysis more

6 UN Doc A/HRC/17/44 (n1) Paras 247–48.
7 Ibid., Para 55.
8 UNSC Res 1973 (17 March 2011) UN Doc S/RES/1973.
9 *See* UN Doc A/HRC/17/44 (n1) Paras 32, 41.
10 Although uncertainty remains regarding the exact circumstances of Gaddafi's death, it is known that he was killed on 20 October 2011 while in custody of rebel militias. *See* 'Death of a Dictator: Bloody Vengeance in Sirte' (*Human Rights Watch*, October 2012) <http://www.hrw.org/sites/default/files/reports/libya1012webwcover_0_0.pdf>.
11 *See* Heidarali Teimouri and Surya P. Subedi, 'Responsibility to Protect and the International Military Intervention in Libya in International Law: What Went Wrong and What Lessons Could be Learnt from It?' (2018) 23 *Journal of Conflict and Security Law* 3, 8–12; HRC, 'Report of the United Nations High Commissioner for Human Rights on the Situation of Human Rights in Libya, Including on the Effectiveness of Technical Assistance and Capacity-building Measures Received by the Government of Libya' (13 January 2017) UN Doc A/HRC/34/42.

manageable, this chapter focuses on four major groups of actors, selected for the key roles that they held in responding to the situation: regional organisations (most particularly, the League of Arab States – LAS – and the African Union – AU), the UNGA and the HRC (as complementary bodies that assumed an interest in the human rights situation in Libya), the UNSC (for its primary role in authorising coercive measures, including the use of force), and NATO (as the body that intervened militarily pursuant to UNSC authorisation). The actions of each of these actors are assessed against existing or emerging international legal norms that are relevant to R2P's implementation, allowing for a unique and detailed analysis of their roles in the application of the R2P doctrine within Libya. Such analysis incorporates extensive examinations of State practice and *opinio juris* pertaining to R2P's development which help to evaluate R2P's legal basis and to identify and address gaps that remain within its framework or that of its component Pillars.

6.2 Regional organisations

Regional organisations played a major role in influencing the international course of events pertaining to the Libyan R2P situation. This section first examines one particular regional reaction, namely, the LAS's suspension of Libya from the body in 2011. It then examines the role of regional organisations more generally in shaping the international community's reaction towards Libya.

6.2.1 Libya's suspension from the League of Arab States

On 26 February 2011, the LAS, as one of the major regional players in the Libyan conflict, adopted Statement 136, which suspended Libya's seat from the body.[12] This marked the first time that a State was suspended from the LAS for actions undertaken against its own people[13] (the only other State to ever be suspended from the LAS prior to this case was Egypt in 1979 for signing a peace agreement with Israel[14]). Although R2P was not invoked in this Statement, it is nevertheless significant that the LAS was reacting on the basis of human rights concerns to a situation widely considered to fall under the doctrine's remit, as evidenced in the Statement's '[denunciation of] the crimes committed against peaceful demonstrations and popular protests in several Libyan cities' as well as in its '[expression of]

12 League of Arab States, 'Statement by Permanent Representatives of the Council of the League of Arab States Regarding the Serious Developments in Libya – LAS Statement 136' (22 February 2011) Paras 1, 8 available at https://bit.ly/2BYsLHz [hereinafter LAS Statement 136].

13 *See* Elin Hellquist, 'Regional Organizations and Sanctions against Members' (*Kolleg-Forschergruppe*, January 2014) at 15 <http://userpage.fu-berlin.de/kfgeu/kfgwp/wpseries/WorkingPaperKFG_59.pdf>.

14 *See* 'Timeline: Arab League' (BBC News, 2011) <http://news.bbc.co.uk/1/hi/world/middle_east/country_profiles/1550977.stm>.

strong disapproval against acts of violence against civilians ... that constitute serious violations of human rights and international humanitarian law'.[15]

Generally, Libya's suspension from the LAS lends support to the use of third-party countermeasures (in this case, by an international organisation) as a means of implementing R2P's Pillar 3.[16] The LAS, in order to uphold community interests, was willing to violate its founding Pact of the League of Arab States (LAS Pact) in order to apply pressure against Libya to bring an end to the mass atrocity situation within the country. Before analysing the specific context of Libya's suspension from the LAS, however, it is worth briefly engaging with the International Law Commission's (ILC) Draft Articles on the Responsibility of International Organizations (DARIO) which, finalised by the ILC in 2011, identify the rules pertaining to the responsibility of international organisations (including on the legal framework for employing countermeasures by such organisations) in a similar manner to the Articles on State Responsibility's (ASR) codification of the laws on State responsibility[17] (discussed in Chapter 2 of this book).[18]

Similar to ASR, DARIO have no conclusive legal status.[19] Unlike ASR, however, they are supported by significantly less practice, thus limiting the extent to which they can be assumed to reflect customary international law.[20] DARIO have also been criticised for attempting to create a 'one-size-fits-all' approach for international organisations by formulating only one set of rules for an extremely diverse array of international organisations.[21] Despite these apparent shortcomings, DARIO have been invoked in international case law and have been accepted as authoritative in such cases, suggesting that they can at least serve as a form of soft law in defining the responsibility of international organisations.[22] Additionally, many of their provisions – including those on countermeasures – are reflective of ASR, which are themselves supported by much higher levels of State practice,

15 LAS Statement 136 (n12) Para 1 (translation by author and Google Translate).
16 *See* Martin Dawidowicz, 'Third-party Countermeasures: A Progressive Development of International Law?' (2016) 29 *Questions of International Law* 3, 5–6 [hereinafter Dawidowicz Third-party Countermeasures].
17 ILC, 'Draft Articles on the Responsibility of International Organizations, with Commentaries' (2011) II(2) Yearbook of the International Law Commission [hereinafter DARIO].
18 *See* Section 2.2.2 of this book.
19 *See* Pierre Klein, 'Responsibility' in Jacob Kantz Cogan, Ian Hurd, and Ian Johnstone (eds) *The Oxford Handbook of International Organizations* (Oxford University Press 2016) 1027–28.
20 *See* Jose E. Alvarez, 'Revisiting the ILC's Draft Rules on International Organization Responsibility' (2011) 105 *American Society of International Law Proceedings* 344, 345–46.
21 *See* Mirka Möldner, 'Responsibility of International Organizations – Introducing the ILC's DARIO' (2012) 16 *Max Planck Yearbook of United Nations Law* 281, 323–24.
22 *See*, for example, *Behrami and Behrami v. France and Saramati v. France, Germany and Norway* (App no 71412/01, 78166/01) ECtHR 2 May 2007 Paras 29–31; *Case of Al-Jedda v. The United Kingdom* (App no 27021/08, 78166/01) ECtHR 7 July 2011 Paras 56, 84. *See also* José Alvarez, 'Misadventures in Subjecthood' (*EJIL: Talk!*, 2010) <http://www.ejiltalk.org/misadventures-in-statehood/>.

opinio juris, and invocation in international case law as detailed in Chapter 2 of this book.[23] With this in mind, DARIO can perhaps help clarify the suggested rules pertaining to the responsibility of international organisations, bearing in mind that these rules are not necessarily conclusive.

In this respect, Article 22(1) DARIO states that:

> [The] wrongfulness of an act of an international organization not in conformity with an international obligation towards a State or another international organization is precluded if and to the extent that the act constitutes a countermeasure taken in accordance with the substantive and procedural conditions required by international law.[24]

This Article essentially allows injured international organisations to employ countermeasures against States or other international organisations that cause them injury through the commission of an internationally wrongful act.[25] The requirement within this Article that countermeasures must be 'taken in accordance with the substantive and procedural conditions required by international law' is elaborated upon within the official commentary to mean that 'one may apply by analogy the conditions that are set out for countermeasures taken by a State against another State in articles 49 to 54 [ASR]'.[26] As such, the rules established by ASR pertaining to countermeasures by States were analogised to international organisations.[27] In this respect, it is recalled from Chapter 2 of this book that Article 49 ASR permits an injured State to undertake countermeasures against another State causing it injury (limited to non-performance of legal obligations towards the State) in order to induce it to rectify its behaviour.[28] Non-injured States, however, are only specifically permitted as per Article 54 ASR to take 'lawful measures' to ensure cessation and reparation by a State that violates an obligation owed to the international community as a whole.[29] The lawfulness of third-State countermeasures, undertaken by non-injured States for breaches of obligations owed to the international community as a whole, were determined to require the further development of the law.[30]

Analogising these rules to DARIO, it can be inferred that international organisations can employ countermeasures against States or international organisations that cause them injury, similarly limited to the non-performance of legal

23 *See* Section 2.2.2 of this book.
24 DARIO (n17) Art 22.
25 *See also,* on this point, Article 51 DARIO, which provides that countermeasures should be undertaken in response to an internationally wrongful act.
26 DARIO (n17) Commentary to Art 22 Para 2.
27 *See* Möldner (n21) 302.
28 ILC, 'Draft Articles on Responsibility of States for Internationally Wrongful Acts, with Commentaries' (2001) II *Yearbook of the International Law Commission* 26, Art 49 [hereinafter ASR]. *See also* Section 2.2.2 of this book.
29 Ibid., Art 54.
30 As elaborated in Section 2.2.2.

obligations. With respect to a breach of an obligation owed to the international community as a whole, however, international organisations are, by extension of Article 54 ASR, only specifically entitled to undertake lawful measures (i.e. they are not expressly permitted to violate their international obligations). This implies that in the Libyan case, the LAS (as a non-injured entity) was only specifically entitled to employ lawful measures (i.e. in accordance with its internal rules and wider international law) in order to address Libya's violation of its R2P Pillar 1 obligations (which also represent obligations owed to the international community as a whole).

In addition to DARIO's above requirements for invoking countermeasures by international organisations, Article 22(2)(b) DARIO further stipulates that countermeasures undertaken by international organisations against their own member-States (thus applicable to the relationship between the LAS and Libya) must not be 'inconsistent with the rules of the organization'.[31] The official commentary to Article 22 stresses that 'given the obligations of close cooperation that generally exist between an international organization and its members, countermeasures are allowed only if the rules of the organization so provide'.[32] This suggests that the LAS's suspension of Libya (as a member-State) in response to its violation of fundamental community interests could only be achieved through a lawfully stipulated process. Dopagne argues that 'the above requirement may appear somewhat bewildering', pointing out that countermeasures are by their very nature 'intrinsically contrary to international law'.[33] He furthermore cites past practice in which international organisations were willing to violate their internal rules in order to induce compliance by member-States with obligations owed to the international community as a whole. Such examples include, most notably, the Universal Postal Union's expulsion of South Africa in 1979 for its apartheid policy,[34] the refusal of the International Atomic Energy Agency (IAEA) to recognise the credentials of the Israeli delegation in 1982 following its military raid on the Osirak nuclear reactor in Iraq,[35] and the International Labour Organization's (ILO) decision

31 DARIO (n17) Art 51.
32 Ibid., Commentary to Art 22 Para 6.
33 Frédéric Dopagne, 'Sanctions and Countermeasures by International Organizations: Diverging Lessons for the Idea of Autonomy' in Richard Collins and Nigel D. White (eds), *International Organizations and the Idea of Autonomy: Institutional Independence in the International Legal Order* (Routledge 2011) 180, 186.
34 The Constitution of the Universal Postal Union does not contain a provision for the expulsion of member-States. Ibid., 181; Universal Postal Union, Resolution C 6/1979 (*United Nations Juridicial Yearbook*, 1979) <http://legal.un.org/docs/?path=../unjuridicalyearbook/pdfs/english/volumes/1979.pdf&lang=E>; Constitution of the Universal Postal Union (adopted on 10 July 1964, entered into force on 1 December 1967) 611 UNTS 7.
35 Article XIX of the Statute of the IAEA allows for the suspension of a member-State which is 'in arrears in the payment of its financial contributions to the Agency' or, through a two-thirds majority vote if it 'has persistently violated the provisions of this Statute or of any agreement entered into by it pursuant to this Statute'. The credentials of the Israeli delegation, however, were refused through a simple majority vote. Dopagne (n33) 181; Statute of the International Atomic Energy Agency (adopted on

in 1999 that the 'Government of Myanmar should cease to benefit from any technical cooperation or assistance from the ILO' because of its forced labour practices.[36]

While this limited practice indicates the willingness of international organisations to engage in third-party countermeasures to induce compliance by their member-States with obligations owed to the international community as a whole, it is arguably neither widespread nor systematic enough to give rise to a customary right in this regard. Such a right may emerge through the continued build-up of State practice and *opinio juris*, and as such, third-party countermeasures by international organisations may come to represent a recognised means of reacting to R2P situations as per the doctrine's Pillar 3. It should also be noted that third-party countermeasures by non-injured international organisations, because they are undertaken multilaterally, presumably enshrine a greater degree of legitimacy than bilateral third-State countermeasures which, although not definitively lawful, enjoy higher levels of State practice and *opinio juris*. This offers an additional incentive for their crystallisation into law.

A careful analysis of the circumstances surrounding Libya's suspension from the LAS reveals that this act represented a third-party countermeasure undertaken by the LAS in order to address Libya's violation of R2P's Pillar 1 (which reflects fundamental community interests).[37] Specifically, Article 18 of the LAS Pact allows for the expulsion (through a unanimous vote) of a State 'not fulfilling the obligations' of the Pact.[38] LAS Resolutions 314 and 318 (1950) further stipulate that the negotiation or conclusion of a peace or other agreement with Israel could similarly lead to expulsion from the body (this provided the legal basis for Egypt's suspension in 1979).[39] While Libya's suspension from the LAS was obviously not premised upon any relationship

29 July 1957, entered into force on 27 August 1957) 276 UNTS 3 Art XIX; 'Resolution Adopted during the 246th Plenary Meeting, on 24 September 1982 (Resolution GC(XXVI)/RES/404)' (*International Atomic Energy Agency*, 18 October 1982) <https://www.iaea.org/About/Policy/GC/GC26/GC26Resolutions/English/gc26res-404_en.pdf>; 'Record of the Two Hundred and Forty-Sixth Plenary Meeting GC(XXVI)/OR.246' (*International Atomic Energy Agency*, 24 September 1982) at 7–10 <https://www.iaea.org/About/Policy/GC/GC26/GC26Records/English/gc26or-246_en.pdf>.

36 The Constitution of the ILO does not contain a provision for the expulsion of member-States. Dopagne (n33) 181; 'Resolution on the Widespread Use of Forced Labour in Myanmar' (*International Labour Organization*, 17 June 1999) Art 3 <http://www.ilo.org/public/english/standards/relm/ilc/ilc87/com-myan.htm>; Instrument for the Amendment of the Constitution of the International Labour Organisation (adopted on 22 June 1972, entered into force on 1 November 1974) 958 UNTS 167.

37 *See* Dawidowicz Third-party Countermeasures (n16) 5–6.

38 Pact of the League of Arab States (adopted 22 March 1945, entered into force 10 May 1945) 70 UNTS 241 Art 18 [hereinafter LAS Pact].

39 *See* Konstantinos D. Magliveras, *Exclusion from Participation in International Organisations: The Law and Practice behind Member States' Expulsion and Suspension of Membership* (Kluwer Law International 1999) 95.

that it held with Israel, it is also highly unlikely that it was justifiable through Article 18 of the Pact because of non-fulfilment of Pact obligations.

First, Article 18 of the LAS Pact refers to the expulsion, but not suspension, of member-States.[40] There is no alternative clause within the Pact that deals specifically with member-State suspension. Kirgis argues that a State can be suspended from an international organisation if it acts in a way that makes it liable to be excluded from the body and if there is no comparable way to achieve suspension.[41] The LAS relied upon such an argument in suspending Egypt's membership in 1979, claiming that 'since it was empowered [through the Pact] to expel a Member, it could, *a fortiori*, suspend one'.[42] However, Magliveras is in notable dissent on this point, highlighting that expulsion and suspension constitute separate legal actions and that 'the former does not presuppose the latter'.[43] He further asserts that the 'fact that the Pact's drafters did not include suspension, should be interpreted as a deliberate decision not to afford this sanction to the League'.[44]

While prior practice of the LAS as an organisation favours Kirgis's interpretation, thus allowing for State suspension through the LAS Pact's Article 18, it remains to be seen which obligation Libya was in breach of. Article 18 of the LAS Pact allows for the exclusion of States 'not fulfilling the obligations' contained within the treaty,[45] obligations that include a prohibition against the use of force 'between two or more member States',[46] non-interference in domestic affairs, and a prohibition against regime change or against undermining governments of other member-States.[47] Human rights obligations and objectives do not appear anywhere within the Pact and do not even constitute any of the stated purposes of the LAS (enshrined within Article 2, these purposes pertain to economic, financial, communication, cultural, nationality, social welfare, and health matters).[48] It was obvious, however, that Libya was suspended specifically for its human rights breaches. LAS Statement 136, for example, which effectuated Libya's suspension, stressed that the suspension would continue until the Libyan authorities responded to the demands stipulated within the Statement, demands which notably called for an 'immediate cessation of violence', a response 'to the legitimate demands of the Libyan people', and the respect for the Libyan people's rights to assembly and expression.[49]

40 LAS Pact (n38) Art 18.
41 Frederic L. Kirgis, 'Book Review and Note: Exclusion from Participation in International Organisations: The Law and Practice behind Member States' Expulsion and Suspension of Membership. By Konstantinos D. Magliveras' (2001) 95 *American Journal of International Law* 734, 735.
42 Magliveras (n39) 98.
43 Ibid.
44 Ibid.
45 LAS Pact (n38) Art 18.
46 Ibid., Art 5.
47 Ibid., Art 8.
48 Ibid., Art 2. *See also* Dawidowicz Third-party Countermeasures (n16) 5–6.
49 LAS Statement 136 (n12) Para 2 (author's translation).

Libya's suspension from the LAS can thus be categorised as a situation in which a third-party countermeasure was invoked by an international organisation as a means of inducing a member-State to uphold its R2P Pillar 1 obligations. At a minimum, this action underscored that R2P reactions need not be dictated solely by the UN, but can also be enriched through the mandates and the expertise of more local actors. Additionally, the lack of international protest to the LAS's suspension of Libya highlights that despite its inherent unlawfulness, States accepted it as a legitimate act (if not contributing to an emerging right to engage in third-party countermeasures).[50] The undertaking of third-party countermeasures, including through the suspension of member-States from regional or international organisations, therefore represents a potential means through which R2P's Pillar 3 can come to be implemented robustly yet non-militarily.

6.2.2 Regional influence on international action

Beyond the LAS's suspension of Libya's seat from the body, relevant regional organisations played a critical role in guiding the international community's overall response to the Libyan conflict, most particularly through propelling the UNSC to authorise the use of force to ensure civilian protection.[51] Specifically, as it became obvious that non-military measures implemented by various international bodies were not being heeded by Libya and were insufficient in inducing it to protect its population,[52] the Gulf Cooperation Council (GCC) became the first regional organisation to advocate a militarised response to the Libyan conflict on 7 March, '[demanding]' that the UNSC 'take all necessary measures to protect civilians, including enforcing a no-fly zone over Libya'.[53] The Organisation of Islamic Cooperation (OIC) followed suit on 8 March, calling upon the UNSC to 'assume its responsibility' in establishing a no-fly zone 'to [protect] civilians from air strikes'.[54] Finally, and most critically, the LAS appealed to the UNSC on 12

50 In the minimal coverage of the LAS's suspension of Libya, no State criticisms were mentioned. *See*, for example, 'Libya Protests: Gaddafi Battles to Control West' (*BBC News*, 23 February 2011) <http://www.bbc.co.uk/news/world-middle-east-12556005>; Kareem Fahim and David Kirkpatrick, 'Qaddafi's Grip on the Capital Tightens as Revolt Grows' (*New York Times*, 22 February 2011) <http://www.nytimes.com/2011/02/23/world/africa/23libya.html?pagewanted=all>.

51 The UNSC's authorisation of the use of force as per Resolution 1973 is discussed in Section 6.4.2 of this chapter.

52 *See* measures implemented by the HRC, UNGA, UNSC and LAS in Sections 6.2.1, 6.3 and 6.4.1. *See also* Geir Ulfstein and Hege Føsund Christiansen, 'The Legality of the NATO Bombing in Libya' (2013) 62 *International and Comparative Law Quarterly* 159, 160.

53 *See* Samir Salama, 'GCC Backs No-fly Zone to Protect Civilians in Libya' (*Gulf News*, 9 March 2011) <https://gulfnews.com/uae/government/gcc-backs-no-fly-zone-to-protect-civilians-in-libya-1.773448>.

54 'Ihsanoglu Support No-fly Decision at OIC Meeting on Libya, Calls for an Islamic Humanitarian Programme in and outside Libya' (*Lauterpacht Centre for International Law*, 8 March 2011) <http://www.lcil.cam.ac.uk/sites/default/files/LCIL/documents/arabspring/libya/Libya_15_Ihsanoglu_Support.pdf>, accessed 3 October 2016.

March 'to bear its responsibilities towards the deteriorating situation in Libya' and to 'impose immediately a no-fly zone' as a 'precautionary measure that allows the protection of the Libyan people and foreign nationals residing in Libya'.[55]

Although none of the GCC, OIC, or LAS specifically referred to R2P while advocating a no-fly zone over Libya, they all stressed civilian protection which reflects the doctrine's essence. They were furthermore responding to a situation that was prominently recognised to lie within the doctrine's scope.[56] The OIC and LAS, by invoking the UNSC's 'responsibility' concurrently with the notion of civilian protection, in effect affirmed the premise of the international community's R2P Pillar 3 responsibility,[57] although neither referred to this responsibility as a legal obligation (i.e. there was no specification that they were invoking the UNSC's legal responsibility as opposed to, for example, a moral responsibility). The GCC employed stronger language by '[demanding]' the UNSC to take action. Even this choice of words, however, although it imparted a particular burden upon the UNSC to ensure civilian protection, fell short of claiming this to be a legal obligation. It seems, therefore, that regional organisations recognised the UNSC's critical role in achieving civilian protection and furthermore held a strong collective expectation for the UNSC to fulfil its responsibility to protect civilians in Libya, although this did not translate into *opinio juris* regarding a duty of the UNSC to take action in R2P situations (i.e. it did not imply the existence of an R2P Pillar 3 obligation).

Here, it should be mentioned that the AU, as another major regional player with respect to Libya, did not join these regional organisations in calling for a no-fly zone, but rather rejected a militarised response to the R2P situation.[58] Importantly, the AU's stance stemmed from a firm conviction that 'only a political solution … will make it possible to promote sustainable peace in Libya'[59] – and thus from an assessment that military measures stood a poor chance of success that

55 'LAS Resolution 7360' (*ICRtoP*, 12 March 2011) Para 1 <http://responsibilitytoprotect.org/Arab%20League%20Ministerial%20level%20statement%2012%20march%202011%20-%20english(1).pdf>.

56 *See*, for example, *supra* note 6 and accompanying text.

57 *See* Catherine Powell, 'Libya: A Multilateral Constitutional Moment?' (2012) 106 *American Journal of International Law* 298, 312–13.

58 'Communiqué of the 265th Meeting of the Peace and Security Council of the African Union, AU Doc PSC/PR/COMM.2(CCLXV)' (*African Union Peace and Security Council*, 10 March 2011) Arts 6, 8 <http://www.peaceau.org/uploads/communique-libya-eng.pdf>.

59 'African Union Decision on the Peaceful Resolution of the Libyan Crisis – Enhancing Africa's Leadership, Promoting African Solutions AU Doc EXT/ASSEMBLY/AU/DEC/(01.2011)' (All Africa, 25 May 2011) Art 3 <https://allafrica.com/stories/201105270681.html>. *See also* 'Press Release: The AU Intensifies its Efforts towards a Political Solution in Libya and Stresses the Importance of the Respect of the Letter and Spirit of Resolution 1973' (*African Union*, 3 May 2011) <https://au.int/sites/default/files/pressreleases/24311-pr-press_release_on_libya_3_05_11.pdf>; 'Decision on the Situation in Libya, AU Doc Assembly/AU/Dec.385(XVII)' (African Union, 30 June–1 July 2011) Art 3 <https://au.int/sites/default/files/decisions/9647-assembly_au_dec_363-390_xvii_e.pdf>.

could threaten the stability of the country and the wider region – rather than from a desire to shield Libya's human rights abuses under the guise of State sovereignty and non-interference. This is critical in that the AU did not reject the principles that underpin R2P's Pillar 3 which call upon the international community to react when a State fails to protect its people from mass atrocity crimes. Rather, it condemned the Libyan government's violations against its people[60] but advised a non-military course of action that it perceived would more effectively achieve civilian protection.

Notwithstanding the AU's opposition to the use of force in Libya, the calls of the GCC, OIC, and LAS for the UNSC to authorise military action in Libya were critical in securing the support of key international players for such a course of action. In the first instance, regional support helped to assuage substantial US concerns regarding the potential costs and casualties that could be entailed within a military option, the prospect of being drawn into an extended conflict, or the possibility of alienating Middle Eastern and Muslim States which were already wary of Western interventionism.[61] At the other end of the spectrum, regional support furthermore induced Russia and China – traditionally opposed to the use of force in international law – not to exercise their veto in this respect.[62] Tellingly, when the UNSC adopted Resolution 1973, which authorised the use of force in Libya,[63] 13 of the 14 UNSC member-States that participated in the discussion following its adoption specifically cited the calls of regional organisations as factors that weighed into their decision-making.[64]

In the Libyan case, therefore, the stances of regional organisations provoked a robust and timely response from the UNSC and are indicative of the influential role that such bodies can assume in guiding the international community's actions in R2P situations.[65] The general value added of regional involvement is that these organisations can facilitate international responses to mass atrocity situations that are uniquely tailored to the context and dynamics of each conflict. With that said, however, it is equally important to bear in mind the potential pitfalls regarding an

60 *See*, for example, 'Communiqué of the 261st Meeting of the Peace and Security Council of the African Union, AU Doc PSC/PR/COMM(CCLXI)' (*African Union Peace and Security Council*, 23 February 2011) Art 2 <http://www.peaceau.org/uploads/psc-communique-on-the-situation-in-libya.pdf>; AU Doc PSC/PR/COM M.2(CCLXV) (n58) Art 5.

61 *See* Alex J. Bellamy and Paul D. Williams, 'The New Politics of Protection? Côte d'Ivoire, Libya and the Responsibility to Protect' (2011) 87 *International Affairs* 825, 843; Luke Glanville, 'Intervention in Libya: From Sovereign Consent to Regional Consent' (2013) 14 *International Studies Perspectives* 325, 335.

62 Ibid.

63 This Resolution is discussed in greater detail in Section 6.4.2 of this chapter.

64 India was the only State not to cite regional support for military intervention as a factor that influenced its decision-making. *See* UNSC 6498th Meeting (17 March 2011) UN Doc S/PV.6498.

65 *See* Bellamy and Williams (n61) 848–49 (describing regional organisations as 'gatekeepers' for international action in response to mass atrocity situations); Glanville (n61) 339–40 (examining the UNSC's increased reliance upon regional organisations in defining its responses to mass atrocity situations).

over-reliance on regional organisations, namely, that these bodies are themselves politicised and may fail to respond adequately (if at all) to R2P situations. This is not to mention the inherent selectivity, as manifested in the Libyan case, that may transpire on behalf of the international community when relevant regional organisations are not in agreement regarding the most appropriate international course of action. In such cases, the question of which regional organisation to follow can come down to a matter of political preference rather than objective determination. Regional organisations should thus be regarded as only one of several sets of actors that can contribute to international reactions to mass atrocity situations.

6.3 UN Human Rights Council and General Assembly

Together, the UN HRC and UNGA responded to the Libyan R2P situation through undertaking a range of non-military measures. On 25 February 2011, the HRC adopted Resolution S-15/1, which called upon the Libyan regime to 'meet its responsibility to protect its population'[66] (thus affirming R2P's Pillar 1) and furthermore established an International Commission of Inquiry on Libya with the mandate to:

> [I]nvestigate all alleged violations of international human rights law in the Libyan Arab Jamahiriya, to establish the facts and circumstances of such violations and of the crimes perpetrated and, where possible, to identify those responsible, to make recommendations, in particular, on accountability measures, all with a view to ensuring that those individuals responsible are held accountable.[67]

Through setting up this Commission of Inquiry, the HRC assumed an investigative and non-coercive role in addressing the R2P situation in Libya. Namely, the Commission's findings offered, as observed by Akande and Tonkin, the potential to make 'authoritative determinations of whether [violations] have taken place and who is responsible',[68] or, in other words, the potential to objectively evaluate, through an independent body, whether mass atrocity crimes had been committed in the Libyan context, and if so, which ones. Its findings were also, importantly, meant to serve as warnings and deterrents to individuals committing (or about to commit) relevant crimes, thereby seeking to prevent the commission of further atrocities.

HRC Resolution S-15/1 furthermore recommended that the UNGA suspend Libya's membership from the HRC for its 'gross and systematic violations of human rights'.[69] On 3 March 2011, the UNGA acted upon the HRC's recommendation

66 HRC Res S-15/1 (3 March 2011) UN Doc A/HRC/RES/S-15/1 Para 2.
67 Ibid., Para 11.
68 Dapo Akande and Hannah Tonkin, 'International Commissions of Inquiry: A New Form of Adjudication?' (*EJIL: Talk!*, 6 April 2012) <http://www.ejiltalk.org/international-commissions-of-inquiry-a-new-form-of-adjudication/>.
69 UN Doc A/HRC/RES/S-15/1 (n66) Para 14.

and adopted Resolution 65/265 without vote, which '[expressed] deep concern about the human rights situation in [Libya]' and '[suspended Libya's] rights of membership in the Human Rights Council'.[70] Through this move, the UNGA exercised a legal right bestowed upon it through UNGA Resolution 60/251, which allows the body to suspend a member-State from the HRC through a two-thirds majority vote if the said State commits 'gross and systematic violations of human rights'.[71]

UNGA Resolution 65/265, which effectuated Libya's suspension from the HRC, did not make specific reference to R2P. Within the discussions that followed its adoption, however, 11 out of the 33 States that delivered statements specifically mentioned that Libya had failed in its obligation to protect its population as per R2P's Pillar 1, indicating widespread support for this aspect of R2P.[72] With respect to a Pillar 3 responsibility of the international community to react, however, States were considerably more divided. Only four States (Hungary, Maldives, Botswana, and Australia) implied that the UNGA's suspension of Libya from the HRC was undertaken as part of a Pillar 3 obligation of the international community, which hardly represents sufficient *opinio juris* to indicate the emergence of such an obligation under customary international law.[73] Counteracted by these sentiments was another small group of States (including Cuba, Nicaragua, Russia, China, Ecuador, Bolivia, and Venezuela) which, although it expressed concern regarding the human rights situation in Libya, was opposed to Libya's suspension from the HRC, or at least held fundamental misgivings surrounding the move due to alleged infringements upon State sovereignty and non-interference.[74] R2P was not specifically cited by these States, although their concerns revolved around a common theme of controversy surrounding the doctrine, namely, that some States perceive it to embody an interventionist tool that can be abused by certain powers under the guise of humanitarianism. While this group of States also represented a minority view, the presence of key players in this camp (most notably, Russia and China as permanent UNSC members) meant that it exerted substantial influence on R2P discourse, which became even more apparent in the Syrian context as discussed in Chapter 7 of this book.

While one small group of States characterised Libya's suspension from the HRC as a means of fulfilling a collective obligation under R2P's Pillar 3, and while another one depicted it as an interventionist measure contrary to established principles of State sovereignty and non-interference, the vast majority of States viewed it instead as a legitimate exercise of the UNGA's right (but not obligation)

70 UNGA Res 65/265 (3 March 2011) UN Doc A/RES/65/265 Preamble, Para 1.
71 UNGA Res 60/251 (3 April 2006) UN Doc A/RES/60/251 Para 8.
72 UNGA, '76th Plenary Meeting' (1 March 2011) UN Doc A/65/PV.76 (comments of Chile, Panama, US, Mexico, Guatemala, New Zealand, Indonesia, Hungary, Maldives, Botswana, and Australia).
73 Ibid., 8, 11, 16, 19.
74 Ibid., 6–7, 12–13, 15–19 (comments of Venezuela, Cuba, Russia, Nicaragua, China, Ecuador, and Bolivia).

to react to the mass atrocity situation in Libya.[75] The United States, for example, claimed that the UNGA 'acted in the noblest *traditions* of the United Nations'.[76] Guatemala stated that Libya's suspension constituted 'an act of solidarity with the people of Libya' and that it also '[strengthened] the mechanisms *at the disposal* of the United Nations to defend and promote human rights at the global level'.[77] Norway maintained that '[b]y taking action today we have exercised the stated will of the Assembly … to *allow for* the suspension of members of the Council that commit gross and systematic violations of human rights'.[78] New Zealand asserted that '[w]e have supported this General Assembly decision to *exercise its power* to suspend the rights of any member of the Council that commits gross and systematic human rights violations'.[79] These States therefore viewed Libya's suspension from the HRC as a mere exercise of the UNGA's competencies to address a mass atrocity situation.

Both the HRC's establishment of a Commission of Inquiry on Libya as well as the UNGA's suspension of Libya from the HRC represent non-military reaction mechanisms that can be invoked to discharge R2P's Pillar 3, namely, that they were both designed to exert pressure on Libya (without the use of force) to cease its commission of atrocities against its population. In adopting these measures, States were in general agreement regarding an obligation of the Libyan State to protect its population as per R2P's Pillar 1, although they were notably divided over aspects pertaining to Pillar 3, namely, whether the international community possessed a duty or even a right to take action in the face of the mass atrocity situation. Significantly, Libya's suspension from the HRC marked the first time that the UNGA invoked its mandate to suspend a member-State from the body because of its human rights violations,[80] reflecting an increased international willingness or even expectation to hold States accountable for mass atrocity crimes committed within their borders. As with the LAS's suspension of Libya from the body, such exclusions of States from international organisations represent a powerful means of signalling international rejection of States' violations of their R2P Pillar 1 obligations and of inducing compliance by these States with the doctrine's principles.

6.4 UN Security Council

6.4.1 Security Council Resolution 1970

On 26 February 2011, the UNSC unanimously adopted Resolution 1970 under Chapter VII which demanded an end to the violence in Libya,[81] referred the

75 Ibid. (*see* comments of US, Mexico, Canada, Colombia, Chile, Guatemala, Panama, Costa Rica, Peru, Norway, Japan, New Zealand, Thailand, Cape Verde and Switzerland).
76 Ibid., 7 (emphasis added).
77 Ibid., 12 (emphasis added).
78 Ibid., 14 (emphasis added).
79 Ibid., 15–16 (emphasis added).
80 *See* Pierre Thielbörger, 'The Status and Future of International Law after the Libya Intervention' (2012) 4 *Goettingen Journal of International Law* 11, 42.
81 UNSC Res 1970 (26 February 2011) UN Doc S/RES/1970 Para 1.

Libyan situation to the International Criminal Court (ICC),[82] and imposed an arms embargo, travel ban, and asset freeze upon specified Libyan individuals and entities.[83] The Resolution furthermore specifically cited 'the Libyan authorities' responsibility to protect its population',[84] thus affirming R2P's Pillar 1. It failed, however, to reference Pillar 3 (whether directly or indirectly), thus framing the Resolution's adoption through the UNSC's exercise of its Chapter VII powers rather than through the body's fulfilment of any sort of responsibility.[85]

Although UNSC Resolution 1970 was not adopted with reference to any international obligation to react to the Libyan R2P situation, it nevertheless demonstrated States' willingness to employ timely and robust measures to address the mass atrocity crimes that were being committed. Its adoption, for example, came only 11 days following the commencement of anti-government protests in Libya, which represents a rather swift international response given the often lengthy and bureaucratic manner through which such decisions are made and implemented. The Resolution furthermore marked only the second instance in which the UNSC referred a situation to the ICC in which the State in question was not a signatory to the ICC Statute[86] (the first time being the referral of the situation in Darfur in 2005[87]). It is also significant that the US and China, both wary of ICC jurisdiction due to concerns regarding the infringement upon State sovereignty, supported such a UNSC referral (both abstained from voting on Darfur in 2005).[88] Therefore, in light of community interests of alleviating a mass atrocity situation, UNSC member-States demonstrated a readiness to adopt timely and decisive measures against Libya as the violating State.

The measures adopted under UNSC Resolution 1970, similar to those implemented by the HRC and UNGA discussed in the previous section, were both lawful and non-military. They were lawful in that they were undertaken through the UNSC's established prerogatives under the UN Charter's Chapter VII. They were also non-military in that they applied pressure on Libya without the use of force to induce it to conform to its Pillar 1 protection responsibilities. This emphasises that there exist a range of methods through which R2P's Pillar 3 can be operationalised, depending upon the situation at hand as well as the remit and respective mandates of each international actor.

82 Ibid., Para 4.
83 Ibid., Paras 9, 15, 17.
84 Ibid., Preamble.
85 *See* Aidan Hehir, 'The Permanence of Inconsistency: Libya, the Security Council, and the Responsibility to Protect' (2013) 38 *International Security* 137, 147.
86 *See* Mahnoush Arsanjani, 'The Rome Statute of the International Criminal Court' (1999) 93 *American Journal of International Law* 22, 27.
87 UNSC Res 1593 (31 March 2005) UN Doc S/RES/1593. This Resolution was adopted prior to R2P's endorsement by States in the 2005 World Summit Outcome document, and hence, R2P was not invoked within it.
88 *See* El Hassan bin Talal and Rolf Schwarz, 'The Responsibility to Protect and the Arab World: An Emerging International Norm?' (2013) 34 *Contemporary Security Policy* 1, 8.

6.4.2 Security Council Resolution 1973

Pursuant to UNSC Resolution 1970, the UNSC adopted Resolution 1973 on 17 March 2011 which observed that the 'situation in the Libyan Arab Jamahiriya continues to constitute a threat to international peace and security' and proceeded to invoke Chapter VII of the UN Charter, and more specifically Article 42 of the Charter under which the use of force can be authorised.[89] This Resolution stressed the 'responsibility of Libyan authorities to protect the Libyan population', thus affirming R2P's Pillar 1.[90] It furthermore made clear that it deemed Libya to have failed to uphold this protection responsibility, as it specifically '[deplored] the failure of the Libyan authorities to comply with resolution 1970', which itself had '[recalled] the Libyan authorities' responsibility to protect its population'.[91] As such, Resolution 1973 proceeded to introduce robust measures against the Libyan State that could be viewed as the international community's assumption of this protection responsibility given host State failure, although, as with other international initiatives discussed thus far, there was no reference to an obligation of the international community to react as per R2P's Pillar 3.

Within the operative text of UNSC Resolution 1973, Paragraph 4 authorised member-States to 'take all necessary measures ... to protect civilians and civilian populated areas under threat of attack in the Libyan Arab Jamahiriya ... while excluding a foreign occupation force of any form on any part of Libyan territory'.[92] Paragraph 6 established 'a ban on all flights in the airspace of the Libyan Arab Jamahiriya in order to help protect civilians'[93] – which effectively instituted a no-fly zone over Libyan airspace – and Paragraph 8 authorised States 'to take all necessary measures to enforce compliance with [this] ban on flights'.[94] The allowance for member-States to 'take all necessary measures', as in Paragraphs 4 and 8, is widely understood in the context of UNSC resolutions to authorise the use of force.[95] The specified purpose for this authorisation was 'to protect civilians [and civilian populated areas]', meaning that force could only be employed to secure this particular objective (and not, for example, to pursue other end goals such as regime change or instating democracy).[96] As a means of preventing abuse, Paragraph 4 prohibited 'a foreign occupation force of any form on any part of Libyan territory'.[97] While this

89 UN Doc S/RES/1973 (n8) Preamble.
90 Ibid.
91 Ibid.
92 Ibid., Para 4.
93 Ibid., Para 6.
94 Ibid., Para 8.
95 *See* Mehrdad Payandeh, 'The United Nations, Military Intervention, and Regime Change in Libya' (2011–2012) 52 *Virginia Journal of International Law* 355, 384–5; Michael N. Schmitt, 'Wings over Libya: The No-fly Zone in Legal Perspective' (2011) 36 *Yale Journal of International Law Online* 45, 45.
96 *See* Christian Henderson, 'International Measures for the Protection of Civilians in Libya and Cote d'Ivoire' (2011) 60 *International and Comparative Law Quarterly* 767, 771–72.
97 UNSC Resolution 1973 (n8) Para 4.

provision did not necessarily preclude the presence of foreign ground troops as part of a military operation undertaken pursuant to Resolution 1973, it at least conditioned that such troops should not attain a level of control within Libyan territory that amounted to an occupation.[98]

UNSC Resolution 1973 marked the first instance in which R2P was invoked in a UNSC resolution that authorised the use of force.[99] This reinforces that despite the doctrine's emphasis upon preventative and non-coercive elements as a means of assuaging certain States' fears that R2P is a reincarnation of humanitarian intervention, military force remains a viable option under the doctrine to be utilised in the most compelling circumstances, namely, when host States manifestly fail to protect their populations in gross violation of their Pillar 1 obligations, and when less interventionist means have not or are not likely to work. In Libya, the UNSC's authorisation of the use of force demonstrated an international commitment to employ the full range of means at the body's disposal to tackle a situation that was deemed to lie within R2P's remit. Furthermore, given that world powers, most particularly the P5, usually entertain divergent national interests, it is significant that their political differences gave way to the imperative to protect civilians and that they were able to cooperate through the UNSC's institutional framework to authorise the use of force as a means of bringing to an end the mass atrocity situation.[100] Despite this international momentum to respond to the Libyan R2P situation, however, deep rifts soon emerged with respect to the implementation of UNSC Resolution 1973. This is discussed in the next section.

6.5 NATO

On 19 March 2011, French, British, and US forces began implementing UNSC Resolution 1973 through targeted airstrikes against Libyan assets and yielded to a NATO military operation on 31 March.[101] By then, there were indications that the primary purpose of the intervention in Libya was shifting beyond mere civilian protection to encompass the pursuit of regime change.[102] Sure enough, when NATO officially concluded its military campaign on 31 October, Libyan President Muammar Gaddafi had been killed by Western-backed Libyan rebels and plans were underway for a political transition within the country.[103] NATO's operations proved to be highly controversial, as it was unclear whether the authorisation within UNSC Resolution 1973 to take 'all necessary measures' to protect civilians

98 *See* Paul R. Williams and Colleen Popken, 'Security Council Resolution 1973 on Libya: A Moment of Legal & Moral Clarity' (2011) 44 *Case Western Reserve Journal of International Law* 225, 246–47.
99 *See* Gary Wilson, 'Applying the Responsibility to Protect to the "Arab Spring"' (2014) 35 *Liverpool Law Review* 157, 164.
100 *See* Thielbörger (n80) 30; Saira Mohamed, 'Taking Stock of the Responsibility to Protect' (2012) 48 *Stanford Journal of International Law* 319, 331.
101 *See supra* note 9.
102 *See infra* note 186 and accompanying text.
103 *See supra* note 10.

could extend to regime change.[104] This issue holds implications upon the implementation of future R2P Chapter VII mandates for civilian protection, namely, how strictly such mandates must be interpreted and what limits, if any, exist with respect to their enforcement.

6.5.1 R2P and regime change

The UNSC has in the past invoked its Chapter VII powers to authorise the pursuit of regime change (including in R2P situations), which suggests that regime change does not in itself represent a misuse of the UNSC's powers. In Haiti, for example, after non-military initiatives failed to restore democratically elected President Aristide following a military coup in 1991, and also given an ensuing humanitarian crisis,[105] the UNSC adopted Resolution 940 under its Chapter VII powers which determined that the situation in Haiti 'continues to constitute a threat to peace and security in the region' and authorised States to use 'all necessary means to facilitate the departure from Haiti of the military leadership'.[106] This Resolution, which clearly promoted regime change, was admittedly limited or controversial on three grounds. First, it emphasised the 'unique character' and 'extraordinary nature' of the situation in Haiti and thus described its response to the situation as an 'exceptional' one.[107] This perhaps limits the precedential status of the Haiti case. Second, Mexico, Uruguay, and China did not consider the situation in Haiti serious enough to constitute a threat to international peace and security, and hence protested the UNSC's right to invoke its Chapter VII powers in order to address it.[108] Third, these same States, along with Cuba, Venezuela, and Brazil, argued that peaceful options for resolving the issue had not been exhausted and that the use of force was therefore unwarranted.[109] In evaluating these criticisms, however, it is important to note that the lawfulness of the pursuit of regime change was not subject to dispute, as none of the States challenged the competence of the UNSC to authorise this mode of action. It is also significant that China and Brazil (as UNSC member-States) abstained from rather than voted against the Resolution despite its being clearly aimed at regime change. The remaining thirteen UNSC member-States voted in favour of the Resolution and

104 *See* Olivier Corten and Vaios Koutroulis, 'The Illegality of Military Support to Rebels in the Libyan War: Aspects of Jus Contra Bellum and Jus in Bello' (2013) 18 *Journal of Conflict and Security Law* 59; Thomas H. Lee, 'The Law of War and the Responsibility to Protect Civilians: A Reinterpretation' (2014) 55 *Harvard International Law Journal* 251; S. Pandiaraj, 'Sovereignty as Responsibility: Reflections on the Legal Status of the Doctrine of Responsibility to Protect' (2016) 15 *Chinese Journal of International Law* 795.

105 *See* Michael D. Ramsey, 'Reinventing the Security Council: The U.N. as a Lockean System' (2003–2004) 79 *Notre Dame Law Review* 1529, 1533–4.

106 UNSC Res 940 (31 July 1994) UN Doc S/RES/940 at Preamble, Para 4.

107 Ibid., Para 2.

108 UNSC 3413th Meeting (31 July 1994) UN Doc S/PV.3413 at 4, 7, 10.

109 Ibid., 4, 6–10.

did not voice any reservations pertaining to the pursuit of regime change following the adoption of a Chapter VII mandate.[110]

Other examples of the UNSC's direct or indirect authorisation of regime change reinforce the UNSC's competence to sanction this practice as a means of addressing situations that threaten or breach international peace and security. For instance, UNSC Resolution 1378, adopted in November 2001 in the context of post-9/11 Afghanistan, supported 'the efforts of the Afghan people to replace the Taliban regime' and emphasised that the 'United Nations should play a central role in supporting the efforts of the Afghan people to establish urgently such a new and transitional administration leading to the formation of a new government'.[111] To put this Resolution into context, it should be noted that it was not adopted under Chapter VII, although it came against the backdrop of the US-led military intervention in Afghanistan which had commenced the month prior as a response to the 9/11 attacks.[112] This intervention, as noted by Kinacioğlu, was premised upon collective self-defence rather than UNSC Chapter VII authorisation.[113] With that said, however, UNSC Resolution 1368, adopted the day after the 9/11 attacks, characterised those attacks as a threat to international peace and security, in addition to affirming the relevance of individual and collective self-defence.[114] Therefore, even if the wider military operations in Afghanistan did not stem specifically from a UNSC Chapter VII mandate, the relevance of the situation to international peace and security was nevertheless established by the UNSC.

UNSC Resolution 1378, which supported 'the efforts of the Afghan people to replace the Taliban regime' as mentioned above, was endorsed unanimously including by traditionally outspoken critics of military intervention such as China, Russia, Iran, and India.[115] As this Resolution was not adopted under Chapter VII, it did not authorise the use of force, nor did it, by default, grant a right for States to engage in regime change in Afghanistan. Nevertheless, the Resolution clearly encouraged the Afghan people to replace their government and thus assumed an unambiguous stance against what was previously an incumbent government. Furthermore, by stating that the 'United Nations should play a central role' in the transition process, the Resolution affirmed the UN's willingness to be directly involved in developments that transpired out of the regime change.

Finally, in 2011, shortly after the adoption of UNSC Resolution 1973 on Libya, the UNSC adopted Resolution 1975 on the situation in Côte d'Ivoire, which the Resolution affirmed 'continues to constitute a threat to international

110 Mexico, Uruguay, Cuba, and Venezuela were not UNSC member-States at the time.

111 UNSC Res 1378 (14 November 2011) UN Doc S/RES/1378 at Preamble, Para 3.

112 *See* Müge Kinacioğlu, 'Forcing Democracy: Is Military Intervention for Regime Change Permissible?' (2012) 1 *All Azimuth* 28, 43; 'Timeline: US intervention in Afghanistan 2001 to 2017' (*Aljazeera*, 22 August 2017) <http://www.aljazeera.com/news/2017/08/2001-2017-intervention-afghanistan-170822035036797.html>.

113 Kinacioğlu (n112) 43.

114 UNSC Res 1368 (12 September 2001) UN Doc S/RES/1368 Para 1.

115 UNSC 4414th Meeting (13 November 2001) UN Doc S/PV.4414; UNSC 4414th Meeting (Resumption 1) (13 November 2001) UN Doc S/PV.4414 (Resumption 1).

peace and security'.[116] Resolution 1975 invoked both Chapter VII and R2P (in the Pillar 1 context) and urged still-sitting President Gbagbo 'to immediately step aside' in favour of democratically elected President Ouattara and '[urged] all Ivorian State institutions … to yield to the authority vested by the Ivorian people in President Alassane Dramane Ouattara'.[117] The Resolution was endorsed unanimously although it contained a clear call for Gbagbo to step down.[118] Resolution 1975 furthermore provided the United Nations Operation in Côte d'Ivoire (UNOCI) with a mandate to employ 'all necessary means … to protect civilians',[119] which was used by UNOCI and French troops to take military action which ultimately led to regime change.[120] This elicited criticisms from India and Russia that the peacekeeping operations violated the principles of neutrality when they engaged in the pursuit of regime change.[121] These criticisms, however, were notably confined and were not voiced by other States. Additionally, it should be appreciated that the pursuit of regime change by a peacekeeping force, which was called upon in UNSC Resolution 1975 to 'impartially [implement] its mandate',[122] is quite distinct from the pursuit of regime change by intervening States following a general UNSC authorisation for member-States to take 'all necessary measures' to protect civilians in response to a situation that threatens or breaches international peace and security as was done in the Libyan case.

The build-up of practice surrounding the explicit endorsement of regime change by the UNSC as a means of addressing situations that threaten or breach international peace and security, including under Chapter VII and while specifically invoking R2P, illustrates that this mode of action is not inherently contrary to the UNSC's legal prerogatives. This conclusion is compatible with the (non-binding[123]) recommendations of the 2001 ICISS report, which offers the following thoughts with respect to the relationship between R2P and regime change:

> The primary purpose of the intervention must be to halt or avert human suffering. Any use of military force that aims from the outset, for example, for the alteration of borders or the advancement of a particular combatant group's claim to self-determination, cannot be justified. Overthrow of regimes is not, as such, a legitimate objective, although disabling that regime's capacity to harm

116 UNSC Res 1975 (30 March 2011) UN Doc S/RES/1975, Preamble.
117 Ibid., Paras 3–4.
118 *See* Matthias Vanhullebusch, 'Regime Change, the Security Council and China' (2015) 14 *Chinese Journal of International Law* 665, 680.
119 UN Doc S/RES/1975 (n116) Para 6.
120 *See* John F. Murphy, 'Responsibility to Protect (R2P) Comes of Age? A Sceptic's View' (2011–2012) 18 *International Law Students' Association Journal of International and Comparative Law* 413, 436.
121 *See* UNSC 6508th Meeting (30 March 2011) UN Doc S/PV.6508, 3 (India); 'Russia Lashes Out at UN Military Action in Cote d'Ivoire' (*Russia Today*, 5 April 2011) < http://www.rt.com/news/cote-ivoire-gbagbo-un/>.
122 UN Doc S/RES/1975 (n116) Para 6.
123 *See* Section 2.3 of this book.

its own people may be essential to discharging the mandate of protection – and what is necessary to achieve that disabling will vary from case to case.[124]

In essence, the report emphasises that the primary purpose of any international action under R2P must be that of human protection. As such, the pursuit of regime change as an end goal in itself is not justified under the doctrine. With that said, however, the report concedes, albeit indirectly, that regime change may be required under certain circumstances in order to achieve the central objective of human protection in an R2P situation, presumably when other means of achieving such protection have not or will not be successful.

The above analysis suggests that the pursuit of regime change in a mass atrocity situation is neither contrary to the UNSC's prerogatives under its Chapter VII powers nor is it incompatible with the R2P doctrine. Ultimately, the acceptability of this course of action as a means of responding to an R2P situation will depend upon the particulars of the authorising UNSC resolution, namely, whether any limits are imposed with respect to its enforcement, and if so, which ones. As such, a detailed examination of UNSC Resolution 1973, which authorised the use of force in the Libyan context, is undertaken in the subsequent sections of this book, with view to determining whether regime change represented a lawful means of discharging its mandate.

6.5.2 Interpretation of UN Security Council resolutions

The lawfulness of NATO's pursuit of regime change in Libya pursuant to UNSC Resolution 1973 requires an examination of the precise authorisation granted within this Resolution, which in turn necessitates a defined process for the interpretation of its relevant provisions. Although UNSC resolutions have long been the subject of proceedings before international courts and tribunals,[125] there remains – and quite ironically – an absence of authoritative rules regarding their interpretation. Instead, the interpretation of UNSC resolutions in international case law has borrowed from the rules of interpretation of treaties, for example as stipulated within Articles 31–32 of the Vienna Convention on the Law of Treaties (VCLT). In brief, Article 31 VCLT states that:

124 'The Responsibility to Protect: The Report of the International Commission on Intervention and State Sovereignty' (*International Commission on Intervention and State Sovereignty*, December 2001) Para 4.33 <http://responsibilitytoprotect.org/ICISS%20Report.pdf> [hereinafter 2001 ICISS Report].

125 See, e.g. as discussed in infra notes 132–134, *Legal Consequences for States of the Continued Presence of South Africa in Namibia (South West Africa) Notwithstanding Security Council Resolution 276* (Advisory Opinion) [1971] ICJ Rep 16 [hereinafter *Namibia* case]; *Prosecutor v Tadić* (Decision on the defence motion of interlocutory appeal on jurisdiction) ICTY-94-1 (2 October 1995) [hereinafter *Tadić* case]; *Accordance with International Law of the Unilateral Declaration of Independence by the Provisional Institutions of Self-Government of Kosovo* (Advisory Opinion) [2010] ICJ Rep 403 [hereinafter *Kosovo* case]; *Al-Jedda* case (n22).

> 1) The terms of a treaty should be interpreted in accordance with their ordinary meaning, bearing in mind the context and the treaty's overall object and purpose; 2) The context includes any agreements or instruments associated with the treaty as agreed to by the parties; 3) Subsequent agreements, subsequent practice, and relevant rules of international law as relevant to the treaty should be taken into account; 4) Special meaning can be assigned to specific terms if the parties so intend.[126]

Article 32 VCLT adds that supplementary means of interpreting treaties, including preparatory work and surrounding circumstances, can corroborate the meaning deduced from the application of Article 31 or can be utilised to overcome any ambiguity, obscurity, unreasonableness, or absurdity resulting from the application of Article 31.[127]

Scholars of international law generally agree that the VCLT's rules for treaty interpretation as per its Articles 31–32 can assist with the interpretation of UNSC resolutions, and that at least some of them can apply by analogy.[128] This is reflected in a passage from the International Court of Justice's (ICJ) 2010 *Kosovo* case, in which the Court affirmed that the relevant provisions of the VCLT 'may provide guidance' in the interpretation of UNSC resolutions.[129] However, these same scholars have been equally careful to stress that treaties and UNSC resolutions are fundamentally different in nature, and that therefore, the rules of treaty interpretation cannot be fully transferable to UNSC resolutions.[130] This is highlighted in the more extended passage from the *Kosovo* case, in which the ICJ observed:

> While the rules on treaty interpretation embodied in Articles 31 and 32 of the Vienna Convention on the Law of Treaties may provide guidance, differences between Security Council resolutions and treaties mean that the interpretation of Security Council resolutions also require that other factors be taken into account. Security Council resolutions are issued by a single, collective body and are drafted through a very different process than that used for the conclusion of a treaty. Security Council resolutions are the product of a voting

126 Vienna Convention on the Law of Treaties (adopted 23 May 1969, entered into force 27 January 1980) 111 UNTS 331, Art 31 [hereinafter VCLT].

127 Ibid., Art 32.

128 *See* Alexander Orakhelashvili, *Collective Security* (Oxford University Press 2011) 40–41; Michael C. Wood, 'The Interpretation of Security Council Resolutions' (1998) 2 *Max Planck Yearbook of United Nations Law Online* 73 at 81, 95 [hereinafter Wood Interpretation]; Michael C. Wood, 'The Interpretation of Security Council Resolutions, Revisited' (2017) 20 *Max Planck Yearbook of United Nations Law Online* 1 at 7–8 and 12–13 [hereinafter Wood Interpretation Revisited]; Efthymios Papastavridis, 'Interpretation of Security Council Resolutions under Chapter VII in the Aftermath of the Iraqi Crisis' (2007) 56 *International and Comparative Law Quarterly* 83, 87–88.

129 *Kosovo* case (n125) Para 94.

130 *See supra* note 128.

> process as provided for in Article 27 of the Charter, and the final text of such resolutions represents the view of the Security Council as a body. Moreover, Security Council resolutions can be binding on all Member States ... , irrespective of whether they played any part in their formulation.[131]

Generally, therefore, it is accepted that the interpretation of UNSC resolutions can borrow from the rules of treaty interpretation as per Articles 31–32 VCLT, although these rules must be tailored to the specific nature of UNSC resolutions as a distinct legal source. Three themes in particular stand out, based upon determinations of international judicial bodies as well as writings of international legal scholars: First, the ordinary meaning of a resolution's relevant provisions should be determined (*Namibia, Tadić, Kosovo*, and *Al-Jedda* cases).[132] This derives from Article 31(1) VCLT and includes, as per Article 31(4) VCLT, any special meaning that may be assigned to certain terms as established by UNSC member-States and/or prior UNSC practice. Second, also as per Article 31(1) VCLT, a resolution's ordinary meaning should be contextualised bearing in mind its object and purpose (*Tadić* and *Kosovo* cases).[133] Third, supplementary means of interpretation, including prior or subsequent resolutions, statements of States, official reports or records, or facts on the ground can be utilised to assist in the interpretation of the above (*Namibia, Tadić, Kosovo*, and *Al-Jedda* cases).[134] This derives from Article 32 VCLT, although Articles 31(2) and 31(3) (which cite the interpretive value of related or subsequent agreements, related instruments, and

131 *Kosovo* case (n125) Para 94.

132 *Namibia* case (n125) Para 114 ('having regard to *the terms of the resolution* to be interpreted' – emphasis added); *Tadić* case (n125) Para 71 (this case engaged in a 'Literal Interpretation of the Statute'. The Statute was itself established pursuant to UNSC Resolution 827); *Kosovo* case (n125) Para 95; *Al-Jedda* case (n22) Para 76 ('[A] United Nations Security Council resolution should be interpreted in the light not only of the language used but also the context in which it was adopted').

133 *Tadić* case (n125) Para 71 (noted the need to 'consider the object and purpose behind the enactment of the Statute' i.e. UNSC Resolution 827); *Kosovo* case (n125) Para 95 ('Having earlier outlined the principal characteristics of Security Council resolution 1244 (1999), ... the Court next observes that three distinct features of that resolution are relevant for discerning its object and purpose').

134 *Namibia* case (n125) Para 114 ('having regard to the terms of the resolution to be interpreted, *the discussions leading to it, the Charter provisions invoked and, in general, all circumstances that might assist in determining the legal consequences of the resolution of the Security Council*' – emphasis added); *Tadić* case (n125) Paras 72–78 (in searching for the object and purpose of the ICTY Statute i.e. UNSC Resolution 827, the ICTY considered a range of sources including the terms of the resolution, previous resolutions, UN Secretary-General reports, and statements of States); *Kosovo* case (n125) Paras 96–100 (in conducting an examination into the object and purpose of UNSC Resolution 1244, the ICJ relied upon supplementary means of interpretation including past resolutions, a report of the UN Secretary-General, and a regulation of the UN Mission in Kosovo); *Al-Jedda* case (n22) Paras 77–86 (the ICJ relied upon supplementary means of interpretation including the language and purpose of several related UNSC resolutions, letters submitted by member-States to the UN, and other circumstances).

subsequent practice) are also relevant in this respect. Scholars of international law have emphasised the elevated role that supplementary materials, for example *travaux*, can hold in the interpretation of UNSC resolutions as compared to treaties, highlighting one area of difference between treaty and UNSC resolution interpretation.[135]

Together, the above three criteria (ordinary meaning, object and purpose, and supplementary materials) can facilitate the interpretive exercise of UNSC Resolution 1973 on Libya to determine whether regime change constituted a legitimate means of enforcing its mandate to employ the use of force. The next three sections of this book are devoted to the separate examination of each of these criteria in this respect.

6.5.3 Ordinary meaning of UNSC Resolution 1973

The search for the limits of the authorisation contained within UNSC Resolution 1973 on Libya commences from an examination of its relevant provisions' ordinary meanings. As mentioned in Section 6.4.2 of this chapter, the authorisation in Paragraphs 4 and 8 of Resolution 1973 for member-States to 'take all necessary measures' is commonly understood in the context of UNSC resolutions to authorise the use of force.[136] Beyond that, however, it is unclear what measures, if any, are either permitted or precluded from the enforcement of such mandates. Some authors advocate an expansive interpretation of the term 'necessary', implying that once the UNSC authorises the use of force, the options for implementing the respective resolution are essentially open-ended as long as they relate to the central objective and are proportionate.[137] However, it is maintained that this interpretation is too wide and could result in large-scale military interventions in situations in which the targeted use of force would be more appropriate. Similarly, however, an interpretation of the opposite extreme is equally unrealistic, namely, one that advances that only military tactics that are absolutely necessary to achieve the objective of civilian protection should be permitted.[138] Such an interpretation is arguably too stringent and cannot be practically adhered to by intervening parties.

Instead, Sarooshi rightly stresses that States should be afforded a degree of flexibility and discretion in enforcing a UNSC Chapter VII mandate, while also adhering to minimum constraints that are binding upon the UNSC itself.[139] This means that implemented measures should reflect the object and purpose of the

135 *See* Wood Interpretation (n128) 94–95; Wood Interpretation Revisited (n128) 35; Papastavridis (n128) 104–06; Bart Duijzentkunst, 'Interpretation of Legislative Security Council Resolutions' (2008) 4 *Utrecht Law Review* 188, 206.

136 *See supra* note 95.

137 *See* Payandeh (n95) 384–85; Ulfstein and Christiansen (n52) 162.

138 *See* Teimouri and Subedi (n11) 27.

139 Danesh Sarooshi, *The United Nations and the Development of Collective Security: The Delegation by the UN Security Council of its Chapter VII Powers* (Clarendon Press 1999) 159.

resolution and should adhere to relevant norms of international law (for example, *jus cogens* norms and fundamental principles of IHL and IHRL[140]). Yee furthermore notes that because the use of force constitutes the most severe infringement upon a State's sovereignty, a narrow interpretation of the term 'necessary' within a UNSC Chapter VII resolution authorising force should always be favoured over a wider one.[141] However, the pursuit of more aggressive measures is not inherently ruled out if such measures are most conducive to fulfilling the resolution's objectives.

With respect to UNSC Resolution 1973, the authorisation for States to take 'all necessary measures' under Paragraphs 4 and 8 was directly tied to the object and purpose of civilian protection.[142] As such, while enforcement measures undertaken pursuant to this Resolution could presumably enjoy a degree of flexibility, they would be expected to conform to this central objective with priority given to less interventionist means (whether or not this was achieved is the subject of the next section). Moreover, a deeper examination of Resolution 1973 reveals the potential to interpret its provisions quite expansively. First, Paragraph 4 authorised protection for both 'civilians' and 'civilian populated areas', meaning that NATO forces were not only allowed to employ force to protect civilians, but also to protect geographical areas in which civilians resided. Presumably, this could have extended protection to military objects – which would have otherwise constituted legitimate targets for Gaddafi forces under IHL – if they were located within civilian-populated areas.[143] It also could have led to the protection of areas controlled by rebels if they were populated by civilians, which would have by default contributed to the protection of opposition forces stationed within civilian-populated areas.[144]

Second, Paragraph 4 of UNSC Resolution 1973 did not authorise protection for civilians or civilian-populated areas 'under attack', but rather those 'under threat of attack' in Libya. This wording is much more open-ended, meaning that there did not have to be an actual or even an imminent attack initiated by Libyan forces in order for member-States to enforce the Resolution.[145] Rather, a mere

140 On international legal norms that bind the UNSC, *see* Orakhelashvili (n128) 57–58; Elena Katselli, 'Holding the Security Council Accountable for Human Rights Violations' (2007) 1 *Human Rights and International Legal Discourse* 301 at 318–19, 323–24; August Reinisch, 'Developing Human Rights and Humanitarian Law Accountability of the Security Council for the Imposition of Economic Sanctions' (2001) 95 *American Journal of International Law* 851, 856–59; T. D. Gill, 'Legal and Some Political Limitations on the Power of the UN Security Council to Exercise its Enforcement Powers under Chapter VII of the Charter' (1995) 26 *Netherlands Yearbook of International Law* 33 at 74, 77–79, 82–83; Dapo Akande, 'The International Court of Justice and the Security Council: Is There Room for Judicial Control of Decisions of the Political Organs of the United Nations?' (1997) 46 *International and Comparative Law Quarterly* 309 at 309, 316, 322.

141 Sienho Yee, 'The Dynamic Interplay between the Interpreters of Security Council Resolutions' (2012) 11 *Chinese Journal of International Law* 613, 617.

142 UN Doc S/RES/1973 (n8) Paras 4, 8.

143 *See* Williams and Popken (n98) 237–38; Ulfstein and Christiansen (n52) 163.

144 *See* Schmitt (n95) 56; Williams and Popken (n98) 238.

145 *See* Ulfstein and Christiansen (n52) 163–64; Williams and Popken (n98) 239.

threat of attack would be sufficient, which could presumably be gauged through troop movements, verbal declarations, or other means, thus opening the door to pre-emptive military engagements against Gaddafi's forces.

Third, the authorisation for States to take 'all necessary measures … to protect civilians and civilian populated areas' was subject to a restriction, namely, that implementing States could not establish 'a foreign occupation force of any form on any part of Libyan territory'.[146] As pointed out by scholars of international law, this provision did not completely preclude the stationing of foreign troops on Libyan soil, but only did so to the extent that they did not become an occupying force.[147] Gray furthermore notes that because this paragraph was specific as to means that member-States could not employ over the course of the Resolution's implementation, it could perhaps be presumed that other means of achieving civilian protection, including regime change, could arguably fall within its remit.[148]

Finally, the 'ordinary meaning' of other provisions within UNSC Resolution 1973 also fail to rule out the possibility of implementation through regime change. For example, Paragraph 2 advocated a solution that 'responds to the legitimate demands of the Libyan people',[149] which arguably could not occur without regime change.[150] The Resolution furthermore strengthened other measures that had been previously decided through UNSC Resolution 1970, including an arms embargo and asset freeze.[151] Combined with the UNSC's referral of the Libyan situation to the ICC in Resolution 1970,[152] such measures isolated the Gaddafi regime to the point where it became difficult to see how a solution other than regime change could accomplish the purpose of Resolution 1973. Indeed, as noted by Payandeh, 'the authorization to use force [had] to be regarded within the overall context of the conflict, which was not only about human rights violations, but also about the realization of the political rights of the Libyan people'.[153] This, in essence, refers to the object and purpose of UNSC Resolution 1973, which is the subject of the next section.

6.5.4 Object and purpose of UNSC Resolution 1973

The next step in evaluating the lawfulness of regime change in Libya is to determine whether and how it can be reconciled with the object and purpose of UNSC Resolution 1973, namely, that of civilian protection. Critics point to the

146 UN Doc S/RES/1973 (n8) Para 4.
147 *See* Williams and Popken (n98) 246–47.
148 Christine Gray, 'The Use of Force for Humanitarian Purposes' in Nigel D. White and Christian Henderson (eds), *Research Handbook on International Conflict and Security Law* (Edward Elgar Publishing Limited 2013) 249–50.
149 UNSC Res 1973 (n8) Para 2.
150 *See* Payandeh (n95) 387–88.
151 UN Doc S/RES/1970 (n81) Paras 9, 17; UNSC Res 1973 (n8) Paras 13, 19.
152 UN Doc S/RES/1970 (n81) Para 4.
153 Payandeh (n95) 388.

subsequent deterioration of the situation in Libya following NATO's termination of its military campaign in October 2011 to contend that regime change not only failed to protect civilians, but was furthermore detrimental to the attainment of this objective. Specifically, Libya descended into civil war post-October 2011. Chaos and violence have overtaken the country, including through the continued commission of mass atrocity crimes by various armed factions and through an ongoing struggle for power between multiple political bodies.[154] The UN High Commissioner for Refugees estimates that as of 2019, there are more than 200,0000 internally displaced persons in Libya and that a further 1.3 million people in the country are in need of humanitarian assistance.[155] These figures invite scepticism regarding whether NATO's pursuit of regime change was aligned with the object and purpose of UNSC Resolution 1973 of civilian protection.

A closer examination of NATO's military intervention in Libya, however, challenges the narrative of critics. Pattison, for example, discusses the 'counterfactual of non-intervention' and maintains that the situation in Libya could have been much worse without NATO's military campaign.[156] Koh furthermore contends that had NATO forces stopped short of regime change, it is likely that Gaddafi's forces would have recuperated and resumed their massacre of civilians,[157] particularly given the clear intent demonstrated by Gaddafi to impose his dominance using brute force.[158] Such a scenario can be likened to that of Syria (discussed in the next chapter), a similar mass atrocity situation that emerged in 2011 out of a violent government response to pro-democratic protests. The international community decided not to intervene militarily against Syria's Assad regime, and the result has been a brutal and ongoing conflict of which scale has far exceeded that of Libya (for example, in terms of civilian casualties, refugees, destroyed infrastructure, and more).[159] Similarly, it is not inconceivable that any scenario that involved Gaddafi staying in power would have led to a bloody outcome far worse than what Libya currently faces, which would run counter to the object and purpose of UNSC Resolution 1973.

Notwithstanding the above, it should be stressed that NATO did commit a grave failure in Libya when it neglected to factor in the need to rebuild the

154 *See supra* note 11. *See also* Neil Clark, 'Western Short-sighted Invasion to Blame for Libya Chaos, Lawlessness' (Reuters, 11 October 2013) <http://rt.com/op-edge/libya-chaos-after-gaddafi-013/>; 'No End in Sight for Libya Violence' (*Aljazeera*, 16 July 2014) <http://www.aljazeera.com/news/middleeast/2014/07/no-end-sight-libya-violence-201471583939888839.html>.

155 'Libya' (*UNHCR*, 2019) <https://www.unhcr.org/libya.html>.

156 James Pattison, 'Perilous Noninterventions? The Counterfactual Assessment of Libya and the Need to be a Responsible Power' (2017) 9 *Global Responsibility to Protect* 219, 221.

157 Harold Koh, 'The War Powers and Humanitarian Intervention' (2016) 53 *Houston Law Review* 971, 983.

158 *See supra* notes 3–4 and accompanying text.

159 *See* Jessica Durando, 'Syria's Civil War: Disturbing Facts Show Cost of Conflict' (*USA Today*, 14 March 2017) <http://www.usatoday.com/story/news/world/2017/03/14/syria-civil-war-facts/99126148/>.

country (either by its own forces or by other entities) following its military intervention. As discussed in Chapter 2 of this book, R2P's initial formulation within the 2001 ICISS report consisted of three interrelated responsibilities to prevent mass atrocity crimes, to react to their commission, and to rebuild affected countries following military intervention.[160] The latter component, however, the responsibility to rebuild, was removed from the doctrine's remit upon R2P's unanimous endorsement in the 2005 World Summit Outcome document, presumably because it entailed a high level of commitment as well as costs that States were hesitant to assume.[161] In the process, however, this omission arguably dealt a blow to R2P's potential efficacy, as rebuilding a country post-intervention represents a vital undertaking to ensuring lasting protection against the resurgence of mass atrocities.[162] The onus of rebuilding furthermore induces intervening States to employ greater care in devising their intervention strategies, as the mere knowledge of a responsibility to rebuild could provoke them to scale back any unnecessary military endeavours (although this could admittedly also have the opposite effect of discouraging them from intervening in the first place[163]). In short, without a responsibility to rebuild that accompanies a responsibility to react, it is difficult to see how R2P can ensure long-lasting protection from mass atrocity crimes.

An imperative for a responsibility to rebuild in the aftermath of R2P military interventions becomes especially clear through an examination of Libya's descent into civil war following NATO's military intervention and regime change. As advanced by Hilpold, it can be argued that from a military standpoint, NATO's intervention in Libya was a success.[164] However, as he correctly identifies, the failure of intervening powers to engage with rebuilding the country imparted disastrous consequences upon the population. Keranen, for example, characterises the international rebuilding strategy in Libya as one of 'disengagement'.[165] She notes that States invested in post-intervention Libya primarily to protect their own national interests – namely, to address issues of border security, terrorism, weapons smuggling, and the refugee crisis – whereas Libyan priorities for rebuilding were relegated to the backseat.[166] To compound this problem, the Central Bank of Libya's assets remained frozen by the UNSC until 16 December 2011,[167] meaning that the

160 *See* Section 2.3 of this book.
161 *See* Albrecht Schnabel, 'The Responsibility to Rebuild' in W. Andy Knight and Frazer Egerton (eds), *The Routledge Handbook of the Responsibility to Protect* (Routledge 2012) 50–51, 57; Peter Hilpold, 'Jus Post Bellum and the Responsibility to Rebuild – Identifying the Contours of an Ever More Important Aspect of R2P' (2015) 6 *Journal of International Humanitarian Legal Studies* 284, 298.
162 *See* Schnabel (n161) 58.
163 This potential negative ramification could be assuaged through the establishment of a Pillar 3 *obligation* to react.
164 Hilpold (161) 300.
165 Outi Keranen, 'What Happened to the Responsibility to Rebuild?' (2016) 3 *Global Governance: A Review of Multilateralism and International Organizations* 331, 340.
166 Ibid., 341.
167 *See* 'Libyan Central Bank Assets Unfrozen to Help Rebuilding Efforts' (*Telegraph*, 17 December 2011) <http://www.telegraph.co.uk/news/worldnews/africaandin

interim government did not possess the sufficient monetary power to invest in State infrastructure or to meet its population's core demands during the first few months of the country's declared liberation. This shortage of funds came at a critical time in which it was crucial for the interim government to assert itself as a legitimate and viable alternative to Gaddafi. On this issue, a Libyan representative declared to the UNSC on 26 September 2011 that '[t]here are numerous factors fuelling instability, but I assert with certainty that one principal factor is the ongoing freeze of Libyan monies and assets'.[168]

It is true, therefore, as characterised by Teimouri and Subedi, that 'the new revolutionary government [in Libya] is replicating the old Jamahiriya of Gaddafi, unable to fulfil its primary responsibility to protect Libyans; therefore, Libya remains an R2P concern'.[169] However, it is important here to discern that the deterioration of the situation in Libya is not a result of NATO's pursuit of regime change *per se*. Rather, as has been demonstrated in this section of the book, had NATO forces stopped short of achieving regime change in Libya, it is highly plausible that the outcome would have been worse with respect to civilian protection, which would run counter to the object and purpose of UNSC Resolution 1973. Instead, Libya's relapse into chaos and violence is more accurately attributable to the international community's non-assumption of its responsibility to rebuild subsequent to NATO's military intervention.[170] This chain of events certainly underscores the importance of a responsibility to rebuild pursuant to R2P reactions – despite the official exclusion of this element from the R2P doctrine – in order to secure a sustainable peace and to safeguard from the resurgence of mass atrocities. As such, renewing emphasis upon this excluded aspect of R2P should be undertaken by the international community as a means of strengthening R2P's efficacy and ensuring that the doctrine is equipped to ensure long-term protection from mass atrocity crimes.

6.5.5 Supplementary tools of interpretation pertaining to UNSC Resolution 1973

Thus far, the analysis of UNSC Resolution 1973 indicates that NATO's pursuit of regime change in Libya contradicted neither its literal text nor its object and purpose. However, an examination of supplementary materials, most notably the statements that States made in the context of the Resolution's adoption, paints a very different picture. Although States generally diverged in their interpretation of Resolution 1973, there seemed to be general agreement that regime change did not represent a legitimate means of enforcing its mandate.

One group of States expressed reservations regarding the potential scope of UNSC Resolution 1973, although these States seemingly understood that its

dianocean/libya/8962887/Libyan-central-bank-assets-unfrozen-to-help-rebuilding-efforts.html>.

168 UNSC 6622nd Meeting (26 September 2011) UN Doc S/PV.6622, 6. *See also* UNSC 6669th Meeting (28 November 2011) UN Doc S/PV.6669, 4.

169 Teimouri and Subedi (n11) 12.

170 *See* Pattison (n156) 224.

enforcement could extend beyond a no-fly zone. India, for example, maintained that there was no 'clarity about details of enforcement measures, including who will participate and with what assets, and how these measures will exactly be carried out'.[171] Similarly, Brazil observed that 'the text of [the Resolution] contemplates measures that go far beyond that call [of a no-fly zone]'.[172] China mentioned that it (along with other UNSC members) 'asked specific questions. However, regrettably, many of those questions failed to be clarified or answered. China has serious difficulty with parts of the resolution.'[173] These States admitted that there were elements of UNSC Resolution 1973 that were not explained prior to the vote. They even contemplated that the enforcement of the Resolution could stretch beyond a no-fly zone. Yet, while they noted their disapproval over such a potential unfolding of events, they did not vote against the Resolution.

As with the first group of States, a second group was similarly opposed to regime change in Libya pursuant to UNSC Resolution 1973. In contrast to the first group, however, States within this group put on record their understanding, prior to the Resolution's adoption, that it would be implemented within a limited context. South Africa, for example, stressed its hope 'that this resolution will be implemented in full respect for both its letter and spirit', expanding on this to mean that it rejected 'any foreign military intervention, whatever its form'.[174] Although this does not exactly speak to the role of regime change under Resolution 1973, it at least highlights that South Africa understood this Resolution within a highly restrictive context. Additionally, Russia noted prior to the Resolution's adoption that 'a whole range of questions raised by Russia and other members of the Council remained unanswered' pertaining to 'how the no-fly zone would be enforced, what the rules of engagement would be and what limits on the use of force there would be.'[175] It furthermore remarked that the draft resolution, throughout the drafting process, 'was morphing before our very eyes, transcending the initial concept as stated by the League of Arab States. Provisions were introduced into the text that could potentially open the door to large-scale military intervention.'[176] However, Russia concluded that '[d]uring negotiations on the draft, statements were heard claiming an absence of any such intentions. We take note of these.'[177] Russia therefore communicated its suspicion regarding a potentially abusive implementation of UNSC Resolution 1973, although it put on record its understanding that this would not transpire, based upon assurances that it reportedly received from intervening powers. Following NATO's intervention in Libya, both Russia and South Africa voiced their clear condemnation of its pursuit of regime change.[178]

171 UN Doc S/PV.6498 (n64) 6.
172 Ibid.
173 Ibid., 10.
174 Ibid.
175 Ibid., 8.
176 Ibid.
177 Ibid.
178 *See*, e.g., UNSC 6531st Meeting (10 May 2011) UN Doc S/PV.6531, 18; UNSC 6627th Meeting (4 October 2011) UN Doc S/PV.6627, 4.

In addition to the above States, Venezuela, Nicaragua, and the African Union also emerged as some of the strongest critics of NATO's pursuit of regime change in Libya, characterising it as an unlawful implementation of UNSC Resolution 1973. Venezuela, for example, expressed its regret that 'certain countries are seeking regime change in Libya, in violation of the Charter of the United Nations. Those actions contravene resolution 1973 (2011), which calls for respect for the sovereignty and territorial integrity of Libya.'[179] Nicaragua asserted:

> Once again we have witnessed the shameful manipulation of the slogan 'protection of civilians' for dishonourable political purposes, seeking unequivocally and blatantly to impose regime change, attacking the sovereignty of a State Member of the United Nations and violating the Organization's Charter.[180]

In similar vein, the African Union noted its 'deep concern' regarding the 'one-sided interpretations' of Resolutions 1970 and 1973 on Libya, as well as the 'consequences that may result for international legality'.[181] These entities, therefore, clearly viewed regime change as an unlawful means of discharging the mandate of UNSC Resolution 1973.

A final group of States accepted or welcomed the notion that regime change would be potentially undertaken in Libya. The UK, for example, asserted that '[t]he central purpose of the resolution is clear: to end the violence, to protect civilians and to allow the people of Libya to determine their own future, *free from the tyranny of the Al-Qadhafi regime*'.[182] Portugal stated in even stronger terms that '[f]or the international community, the regime that has ruled Libya for more than 40 years has come to an end by the will of the Libyan people'.[183] Germany, even though it expressed reservations with respect to 'large-scale loss of life' and 'protracted military conflict', emphasised that:

> Our intention is to stop the violence in the country and to send clear messages to Al-Qadhafi and his regime that their time is over. Muammar Al-Qadhafi must relinquish power immediately. His regime has lost all legitimacy and can no longer be an interlocutor for us.[184]

These statements revealed clear indications that certain States viewed regime change to be inevitable within Libya. Interestingly, France and the US, as two of the three States (alongside the UK) that led the military action against Libya, maintained more neutral tones and refrained from explicitly articulating an intention for pursuing regime change. However, France did mention that Resolution

179 UNSC 6531st Meeting (Resumption 1) (10 May 2011) UN Doc S/PV.6531 (Resumption 1), 19.
180 UN Doc S/PV.6531 (n178) 34.
181 UNSC 6555th Meeting (15 June 2011) UN Doc S/PV.6555, 4.
182 UN Doc S/PV.6498 (n64) 4 (emphasis added).
183 Ibid., 8.
184 Ibid., 4.

1973 authorised States to take 'all measures necessary, over and above the no-fly zone, to protect civilians and territories',[185] which left the interpretation open-ended. The US similarly declared that the 'future of Libya should be decided by the people of Libya',[186] with the implicit understanding that the people would not choose Gaddafi.

Ironically, however, these same States that advocated regime change in Libya did not necessarily believe that such a course of action lay within the remit of UNSC Resolution 1973. Instead of justifying their pursuit of regime change with reference to the Resolution's ordinary meaning and object and purpose – in line with the analysis conducted in the previous two sections of this book – they instead maintained that regime change was undertaken outside the context of Resolution 1973 but nevertheless constituted a necessary outcome from a humanitarian point of view. For example, then-US President Obama stated on 28 March 2011:

> [There] is no question that Libya – and the world – would be better off with Qaddafi out of power. I, along with many other world leaders, have embraced that goal, and will actively pursue it through non-military means. But broadening our military mission to include regime change would be a mistake.[187]

Here, Obama was explicit that the US was pursuing regime change as an end goal in Libya. Nonetheless, he was careful to distinguish that this course of action was not being undertaken as part of the broader military intervention (which was authorised by Resolution 1973), but rather through 'non-military means', and even maintained that pursuing regime change as part of the military mission would be a 'mistake'. This indicates that the US's interpretation of the authorisation to use 'all necessary measures' under Resolution 1973 did not encompass the right to resort to regime change.

On 14 April 2011, US, UK, and French leaders published a joint article in which they stated that 'our mandate under U.N. Security Council Resolution 1973 … is not to remove Qaddafi by force. But it is impossible to imagine a future for Libya with Qaddafi in power.'[188] They proceeded to insist that 'so long as Qaddafi is in power, NATO must maintain its operations so that civilians remain protected'.[189] Again, this article reveals that intervening powers did not believe that regime change represented an acceptable means of discharging the mandate of UNSC Resolution 1973. As such, they embraced regime change as an end goal

185 Ibid., 3.
186 Ibid., 5.
187 'Obama's Libya Speech' (*Washington Post*, 28 March 2011) <http://www.washingtonpost.com/blogs/right-turn/post/obamas-libya-speech/2011/03/04/AFOOTDrB_blog.html?utm_term=.0ad6c06cc215>.
188 Barack Obama, David Cameron, and Nicolas Sarkozy, 'Libya's Pathway to Peace' (*New York Times*, 14 April 2011) <https://www.nytimes.com/2011/04/15/opinion/15iht-edlibya15.html>.
189 Ibid.

for NATO's Libya intervention while simultaneously acknowledging that this outcome was not sanctioned by the Resolution.

In essence, it appears that the US, UK, and French leaders were invoking an 'illegal yet legitimate' justification, similar to that utilised for the Kosovo intervention of 1999; i.e., that while regime change was not sanctioned by UNSC Resolution 1973, and while it stretched the mandate contained within it, it constituted a necessary endeavour to avert large-scale human loss. Their choice to advance political rather than legal arguments most probably reflected their reluctance to establish regime change as an acceptable means of discharging UNSC Chapter VII resolutions authorising coercive military action (which could be employed, for example, by their political rivals). In this manner, however, they effectively limited the precedential value of the Libyan case as an example in which regime change was undertaken, arguably as a last resort and in response to a compelling R2P situation, pursuant to a UNSC Chapter VII mandate authorising the use of force. Their indirect justification of their pursuit of regime change furthermore reveals a significant failure to realise the aims of the R2P doctrine, which was meant to reconcile legal and moral dimensions pertaining to the use of force in mass atrocity situations and to ensure that the international community is legally equipped with the tools to effectively deal with such cases.

The divisiveness of NATO's pursuit of regime change in Libya is likely to impart repercussions with respect to future UNSC responses to R2P situations. This is particularly so given that Russia and China, as two of the States that opposed NATO's implementation of UNSC Resolution 1973, are veto-wielding permanent members of the UNSC and, as such, enjoy a disproportionate power to shape international discourse on the adoption and implementation of UNSC Chapter VII mandates. Given the Libyan experience, it is likely that Russia and China will increasingly demand more specific delineations of Chapter VII mandates, including of the means that are acceptable and/or excluded from their enforcement. While this in itself is not a negative development, it is furthermore likely that Russia and China will increasingly oppose what they deem more interventionist measures, and hence, they may be unwilling to authorise the full range of means at the UNSC's disposal to respond to R2P situations even if such measures are necessary to address the perpetration of mass atrocity crimes. This is indeed what transpired in the Syrian context when Russia, referring to what it regarded as an abusive intervention in Libya, declared pursuant to its veto on 4 October 2011 that '[t]he situation in Syria cannot be considered in the Council separately from the Libyan experience'.[190] As such, while in the long term, Russia and China's renewed distrust in the implementation of Chapter VII mandates authorising the use of force may propel a greater degree of clarity with respect to the drafting of such mandates, it may also conversely hinder the authorisation of more robust measures to react to R2P situations when such measures are required.

190 UN Doc S/PV.6627 (n178) 4. The corresponding draft resolution on Syria, however, did not invoke Chapter VII, nor did it, by default, authorise the use of force. *See* UNSC Draft Resolution (4 October 2011) UN Doc S/2011/612. *See also* Section 7.2.2 of this book.

6.6 Conclusion

There is no doubt that the Libyan mass atrocity situation represents a major R2P case. Scholarly evaluations of the international community's response as per the doctrine, however, have been wide-ranging. One group of scholars, for example, upholds the Libyan example as a prototype for how R2P should be executed in practice. Evans describes it as 'a textbook case of the RtoP norm working exactly as it was supposed to, with nothing else in issue but stopping continuing and imminent mass atrocity crimes'.[191] Chorin further asserts that 'the Libya intervention appears to have been as successful an implementation of R2P as could have been expected'.[192] These authors therefore view the international community's timely and decisive response to the Libyan mass atrocity situation as a model R2P case.

Other scholars, however, are more cautious in their assessment of the international reaction towards the Libyan R2P situation.[193] In particular, NATO's pursuit of regime change tarnished the legitimacy of the operations in the eyes of many.[194] Others point out that the Libyan case was unique, given the Gaddafi regime's clear display of intent to commit mass atrocities, regional organisations' strong support for military intervention, and the existence of reasonable prospects for the success of such an intervention.[195] National interests such as oil, refugee flow into Europe, and election considerations also undoubtedly enhanced the decision-making calculus.[196] As such, these scholars point out that it is highly unlikely that such circumstances favouring robust international action (including military intervention) will consistently converge in future mass atrocity situations, meaning that the international community's decision to engage heavily in Libya was likely predicated upon the particulars of this case rather than signifying a turning point in the international community's discharge of its R2P Pillar 3 responsibility. This point becomes highly evident in the discussion in Chapter 7 of this book on the mass atrocity situation in Syria, to which the international community assumed a very different approach.

Despite the degree of caution that must be exercised in evaluating the Libyan R2P case, some observations can nevertheless be gleaned with respect to the doctrine's application within it. First, there were multiple and widespread affirmations of the legally binding nature of R2P's Pillar 1 which calls upon host States to

191 Gareth Evans, 'Interview: The R2P Balance Sheet after Libya' (*E-International Relations,* September 2011) at 40 <http://www.e-ir.info/wp-content/uploads/R2P.pdf>.
192 Ethan Chorin, 'NATO's Libya Intervention and the Continued Case for a "Responsibility to Rebuild"' (2013) 31 *Boston University International Law Journal* 365, 376.
193 *See*, for example, Hehir (n85).
194 As discussed in Section 6.5 of this chapter.
195 *See*, for example, Sari Bernstein, 'The Responsibility to Protect after Libya: Humanitarian Prevention as Customary International Law' (2012) 38 *Brooklyn Journal of International Law* 305, 337–38.
196 *See* Mohamed (n100) 333–34; Jason W. Davidson, 'France, Britain and the Intervention in Libya: An Integrated Analysis' (2013) 26 *Cambridge Review of International Affairs* 310 at 315–16, 319–20, 323–24.

protect their populations. Libya's responsibility to protect its population, for example, was specifically referenced in UNSC Resolutions 1970 and 1973 as well as in HRC Resolution S-15/1,[197] with the clear implications that Libya's failure in this regard constituted a breach of its obligations under international law. Furthermore, a large and diverse set of States, particularly in the context of UNGA proceedings on Resolution 65/265, noted that Libya's failure to meet its responsibility to protect made it liable to have action taken against it by the international community.[198] Such statements provide evidence of State practice and *opinio juris* regarding the legally binding nature of R2P's Pillar 1.

Second, the Libya case affirms that the discharge of R2P's Pillar 3 remains a right although not an obligation upon the international community. None of the aforementioned resolutions, for example, referenced a responsibility or an obligation of the international community to intervene in Libya (even if not militarily). Only a handful of States cited such a Pillar 3 obligation within discussions of these resolutions, hardly amounting to sufficient State practice or *opinio juris* to indicate the emergence of a Pillar 3 obligation under customary international law.[199] Instead, the international community's reactions towards the Libya situation underscore that it engaged with the R2P case out of a mere right or moral responsibility at best.

Third, the diversity of the actors that played a role in responding to the Libyan mass atrocity situation – inclusive of the HRC, UNGA, UNSC, and regional and/or international organisations such as the LAS, OIC, GCC, AU, and NATO – highlights that there is no one specific bearer of responsibility under R2P's Pillar 3. Rather, the doctrine can be implemented through a range of international actors, each of which can adopt measures in line with its respective mandate and sphere of influence. Fourth, and in similar vein, the range of reaction mechanisms employed in response to the Libyan R2P situation emphasises that R2P, far from being a military tool, can be enforced through a host of non-military means. In Libya, such non-military measures included its suspension from the HRC and the LAS, the HRC's establishment of a Commission of Inquiry, and the UNSC's referral of the situation to the ICC as well as its imposition of an arms embargo, travel ban, and asset freeze. These measures were undertaken in accordance with established legal procedure, with the exception of Libya's suspension from the LAS which arguably constituted a third-party countermeasure. This particular move by the LAS provides limited support for an emerging right of third-party countermeasures to induce compliance with fundamental community interests such as the eradication of mass atrocity situations, and represents a promising means of strengthening the R2P framework.

Finally, the discourse surrounding the lawfulness of NATO's pursuit of regime change in Libya under UNSC Resolution 1973 reveals the need for further engagement with the relationship between R2P and regime change. An analysis of

197 *See supra* notes 66, 84, and 90.
198 *See supra* note 72.
199 *See supra* note 73.

Resolution 1973 revealed that regime change could be reconciled with its relevant provisions' ordinary meaning as well as with its object and purpose of civilian protection. Upon examination of supplementary means of interpretation, however, most notably the statements made by States following the Resolution's adoption, it becomes apparent that States both in favour of and against regime change agreed that this course of action did not lie within the Resolution's mandate. Rather than justifying regime change under Resolution 1973, intervening NATO States instead advanced that it was illegal yet legitimate, thus incompatible with the Resolution although necessary from a humanitarian perspective. The discrepancy in these positions highlights the need to examine more carefully the existing or ideal relationship between R2P and regime change, specifically whether linking the two concepts will facilitate a more robust framework for human protection or whether it will conversely jeopardise the very acceptance of R2P on the international stage. In the near future, it is predicted that the Libya experience will push certain States (including Russia and China as P5 members) to demand greater clarity prior to authorising measures under the UNSC's Chapter VII powers and to be more opposed to measures that they deem more interventionist (for example, regime change). While this may propel greater legal certainty with respect to the implementation of Chapter VII mandates, it may also hinder the adoption of robust measures when such measures are arguably required to address mass atrocity situations.

7 The application of R2P to the Syria Case

7.1 Introduction

Syria has been under the rule of the Assad family since 1970, first under Hafez al-Assad from 1970 until his death in 2000, and then his son Bashar al-Assad from 2000 until present day. Under their joint control over Syria, the country was governed under emergency law until 2011 (after the emergency law was repealed, it was replaced by a very similar law disguised as counterterrorism legislation) and all forms of opposition were banned.[1] International human rights organisations such as Amnesty International and Human Rights Watch consistently reported rampant corruption, torture, arbitrary detention, and curtailed civil liberties, prompting Human Rights Watch to declare in 2010 that 'Syria's authorities were among the worse [*sic*] violators of human rights last year'.[2]

In mid-March 2011, approximately one month after the Libyan uprising against Muammar Gaddafi commenced, the Syrian people also began a non-violent popular uprising against President Assad's rule. Assad's initial reaction to these protests was hopeful, as he indicated that he would implement reforms and transform Syria into a more representative and democratic State.[3] Simultaneously, however, his military responded to peaceful demonstrations with brutal force, attempting to

1 HRC, 'Report of the United Nations High Commissioner for Human Rights on the Situation of Human Rights in the Syrian Arab Republic' (15 September 2011) UN Doc A/HRC/18/53 Para 22; Omar al-Shaaro, 'President Al-Assad Endorses Anti-terrorism Legislation' (*Day Press News*, 2 July 2012) <http://www.dp-news.com/en/detail.aspx?articleid=125126>.

2 *See* 'World Report' (*Human Rights Watch*, 2010) at 555–61 <https://www.hrw.org/sites/default/files/world_report_download/wr2010_0.pdf>; 'Syria among Worst for Rights Abuses: HRW Report' (*Reuters*, 24 January 2011) <https://www.reuters.com/article/us-syria-rights/syria-among-worst-for-rights-abuses-hrw-report-idUSTRE70N5S620110124>.

3 *See*, for example, 'Bashar al-Assad Speech at Syrian People's Assembly' (*Voltaire Network*, 30 March 2011) <http://www.voltairenet.org/Bashar-al-Assad-Speech-at-Syrian>; Bashar Al-Assad, 'Speech by President Bashar al-Assad to Ministers After the Swearing-In of Syria's New Government' (*Al-Bab*, 16 April 2011) <http://al-bab.com/albab-orig/albab/arab/docs/syria/bashar_assad_speech_110416.htm>; 'Speech by President Bashar al-Assad at Damascus University' (*Voltaire Network*, 20 June 2011) <http://www.voltairenet.org/article170602.html>.

crush all forms of dissent through killing, arbitrarily detaining, and torturing non-violent protestors.[4] In July 2011, UN Special Advisers on the Prevention of Genocide and on the Responsibility to Protect issued a joint press release claiming 'a serious possibility that crimes against humanity may have been committed and continue to be committed in Syria'.[5] Then-UN High Commissioner for Human Rights Navi Pillay similarly described to the UN Human Rights Council (HRC) in August 2011 'a pattern of widespread or systematic human rights violations by Syrian security and military forces, including murder, enforced disappearances, torture, deprivation of liberty, and persecution ... [which may] amount to crimes against humanity'.[6]

The Assad regime's violent crackdown against non-violent protests paved the way for the emergence of armed opposition groups as early as July 2011, and the situation was characterised as a non-international armed conflict (NIAC) in August 2012 by the Independent International Commission of Inquiry on Syria[7] (established by the HRC to investigate alleged violations of international human rights law perpetrated over the course of the conflict[8]). To date, this Commission has affirmed that the Syrian regime committed, among others, crimes against humanity of murder, torture, rape, and enforced disappearance, as well as war crimes of murder, torture, rape, arbitrary arrest and detention, indiscriminate attacks, attacking protected objects, employing chemical weapons, and forcible displacement, thus making R2P directly relevant to the situation at hand.[9] It furthermore documented the commission of mass atrocity crimes by non-State armed groups[10] – including war crimes, crimes against humanity, and even genocide –

4 *See* Jess Gifkins, 'The UN Security Council Divided: Syria in Crisis' (2012) 4 *Global Responsibility to Protect* 377, 377–79.

5 'Special Advisers of the United Nations Secretary-General on the Prevention of Genocide, Francis Deng, and on the Responsibility to Protect, Edward Luck, on the Situation in Syria' (*Office of the Special Adviser on the Prevention of Genocide*, 21 July 2011) <http://www.un.org/en/genocideprevention/documents/media/statements/2011/English/2011-07-21-OSAPG%20statement%20Syria%2022%20July%202011%20FINAL.pdf>.

6 'Statement by Ms. Navi Pillay, UN High Commissioner for Human Rights to the Human Rights Council 17th Special Session on "Situation of Human Rights in the Syrian Arab Republic" in Geneva' (*Relief Web*, 22 August 2011) <http://reliefweb.int/report/syrian-arab-republic/statement-ms-navi-pillay-un-high-commissioner-human-rights-human-rights>.

7 *See* HRC, 'Report of the Independent International Commission of Inquiry on the Syrian Arab Republic' (16 August 2012) UN Doc A/HRC/21/50 Para 12; Jeffrey White, 'Asad's Armed Opposition: The Free Syrian Army' (*Washington Institute*, 30 November 2011) <http://www.washingtoninstitute.org/policy-analysis/view/asads-armed-opposition-the-free-syrian-army>.

8 *See* HRC Res S-17/1 (23 August 2011) UN Doc A/HRC/RES/S-17/1 Art 12.

9 *See*, for example, UN Doc A/HRC/21/50 (n7); HRC, 'Report of the Independent International Commission of Inquiry on the Syrian Arab Republic' (5 February 2013) UN Doc A/HRC/22/59; HRC, 'Report of the Independent International Commission of Inquiry on the Syrian Arab Republic' (9 August 2018) UN Doc A/HRC/39/65.

10 *See*, for example, HRC, 'Report of the Independent International Commission of Inquiry on the Syrian Arab Republic' (13 August 2014) UN Doc A/HRC/27/60

most particularly by UN-sanctioned and proscribed groups such as the so-called Islamic State (ISIS or ISIL) and Al-Nusra Front (ANF).[11] In March 2017, then-UN High Commissioner for Human Rights Zeid Ra'ad Al Hussein characterised the situation in Syria as the 'worst man-made disaster the world has seen since World War II',[12] and the conflict remains ongoing as of the writing of this book.

Despite this grave state of affairs, however, the international response to the Syrian R2P situation has been gravely lacking, most notably due to the UNSC's paralysis as a result of persistent Russian – and to a lesser extent Chinese – vetoes. A limited response in the form of a US-led military intervention transpired in September 2014 to counteract the threats posed by ISIS and ANF.[13] No similar action, however, has been forthcoming to address the atrocities perpetrated by the Assad regime.

Similarly to Chapter 6 on Libya, this chapter examines how R2P influenced the course of events in Syria and how developments within Syria in turn impart lessons regarding the interpretation and application of the doctrine. The focus here, as with Libya, lies in R2P's Pillars 1 and 3; given the rapid deterioration of the situation in Syria as well as the Assad regime's deliberate failure to protect its population from mass atrocity crimes, it was arguably imperative for the international community to assume its Pillar 3 responsibilities at the exclusion of assistance-giving as per Pillar 2. This chapter is structured around the major actors that influenced (whether positively or negatively) the Syrian conflict's trajectory, incorporating analysis on a range of dimensions (both military and non-military) that these actors' (in)action assumed. The actors that receive principal consideration include the UNSC (for its primary role in maintaining international peace and security), the League of Arab States (LAS – as the main regional actor), non-State actors (as key parties to the conflict), and the US-led Coalition against ISIS and ANF (as a military intervener in Syria). Given the international community's overall lacking response to the Syrian conflict, this chapter emphasises how R2P could have (or should have) been invoked in Syria in order to effectively respond to the mass atrocity situation, and more broadly, how the doctrine must progress in order to address the remaining gaps that hinder its full enforcement.

Paras 29, 36–38, 61–74, 92, 95, 135; HRC, 'Rule of Terror: Living under ISIS in Syria' (19 November 2014) UN Doc A/HRC/27/CRP.3 Paras 46, 50–52, 56–57, 63; UN Doc A/HRC/39/65 (n9) Paras 24, 31, 89; 'Syria: Abductions, Torture and Summary Killings at the Hands of Armed Groups' (*Amnesty International*, 5 July 2016) <https://www.amnesty.org/en/latest/news/2016/07/syria-abductions-torture-and-summary-killings-at-the-hands-of-armed-groups/>.

11 *See* Kathy Gilsinan, 'How Syria's Uprising Spawned a Jihad' (*Atlantic*, 16 March 2016) <https://www.theatlantic.com/international/archive/2016/03/syria-civil-war-five-years/474006/>.

12 'Syria Worst Man-made Disaster Since World War II – Zeid' (*UN Office of the High Commissioner*, 14 March 2017) <https://www.ohchr.org/EN/NewsEvents/Pages/DisplayNews.aspx?NewsID=21373&LangID=E>.

13 *See* Craig Whitlock, 'U.S. Begins Airstrikes against Islamic State in Syria' (*Washington Post*, 23 September 2014) <https://www.washingtonpost.com/world/national-security/us-begins-airstrikes-against-islamic-state-in-syria/2014/09/22/8b677e26-42b3-11e4-b437-1a7368204804_story.html?utm_term=.0a974d07dc7e>.

7.2 UN Security Council

The UNSC's approach towards Syria stood in stark contrast to that of Libya. In Libya, the UNSC almost immediately invoked R2P and adopted measures through its Chapter VII powers, culminating in the authorisation for the use of force through Resolution 1973.[14] In Syria, on the other hand, the UNSC's response was slow and ineffective, primarily as a result of 12 vetoes (to date) exercised by Russia and China that obstructed the body from authorising coercive measures under Chapter VII. This section first offers an overview of the UNSC's engagement with R2P in the Syrian context. It then examines Russia and China's invocation of the veto throughout the conflict with reference to the R2P doctrine. Finally, this section undertakes a thematic analysis of some of the key areas of the conflict in which the UNSC engaged (or attempted to engage), namely, general measures, chemical weapons, humanitarian access, accountability, and civilian protection, and discusses how the international response towards each of these categories could have been strengthened as per R2P's Pillar 3. Specifically, it argues that given the UNSC's paralysis and ineffectiveness on Syria, the onus of discharging R2P's Pillar 3 should have transferred to other international actors inclusive of States and international organisations, which should have employed all means at their disposal to counter the R2P situation, including through their pursuit of lawful measures, third-party countermeasures, and UNGA recommendations under Uniting for Peace (UforP).

7.2.1 R2P in the UN Security Council

At face value, the UNSC seemed restrained in its invocation of R2P in the Syrian context, particularly when compared to the Libyan case in which R2P featured prominently in the body's response to the mass atrocities being committed. The first draft resolution considered by the UNSC on Syria on 4 October 2011 did affirm R2P's Pillar 1 through '[recalling] the Syrian Government's primary responsibility to protect its population'.[15] Following this draft resolution's veto by Russia and China, however, R2P was not cited in any further UNSC resolutions or draft resolutions on Syria until February 2014 with the adoption of Resolution 2139.[16] Thereon after, as detailed in subsequent sections, references to R2P returned to six additional UNSC resolutions on Syria and in particular those centring on humanitarian access, although these references were also notably confined to the doctrine's Pillar 1 dimension.[17]

14 *See* Section 6.4 of this book.
15 UNSC Draft Resolution (4 October 2011) UN Doc S/2011/612 Preamble.
16 UNSC Res 2139 (22 February 2014) UN Doc S/RES/2139 Para 9.
17 *See* UNSC Res 2165 (14 July 2014) UN Doc S/RES/2165; UNSC Res 2254 (18 December 2015) UN Doc S/RES/2254; UNSC Res 2258 (22 December 2015) UN Doc S/RES/2258; UNSC Res 2332 (21 December 2016) UN Doc S/RES/2332; UNSC Res 2393 (19 December 2017) UN Doc S/RES/2393; UNSC Res 2449 (13 December 2018) UN Doc S/RES/2449. *See also* Section 7.2.5 of this chapter.

The above trends could suggest that international resolve towards the principles underpinning R2P diminished within the Syrian context as compared to the Libyan one. However, a more nuanced analysis reveals that levels of State practice and *opinio juris* for R2P's Pillars 1 and 3 remained unchanged, namely, that Pillar 1 continued to be upheld as an obligation of the host State (in this case, Syria) while Pillar 3 continued to represent a source of contention and in any case was rejected as imposing any legal obligation upon the international community to react to the commission of mass atrocity crimes. The debate surrounding the 4 October 2011 vetoed UNSC draft resolution on Syria (which invoked R2P's Pillar 1) is particularly instructive in this respect. This draft resolution received the affirmative votes of nine States, highlighting that a majority of UNSC member-States agreed (or at least acquiesced) to the inclusion of R2P's Pillar 1 within it. As for the two of the UNSC's permanent five (P5) member-States that vetoed the draft resolution (Russia and China), as well as the four non-permanent member-States that abstained from voting (India, Brazil, Lebanon, and South Africa), an analysis of their stances reveals that their points of contention revolved exclusively around the proposed implementation of the draft resolution, thus centring on R2P's Pillar 3 rather than its Pillar 1.

Russia, for example, stressed that '[t]he situation in Syria cannot be considered in the Council separately from the Libyan experience' and that, in similar vein, it was 'alarmed by statements that compliance with Security Council resolutions on Libya in the [North Atlantic Treaty Organization – NATO] interpretation is a model for the future actions of NATO in implementing the responsibility to protect'.[18] As such, Russia's grounds for opposing the 4 October 2011 UNSC draft resolution on Syria were directed towards the international community's implementation of R2P in Libya (i.e. concerns regarding Pillar 3). It was not, however, opposed to the principles underlying Pillar 1 which specify host State responsibilities to protect their populations from mass atrocity crimes. For example, Russia declared that 'the violence [in Syria] is unacceptable, and we condemn the repression of protests by peaceful demonstrators'.[19] It furthermore offered explicit support for R2P's Pillar 1 in a separate UNSC discussion on the protection of civilians that was convened five months prior in May 2011, proclaiming that 'the Governments of States involved in conflicts bear the primary responsibility for protecting the population living on their territory'.[20] This statement notably came after the Syrian R2P situation had commenced and furthermore followed NATO States' affirmations regarding their end goals for regime change in Libya.[21]

China, as the other P5 member that vetoed the 4 October 2011 UNSC draft resolution on Syria, emphasised that any proposed international measures for Syria should '[comply] with the Charter of the United Nations and the principle of

18 UNSC 6627th Meeting (4 October 2011) UN Doc S/PV.6627, 4.
19 Ibid., 4.
20 UNSC 6531st Meeting (10 May 2011) UN Doc S/PV.6531, 9.
21 *See* Section 6.5.5 for an overview of intervening States' references to regime change in the context of the Libyan intervention.

non-interference in the internal affairs of States', and furthermore made clear that it was vested in preserving the '[full] respect [of] Syria's sovereignty, independence and territorial integrity'.[22] China's concerns, therefore, revolved around the potential for international action to impinge upon Syria's sovereignty and territorial integrity, which notably pertain to the international community's reaction as per R2P's Pillar 3. It did not, importantly, challenge the premise of Syria's obligation as the host State to protect its population as per R2P's Pillar 1. Instead, China acknowledged in a separate UNSC discussion on the protection of civilians in May 2011 that the 'responsibility to protect civilians lies first and foremost with the Government of the country concerned',[23] thus affirming its commitment to Pillar 1. Similarly, Brazil, South Africa, Lebanon, and India delivered statements to the effect that they were opposed to or distrustful of international action in the Syrian R2P context, although they condemned the repressive practices of the Syrian State and/or expressed their support for R2P's Pillar 1.[24]

It is true that following the 4 October 2011 vote, there was a complete silence on R2P within UNSC discussions on Syria until February 2014, with the exception of a reference that Rwanda made to the doctrine in a September 2013 meeting.[25] This silence, however, rather than indicating a fundamental shift in States' attitudes towards the doctrine, can perhaps best be attributed to political prudence; given Russia's – and, to a second extent, China and other States' – distrust of the doctrine's implementation in Libya and their opposition to the adoption of any coercive measures against Syria,[26] specific mention of R2P was likely sacrificed in the Syrian case in order to facilitate consensus surrounding non-military means of responding to the situation. Continued support for the doctrine, however, at least with respect to its Pillar 1, is evidenced through the aforementioned affirmations by traditional R2P sceptics as well as through its re-inclusion into UNSC resolutions and discussions on Syria on a regular basis beginning in 2014.

Therefore, far from constituting a shift from the Libya case in State practice and *opinio juris* pertaining to the R2P doctrine, the UNSC's overall reaction to the mass atrocity situation in Syria indicates that States continued to uphold R2P's Pillar 1 as an obligation of host States although they remained divided over the implementation of Pillar 3. In particular, NATO's pursuit of regime change in Libya made certain States, most notably Russia and China as two P5 member-

22 UN Doc S/PV.6627 (n18) 5.
23 UN Doc S/PV.6531 (n20) 20.
24 *See* ibid., 10, 17, 22 (comments of India, South Africa, and Lebanon); UNSC 6590th Meeting (26 July 2011) UN Doc S/PV.6590, 21 (comments of Brazil); UN Doc S/PV.6627 (n18) 6–7, 11–12 (comments of India, South Africa, and Brazil); UNSC 6650th Meeting (9 November 2011) UN Doc S/PV.6650 at 15–17, 22 (comments of Brazil, India, and South Africa).
25 Rwanda's reference to R2P was made following the UNSC's adoption of Resolution 2118 in September 2013 in response to the Ghouta chemical attack (discussed further in Section 7.2.4 of this chapter). Its comment centred on R2P's Pillar 3, namely, that 'the primary responsibility of this global body is the responsibility to protect'. UNSC 7038th Meeting (27 September 2013) UN Doc S/PV.7038, 14.
26 Discussed further in the next section of this chapter.

States, cautious of authorising any action in connection with R2P that could potentially lead to military intervention.[27] This, unfortunately, resulted in the near-total paralysis of the international community in dealing with the Syrian R2P situation, bringing to the fore some of the doctrine's compelling weaknesses. One such weakness, namely, the potential for the permanent veto to obstruct international action, is discussed in the next section.

7.2.2 The permanent veto

Despite the rapid deterioration of the situation in Syria, a robust UNSC response was obstructed through the exercise of the veto on 12 separate occasions by Russia and China as two of the UNSC's P5. Together, both Russia and China vetoed six draft resolutions on 4 October 2011, 4 February 2012, 19 July 2012, 22 May 2014, 5 December 2016, and 28 February 2017.[28] Russia alone vetoed another six draft resolutions on 8 October 2016, 12 April 2017, 24 October 2017, 16 November 2017, 17 November 2017, and 10 April 2018.[29] Admittedly, the right to the veto as stipulated within Article 27(3) of the UN Charter is not subject to any relevant limitations, implying that it can be employed by the P5 without restraint.[30] With that said, however, two legal arguments were advanced in Chapter 5 of this book against the unrestricted use of the veto in R2P situations. These arguments can facilitate building a case regarding the abusiveness of Russian and Chinese vetoes in the Syrian context, and consequently, can help justify the circumvention of these vetoes through other means available to the international community, most notably through the pursuit of lawful measures, third-party countermeasures, and the UforP mechanism.

27 *See* Geir Ulfstein and Hege Føsund Christiansen, 'The Legality of the NATO Bombing in Libya' (2013) 62 *International and Comparative Law Quarterly* 159, 169–71; Andrew Garwood-Gowers, 'The Responsibility to Protect and the Arab Spring: Libya as the Exception, Syria as the Norm?' (2013) 36 *University of New South Wales Law Journal* 594, 612. *See also* Section 6.5 of this book on NATO's pursuit of regime change in Libya.

28 UN Doc S/2011/612 (n15); UNSC Draft Resolution (4 February 2012) UN Doc S/2012/77; UNSC Draft Resolution (19 July 2012) UN Doc S/2012/538; UNSC Draft Resolution (22 May 2014) UN Doc S/2014/348; UNSC Draft Resolution (5 December 2016) UN Doc S/2016/1026; UNSC Draft Resolution (28 February 2017) UN Doc S/2017/172.

29 UNSC Draft Resolution (8 October 2016) UN Doc S/2016/846; UNSC Draft Resolution (12 April 2017) UN Doc S/2017/315; UNSC Draft Resolution (24 October 2017) UN Doc S/2017/884; UNSC Draft Resolution (16 November 2017) UN Doc S/2017/962; UNSC Draft Resolution (17 November 2017) UN Doc S/2017/970; UNSC Draft Resolution (10 April 2018) UN Doc S/2018/321.

30 Article 27 of the UN Charter only specifies that 'in decisions under Chapter VI, and under paragraph 3 of Article 52, a party to a dispute shall abstain from voting'. This does not, however, apply to decisions taken under Chapter VII of the UN Charter. Charter of the United Nations (adopted 24 October 1945) 1 UNTS XVI Art 27 [hereinafter UN Charter].

One argument calling for limitations to the permanent veto was proposed by Carswell through a combined reading of Articles 1, 2, and 24 of the UN Charter. This argument holds that the P5 are under an obligation to discharge their responsibility to maintain international peace and security in good faith, and that a veto could accordingly be deemed abusive if it breaches this good faith obligation.[31] With respect to Syria, the rationales of Russia and China in exercising their 12 vetoes were that the corresponding draft resolutions were biased against the Syrian State and that they opened the door to military intervention and regime change, a course of action that they opposed.[32] Contrary to these allegations, however, the 12 vetoed draft resolutions on Syria were highly restrictive in the measures that they stipulated and did not pave the way for military intervention or regime change (although, with that said, it should be stressed that it is well within the UNSC's competency to authorise either course of action under its Chapter VII powers[33]). As outlined in Table 7.1, only three of the 12 vetoed draft resolutions invoked Chapter VII, which represents the precursor to the authorisation of the use of force. A brief glance at the texts of even these three draft resolutions leaves little doubt that the reference to Chapter VII was not to authorise, or even to facilitate, the use of force.

The 22 May 2014 draft resolution, for example, invoked Chapter VII in the context of referring the Syrian situation to the International Criminal Court (ICC).[34] The 19 July 2012 draft resolution outlined non-military measures to monitor and alleviate the situation. It threatened that 'if the Syrian authorities have not fully complied with paragraph 4 above within ten days, then it shall impose immediately measures under Article 41 of the UN Charter'.[35] Paragraph 4 to which this provision referred called for the implementation of Kofi Annan's Six Point Plan,[36] which was itself agreed to by the Syrian authorities.[37] Hence, the threat of further measures as per this draft resolution was contingent upon Syria's adherence to a plan to which it had already consented, rather than to one that was imposed coercively. Furthermore, it should be pointed out that this draft resolution resolved to adopt additional measures under Article 41 of the UN Charter in the case of Syria's noncompliance, which, significantly, entails only 'measures not involving the use of armed force'.[38] In order to refer to the use of force, the UNSC would have had to cite instead Article 42 of the Charter.[39] Similarly, the 28

31 *See* Section 5.3.1 of this book.
32 *See*, for example, UNSC 6810th Meeting (19 July 2012) UN Doc S/PV.6810 at 9, 13; UNSC 7180th Meeting (22 May 2014) UN Doc S/PV.7180, 13.
33 *See* Yasmine Nahlawi, 'The Legality of NATO's Pursuit of Regime Change in Libya' (2018) 5 *Journal on the Use of Force and International Law* 295. *See also* Section 6.5.1 of this book.
34 UN Doc S/2014/348 (n28).
35 UN Doc S/2012/538 (n28) Para 14.
36 *See* UNSC Res 2042 (14 April 2012) UN Doc S/RES/2042 Annex.
37 *See* 'Syria "Accepts" Annan Plan to End Crisis' (*Aljazeera*, 28 March 2012) <https://www.aljazeera.com/news/middleeast/2012/03/2012327104152892450.html>.
38 UN Charter (n30) Art 41.
39 Ibid., Art 42.

Table 7.1 Overview of the 12 vetoes exercised to date in the UNSC with respect to the Syrian R2P situation.

Date	*Document number*	*Vote (for-against-abstain)*	*Vetoing party/ies*	*Ch VII?*
4 Oct 2011	S/2011/612	9-2-4	Russia & China	No
4 Feb 2012	S/2012/77	13-2-0	Russia & China	No
19 Jul 2012	S/2012/538	11-2-2	Russia & China	Yes
22 May 2014	S/2014/348	13-2-0	Russia & China	Yes
8 Oct 2016	S/2016/846	11-2-2	Russia	No
5 Dec 2016	S/2016/1026	11-3-1	Russia & China	No
28 Feb 2017	S/2017/172	9-3-3	Russia & China	Yes
12 Apr 2017	S/2017/315	10-2-3	Russia	No
24 Oct 2017	S/2017/884	11-2-2	Russia	No
16 Nov 2017	S/2017/962	11-2-2	Russia	No
17 Nov 2017	S/2017/970	12-2-1	Russia	No
10 Apr 2018	S/2018/321	12-2-1	Russia	No

February 2017 draft resolution noted that the UNSC was '[acting] under Chapter VII of the Charter of the United Nations, *and taking measures under its Article 41*',[40] which, as above, assumes only a non-military scope. Other draft resolutions that did not invoke Chapter VII also made it clear that they did not authorise the use of force. For example, the draft resolution of 4 February 2012 stated that 'nothing in this resolution authorizes measures under Article 42 of the Charter' (e.g. the use of force),[41] while those of 8 October and 5 December 2016 both stressed that 'there is no military solution to the conflict in Syria'.[42]

Given the above analysis, it is difficult to accept Russia and China's allegations that the 12 vetoed draft resolutions paved the way for military intervention and regime change in Syria. Instead, it seems that such pretences were offered by these States to justify their vetoes, which were in reality undertaken in bad faith for political expediency. Russia, for example, enjoys longstanding and extensive economic, military, and security ties with Syria, inclusive of weapons deals and business investments.[43] Essentially, Syria provides Russia a foothold into the Middle East, including, importantly, through hosting the only Russian naval military base outside the former Soviet Union (a resupply base in Tartus on the Mediterranean Sea).[44] This is not to mention that Russia ultimately intervened directly (militarily) in the Syrian conflict in September 2015 in support of the Assad regime under the premise of intervention by

40 UN Doc S/2017/172 (n28) Preamble (emphasis added).
41 UN Doc S/2012/77 (n28) Preamble.
42 UN Doc S/2016/846 (n29) Preamble.
43 *See* Anna Borshchevskaya, 'Russia's Many Interests in Syria' (*Washington Institute*, 24 January 2013) <http://www.washingtoninstitute.org/policy-analysis/view/russias-many-interests-in-syria>.
44 Ibid.

invitation of the host State,[45] and may have been implicated in the commission of war crimes itself through these military operations.[46]

China too, although maintaining a more consistent foreign policy of non-interference and preservation of State sovereignty which it asserted in other conflict situations such as Kosovo and Libya,[47] retains underlying interests in the Syrian conflict with view to preserving the status quo. Aside from economic and security ties that it has long held with Syria, China seized upon the Syrian conflict as an opportunity to bolster its position globally and to gain influence within the Middle East specifically.[48] It also sought economic gains through forging closer ties with key States involved in the conflict including Russia, Iran, and Saudi Arabia.[49] As such, despite the Assad regime's flagrant violations of international law as well as its failure to uphold its primary responsibility to protect its population from mass atrocity crimes as per R2P, Russia and China saw in their best interests to assume a protective role over the regime. Weighing their rhetoric against the provisions of the vetoed draft resolutions and taking into account their deeply vested interests in Syria leads to the very reasonable conclusion that their vetoes were exercised in bad faith (contrary to Article 2(2) of the UN Charter) and as such can be characterised as abusive.

The second argument proposed in Chapter 5 of this book against the unrestricted use of the veto in R2P situations lies in Article 41 of the International Law Commission's Articles on State Responsibility (ILC's ASR), which, although not conclusively binding, offers some indication of how international law is or will be progressing with regards to third-State obligations to respond serious *jus cogens* violations. It was maintained in Chapter 5 that this Article can be interpreted to limit the right of the P5 to veto a UNSC draft resolution addressing an R2P situation unless they can demonstrate that they are pursuing alternative means of responding to the situation that are at least as likely to be as effective as the

45 A legal analysis of this military intervention, however, lies outside the scope of the present discussion. Andrew Osborn and Phil Stewart, 'Russia Begins Syria Air Strikes in its Biggest Mideast Intervention in Decades' (*Reuters*, 1 October 2015) <https://www.reuters.com/article/us-mideast-crisis-russia/russia-begins-syria-air-strikes-in-its-biggest-mideast-intervention-in-decades-idUSKCN0RU0MG20151001>.

46 *See*, for example, HRC, 'Report of the Independent International Commission of Inquiry on the Syrian Arab Republic' (1 February 2018) UN Doc A/HRC/37/72 Paras 78–79; 'Russia/Syria: War Crimes in Month of Bombing Aleppo' (*Human Rights Watch*, 1 December 2016) <https://www.hrw.org/news/2016/12/01/russia/syria-war-crimes-month-bombing-aleppo>.

47 *See* 'China's Initiation of the Five Principles of Peace Co-Existence' (*Ministry of Foreign Affairs of the People's Republic of China*, 2014) <https://www.fmprc.gov.cn/mfa_eng/ziliao_665539/3602_665543/3604_665547/t18053.shtml>; Mauro Barelli, 'Preventing and Responding to Atrocity Crimes: China, Sovereignty and the Responsibility to Protect' (2018) 23 *Journal of Conflict and Security Law* 173.

48 *See* Samuel Ramani, 'China's Syria Agenda' (*The Diplomat*, 22 September 2016) <https://thediplomat.com/2016/09/chinas-syria-agenda/>; Daniel Pena, 'China's Syria Strategy' (*Huffington Post*) <https://www.huffingtonpost.com/daniel-pena/china-syria_b_3923162.html>.

49 Ibid.

measures proposed by the draft resolution.[50] White's analysis is useful here, as he suggests that the 'continued commission of core crimes' following the use of a veto is a primary indicator that this veto '[constituted] a dereliction of the duty to protect placed on the UNSC by R2P'.[51] In this respect, the abusive nature of Russia and China's vetoes on Syria is best evidenced in the prolongation of the R2P situation, which has been ongoing for over eight years. Resolutions that managed to be adopted by the UNSC (for example, calling for an end to the use of chemical weapons and barrel bombs,[52] for the facilitation of humanitarian access,[53] and for the observance of ceasefires[54]), as detailed in subsequent sections, were watered down in order to enlist Russian and Chinese support. Consequently, they were lacking in enforceability and were unsurprisingly systematically violated as part of the conflict's wider deterioration.

Finally, the attitudes of States towards the exercise of a veto can represent a powerful means of assessing its legitimacy. Such attitudes can be gauged through a UNSC procedural vote as suggested by Carswell as well as Melling and Dennett,[55] through a UNGA majority vote as advocated by Judge Alvarez in his dissenting opinion in the *Competence* case,[56] or even through an informal assessment of general State reactions (for example, widespread and overwhelming criticisms of a veto by States can serve as compelling indicators regarding its illegitimacy). In this respect, it is worth mentioning that the 12 Russian and Chinese vetoes on Syria were met with strong protests by States and were thus widely perceived as illegitimate abuses of power. Within the UNSC, and more specifically within the 12 meetings in which the Russian and Chinese vetoes were exercised,[57] the US, UK,

50 *See* Section 5.3.1 of this book.

51 Nigel D. White, 'Commentary: International Institutions and their Role in R2P' in Richard Barnes and Vassilis Tzevelekos (eds), *Beyond Responsibility to Protct: Generating Change in International Law* (Intersentia 2016) 150.

52 *See*, for example, UNSC Res 2118 (27 September 2013) UN Doc S/RES/2118 Paras 4–5; UN Doc S/RES/2139 (n16) Para 3; UNSC Res 2209 (6 March 2015) UN Doc S/RES/2209 Paras 3–4; UNSC Res 2235 (7 August 2015) UN Doc S/RES/2235 Paras 2–3; UNSC Res 2314 (31 October 2016) UN Doc S/RES/2314 Para 2; UNSC Res 2319 (7 August 2015) UN Doc S/RES/2319 Para 3.

53 *See*, for example, UN Doc S/RES/2139 (n52) Para 6; UN Doc S/RES/2165 (n17) Paras 2, 6; UN Doc S/RES/2254 (n17) Para 12; UNSC Res 2268 (26 February 2016) UN Doc S/RES/2268 Para 5; UN Doc S/RES/2332 (n17) Para 2; UN Doc S/RES/2393 (n17) Para 2; UN Doc S/RES/2449 (n17) Para 3.

54 *See*, for example, UN Doc S/RES/2254 (n17) Para 5; UN Doc S/RES/2268 (n53) Para 3; UNSC Res 2401 (24 February 2018) UN Doc S/RES/2401 Para 1.

55 Andrew J. Carswell, 'Unblocking the UN Security Council: The *Uniting for Peace* Resolution' (2013) 18 *Journal of Conflict and Security Law* 453, 472–73; Graham Melling and Anne Dennett, 'The Security Council Veto and Syria: Responding to Mass Atrocities through the "Uniting for Peace" Resolution' (2017) 57 *Indian Journal of International Law* 285, 303.

56 *Competence of the General Assembly for the Admission of a State to the United Nations* (Dissenting Opinion of Judge Alvarez) [1950] ICJ Rep 12, 20.

57 *See* UN Doc S/PV.6627 (n18); UNSC 6711th Meeting (4 February 2012) UN Doc S/PV.6711; UN Doc S/PV.6810 (n64); UN Doc S/PV.7180 (n32); UNSC 7785th Meeting (8 October 2016) UN Doc S/PV.7785; UNSC 7825th Meeting (5

and France were the most vocal in protesting the vetoes, although they were joined in this respect by 18 other States, namely, Colombia, Germany, Guatemala, Rwanda, Jordan, Luxembourg, Chile, Australia, Lithuania, South Korea, Ukraine, New Zealand, Spain, Uruguay, Sweden, Poland, the Netherlands, and Kuwait.[58] Nine of these States (US, UK, France, Luxembourg, Ukraine, New Zealand, Sweden, Poland, and the Netherlands) departed from accepted protocol (whereby States make only indirect references to other States when voicing disagreement) to specifically naming and shaming Russia and/or China as the vetoing parties.[59] Such condemnations became more pronounced with successive vetoes, indicating States' increased collective outrage regarding the unchecked manner in which Russia and China were employing their veto to obstruct UNSC action on Syria. Eight States (Rwanda, Jordan, Luxembourg, Chile, Australia, Ukraine, France, and Kuwait[60]) furthermore called upon the UNSC to give serious consideration to a code of conduct advanced by France in 2013 which calls upon the P5 to 'voluntarily regulate their right to exercise their veto' in mass atrocity (R2P) situations.[61] In this manner, the persistent Russian and Chinese vetoes underscored a more general problem regarding the implementation of R2P.

Importantly, condemnations of Russia and China's exercise of the veto in the Syrian context extended beyond the UNSC. For example, in a rare move by the UNGA on 7 August 2012 (after Russia and China's third set of vetoes), the body adopted Resolution 66/253B which '[deplored] the failure of the Security Council to agree on measures to ensure the compliance of Syrian authorities with its decisions'.[62] This Resolution, adopted by 133 votes to 12 with 31 abstentions, exposed deep-seated frustrations by States regarding the UNSC's inability to take concrete action to alleviate the R2P situation in Syria. Again on 18 December 2013, the body adopted Resolution 68/182 by 127 votes to 13 with 47 abstentions which:

> [Reminded] the Security Council of its primary responsibility for the maintenance of international peace and security and to take measures to put an end to all serious violations of international humanitarian law and all serious violations and abuses of international human rights law committed in the Syrian Arab Republic.[63]

December 2016) UN Doc S/PV.7825; UNSC 7893rd Meeting (28 February 2017) UN Doc S/PV.7893; UNSC 7922nd Meeting (12 April 2017) UN Doc S/PV.7922; UNSC 8073rd Meeting (24 October 2017) UN Doc S/PV.8073; UNSC 8105th Meeting (16 November 2017) UN Doc S/PV.8105; UNSC 8107th Meeting (17 November 2017) UN Doc S/PV.8107; UNSC 8228th Meeting (10 April 2018) UN Doc S/PV.8228.

58 Ibid.

59 Ibid.

60 Ibid.

61 Laurent Fabius, 'A Call for Self-Restraint at the U.N.' (*New York Times*, 4 October 2013) <http://www.nytimes.com/2013/10/04/opinion/a-call-for-self-restraint-at-the-un.html>.

62 UNGA Res 66/253B (7 August 2012) UN Doc A/RES/66/253B Preamble.

63 UNGA Res 68/182 (30 January 2014) UN Doc A/RES/68/182 Para 12.

Using stronger language on 9 December 2016, the UNGA adopted Resolution 71/130 by 122 votes to 13 with 36 abstentions which '[expressed] alarm that the responsibility of the Security Council to ensure prompt and effective action has not been further discharged with regard to the Syrian Arab Republic',[64] and furthermore '[urged] the Security Council to further exercise its responsibility for the maintenance of international peace and security by taking additional measures to address the crisis in the Syrian Arab Republic'.[65] In this manner, international disapproval regarding Russia and China's abusive vetoes within the UNSC on Syria was manifested at the UN institutional level.

Overall, the content of the vetoed UNSC draft resolutions (which were devoid of coercive measures such as the authorisation of the use of force or regime change), Russian and Chinese vested interests in Syria, the prolongation of the Syrian conflict, and the overwhelming protests of States both within and outside the UNSC against Russian and Chinese vetoes present strong justification for characterising these vetoes as abusive. It can furthermore be reasonably argued that these vetoes prevented the UNSC from adequately discharging its primary responsibility to maintain international peace and security as per Article 24 of the UN Charter, as well as from responding effectively to the Syrian R2P situation. In this case, therefore, the international community – inclusive of States and international organisations – should have looked beyond the UNSC to discharge its Pillar 3 responsibility to protect, for example through the adoption of lawful measures in line with States' and international organisations' respective mandates, through the undertaking of third-party countermeasures as a means of prompting the further development of international law in this respect,[66] or through the invocation of UforP through which the UNGA could recommend a range of measures up to and including the use of force.[67] Such international mobilisation would reinforce that the international community's Pillar 3 responsibility exists irrespective of UNSC action or lack thereof, and, that by default, this Pillar 3 responsibility is not directed towards any one particular actor, but should rather be shouldered by the international community as a whole. The remainder of the section discusses in detail how the UNSC failed to fulfil its Pillar 3 responsibility in various contexts throughout the Syrian conflict, and how instead, reactions by other international actors could have manifested as a means of overcoming these failures.

7.2.3 General measures

Over the first one-and-a-half years of the Syrian conflict, the UNSC was concerned primarily with what can be termed 'general measures' to alleviate the R2P

64 UNGA Res 71/130 (19 December 2016) UN Doc A/RES/71/130 Preamble.

65 Ibid., Para 10.

66 Recall from Section 2.2.1 of this book that while extensive State practice exists pertaining to the use of third-State countermeasures, the ILC declined to comment on their lawfulness, leaving this question instead to the 'further development of international law'.

67 As detailed in Section 5.3.2.1.

situation. Throughout this period, the body adopted three resolutions – 2042, 2043, and 2059[68] – that sought to implement a 'Six Point Plan' for the cessation of hostilities developed by Kofi Annan as a joint UN-LAS Special Envoy to Syria,[69] as well as to establish a UN Supervision Mission in Syria (UNSMIS) to monitor this cessation of hostilities.[70] Both initiatives were introduced with the consent of the Syrian authorities, although neither one succeeded: UNSMIS was terminated through UNSC Resolution 2059 due to 'operational implications of the increasingly dangerous security situation in Syria',[71] and Kofi Annan resigned in August 2012 from his position as Joint Special Envoy to Syria in large part due to the failure of the international community to provide sufficient backing to his initiatives.[72] Therefore, while the UNSC paid lip service regarding the imperative for a cessation of hostilities in Syria, it did not enforce such a cessation of hostilities nor did it hold violating parties (primarily, the Assad regime[73]) to account for its breach.

In addition to the above three UNSC resolutions on Syria, Russia and China together vetoed another three draft resolutions throughout the first year and a half of the conflict, specially on 4 October 2011, 4 February 2012, and 19 July 2012.[74] These draft resolutions sought to introduce generic non-military measures as a means of pressuring all groups, but particularly the Assad regime, to cease the commission of violations of international law, including by calling for an end to the violence, accountability, an inclusive political process, the appointment of a Joint Special Envoy, and restraint over arms sales. They did not seek to implement any coercive measures, not even non-military ones such as sanctions or an arms embargo which in many respects constitute standard first-line responses to situations that threaten or breach international peace and security. Even the invocation of Chapter VII in the 19 July 2012 draft resolution was presumably made under Article 41 rather than 42 of the UN Charter.[75]

At this key stage of the Syrian R2P situation, targeted and robust UNSC action may have succeeded in imparting lasting effects in terms of curbing atrocities and preventing Syria's further descent into war. Given the body's ineffectiveness,

68 UN Doc S/RES/2042 (n36); UNSC Res 2043 (21 April 2012) UN Doc S/RES/2043; UNSC Res 2059 (20 July 2012) UN Doc S/RES/2059.
69 *See* UN Doc S/RES/2042 (n36) Annex; 'Syria "accepts" Annan plan to end crisis' (n37).
70 UN Doc S/RES/2042 (n36) Para 5; UN Doc S/RES/2043 (n68) Para 5.
71 UN Doc S/RES/2059 (68) Para 1.
72 Matthew Weaver and Brian Whitaker, 'Syria Crisis: Kofi Annan Resigns as Peace Envoy' (*Guardian*, 2 August 2012) <https://www.theguardian.com/world/middle-east-live/2012/aug/02/syria-crisis-damascus-massacres-live>.
73 *See* Ruth Sherlock and David Blair, 'Syria: Kofi Annan Attacks UN Security Council for "Finger Pointing and Name-Calling"' (*Telegraph*, 2 August 2012) <https://www.telegraph.co.uk/news/worldnews/middleeast/syria/9448021/Syria-Kofi-Annan-attacks-UN-Security-Council-for-finger-pointing-and-name-calling.html>.
74 UN Doc S/2011/612 (n15); UN Doc S/2012/77 (n28); UN Doc S/2012/538 (n28).
75 *See supra* notes 35–39 and accompanying text.

however, States and international organisations should have assumed a greater role in seeking human protection outside the confines of the UNSC. This could have occurred, for example, through the adoption of lawful measures (e.g. public condemnations, the severing of diplomatic ties, and diplomatic initiatives) or third-party countermeasures (e.g. the imposition of sanctions, asset freezes, and arms embargos). The limited pursuit of such measures was undertaken by various States and international organisations throughout 2011 and 2012, although they were not as timely or as extensive as required to exert sufficient pressure on Syria to change course.[76] UforP is also relevant in this respect, as its invocation could have delivered UNGA recommendations encompassing of the above measures. Of course, while UNGA recommendations under UforP would not have created binding obligations upon States to respond to the R2P situation, they would have at least presented a legal justification for States to undertake specified measures should they have wished to do so, and perhaps would have incentivised a greater range of States to adopt such measures.

7.2.4 Chemical weapons

Chemical weapons were employed within the Syrian context primarily by the Assad regime as early as December 2012.[77] Although they have not been responsible for the majority of deaths within the conflict, nor do they represent the primary means of perpetuating the R2P situation,[78] they have nevertheless been the subject of significant international focus as detailed within this section. In terms of the relevance of chemical weapons use to R2P, it should be noted that Article 8 of the ICC Statute, which defines war crimes, prohibits in both international and non-international armed conflicts '[e]mploying poison or poisoned weapons' as well as '[e]mploying asphyxiating, poisonous or other gases, and all analogous liquids, materials or devices'.[79] Notably, this phrasing does not specifically identify chemical weapons use as a war crime. Cottier and Schabas each explain that this omission is due to controversy that arose during

76 For an extensive overview of the international response to the Syrian conflict, *see* 'Timeline of the International Response to the Situation in Syria' (*Global Centre for the Responsibility to Protect*, 2016) <http://www.globalr2p.org/media/files/timeline-of-international-response-to-syria-28.pdf>. *See also* Susan Breau, *The Responsibility to Protect in International Law: An Emerging Paradigm Shift* (Routledge 2016) 257–59.

77 *See* Ashish Kumar Sen, 'A Brief History of Chemical Weapons in Syria' (*Atlantic Council*, 9 April 2018) <http://www.atlanticcouncil.org/blogs/new-atlanticist/a-brief-history-of-chemical-weapons-in-syria>; UNSC, 'Letter Dated 26 October 2017 from the Secretary-General Addressed to the President of the Security Council' (26 October 2017) UN Doc S/2017/904 Para 46.

78 *See* Yasmine Nahlawi, 'The Responsibility to Protect and Obama's Red Line on Syria' (2016) 8 *Global Responsibility to Protect* 76, 95–97.

79 Rome Statute of the International Criminal Court (adopted 17 July 1998, entered into force 1 July 2002) 2187 UNTS 3 Arts 8(2)(b) and 8(2)(e) [hereinafter ICC Statute] Arts 8(2)(b) and 8(2)(e).

the drafting of the ICC Statute, whereby developed States protested the inclusion of nuclear weapons into Article 8 and developing States in turn protested the inclusion of biological and chemical weapons, calling them the 'poor man's atomic bomb'.[80] As a result, all three categories of crimes were eliminated (by name) from the Article.[81] However, Cottier concedes that the wording of the respective provisions can be understood to apply directly to chemical weapons,[82] a notion that is met with widespread support of international legal scholars.[83] In this sense, the use of chemical weapons in an armed conflict would constitute a war crime and in turn trigger the applicability of R2P.

In August 2012, then-US President Obama proclaimed that chemical weapons use in Syria constituted a 'red line' that would lead to consequences if crossed.[84] Following the Assad regime's launch of a major chemical attack on Ghouta, Syria on 21 August 2013 which claimed over 1,000 civilian casualties,[85] Western powers (primarily headed by the US) threatened to intervene militarily to 'respond to the Assad regime's use of chemical weapons through a targeted military strike'.[86] Specifically, Obama announced that he was 'comfortable going forward without the approval' of the UNSC, which he wrote off as 'completely paralyzed and unwilling to hold Assad accountable'.[87] The situation was subsequently defused through the adoption of US- and Russian-negotiated UNSC Resolution 2118 in September 2013, which (not under Chapter VII) condemned the Ghouta chemical attack, declared chemical weapon use to constitute a threat to international peace and security, called for the destruction of Syria's chemical weapons programme as per procedures established by the Organisation for the Prohibition

80 Michael Cottier, 'Preliminary Remarks on Subparagraphs (xvii)–(xx): Prohibited Weapons: Drafting History' in Otto Triffterer (ed.), *Commentary on the Rome Statute of the International Criminal Court* (Nomos Verlagsgesellschaft Baden-Baden 1999) 241. *See also* William Schabas, *An Introduction to the International Criminal Court* (2nd edn, Cambridge University Press 2004) 137–38.
81 Ibid.
82 Cottier (n80) 241.
83 *See*, for example, Carsten Stahn, 'Between Law-breaking and Law-making: Syria, Humanitarian Intervention and "What the Law Ought to be"' (2013) 19 *Journal of Conflict and Security Law* 25, 29; Michael Bothe, 'War Crimes' in Antonio Cassese, Paola Gaeta, and John R.W.D. Jones (eds), *The Rome Statute of the International Criminal Court: A Commentary* (Oxford University Press 2002) 407; Sandesh Sivakumaran, *The Law of Non-international Armed Conflict* (Oxford University Press 2012) 396.
84 'Remarks by the President to the White House Press Corps' (*The White House,* 20 August 2012) <http://www.whitehouse.gov/the-press-office/2012/08/20/remarks-president-white-house-press-corps>.
85 'Syria Conflict: Chemical Attacks Kill Hundreds' (BBC News, 21 August 2013) <http://www.bbc.co.uk/news/world-middle-east-23777201>.
86 *See* 'Remarks by the President in Address to the Nation on Syria' (*The White House,* 10 September 2013) <http://www.whitehouse.gov/the-press-office/2013/09/10/remarks-president-address-nation-syria>.
87 'Statement by the President on Syria' (*The White House: Office of the Press Secretary,* 31 August 2013) <http://www.whitehouse.gov/the-press-office/2013/08/31/statement-president-syria>.

of Chemical Weapons (OPCW), and threatened further measures under Chapter VII in the case of non-compliance with this Resolution.[88]

Given the UNSC's characteristic paralysis on the situation in Syria, it is quite significant that the body was able to generate consensus that facilitated the adoption of Resolution 2118. Equally noteworthy is that this momentum to address chemical weapons use in Syria persisted within the UNSC until the end of 2016, during which time the body adopted four additional resolutions on the subject – Resolution 2209 in March 2015, Resolution 2235 in August 2015, Resolution 2314 in October 2016, and Resolution 2319 in November 2016 – which condemned their use; called for accountability for the respective perpetrators; established a Joint Investigative Mechanism (JIM) in collaboration with the OPCW to 'identify to the greatest extent feasible individuals, entities, groups, or governments who were perpetrators, organisers, sponsors or otherwise involved in the use of chemicals as weapons … in the Syrian Arab Republic'; and renewed JIM on two separate occasions.[89] While this seems at face value a success in the international community's response to the Syrian R2P situation, a deeper analysis of the chemical weapons dimension reveals yet another UNSC failure in this respect.

First, the resolutions adopted by the UNSC on chemical weapons use in Syria were set for failure. They did not, for example, invoke Chapter VII, nor did they stipulate clear consequences for their breach. Rather, Resolution 2118 vaguely '[decided], in the event of non-compliance with this resolution,… to impose measures under Chapter VII of the United Nations Charter'.[90] Despite repeated instances of chemical weapons use in Syria following this Resolution's adoption,[91] however, such Chapter VII authorisations were not forthcoming. Instead, subsequent Resolutions similarly threatened the adoption of additional measures under Chapter VII in the event of their breach,[92] although follow-through was again lacking despite continued allegations of chemical weapons use.[93] Ultimately, this political manoeuvring by the UNSC can be attributed to Russia and China's vehement opposition to the invocation of Chapter VII in the context of the Syrian conflict. Given these States' demonstrated predisposition to veto draft resolutions

88 UN Doc S/RES/2118 (n52).
89 *See* UN Doc S/RES/2209 (n52); UN Doc S/RES/2235 (n52); UN Doc S/RES/2314 (n52); UN Doc S/RES/2319 (n52).
90 UN Doc S/RES/2118 (n52) Para 21.
91 *See*, for example, OPCW, 'Second Report of the OPCW Fact-Finding Mission in Syria: Key Findings' (10 September 2014) Doc S/1212/2014; OPCW, 'Third Report of the OPCW Fact-Finding Mission in Syria: Key Findings' (18 December 2014) Doc S/1230/2014.
92 UN Doc S/RES/2209 (n52) Para 7; UN Doc S/RES/2235 (n52) Para 15; UN Doc S/RES/2314 (n52) Para 2; UN Doc S/RES/2319 (n52) Para 3.
93 *See*, for example, OPCW, 'Report of the OPCW Fact-finding Mission in Syria Regarding Alleged Incidents in Marea, Syrian Arab Republic August 2015' (29 October 2015) Doc S/1320/2015; OPCW, 'Report of the OPCW Fact-finding Mission in Syria Regarding Alleged Incidents in the Idlib Governorate of the Syrian Arab Republic between 16 March and 20 May 2015' (29 October 2015) Doc S/1319/2015.

that sought to impose concrete measures against the Assad regime, it can only be surmised that such empty provisions threatening further action under Chapter VII were incorporated into the respective resolutions not to facilitate further action against chemical weapons perpetrators in Syria (primarily, the Assad regime) in the case of non-compliance, but rather, to delay and quash the prospect of coercive measures being imposed under Chapter VII. Therefore, although the UNSC remained in theory seized of the chemical weapons issue between 2014 and 2016, such weapons continued to be employed against the civilian population with impunity.

Second, UNSC involvement with respect to chemical weapons use in Syria came to an abrupt halt in 2017. Between 2017 and 2018, Russia vetoed six draft resolutions (China also exercised its veto on one of these occasions) which called for the imposition of an asset freeze and travel ban against individuals connected to chemical attacks in Syria, the prevention of the sale of chemical weapons-related materials to Syria, the renewal of JIM, and the establishment of a UN Independent Mechanism of Investigation (UNIMI) with a similar mandate to JIM (following the UNSC's failure to renew the latter due to the exercise of three Russian vetoes in October and November 2017).[94] In the midst of this UNSC paralysis, the Assad regime committed two particularly egregious chemical attacks, one against the town of Khan Sheikhoun on 4 April 2017, which killed almost 100 civilians, and another against the city of Douma on 7 April 2018, which killed dozens of civilians.[95] Rather than being met with a concerted Chapter VII UNSC response as pledged within the various UNSC resolutions on chemical weapons use in Syria,[96] these attacks were instead responded to by individual States in the form of unauthorised military interventions. The attack against Khan Sheikhoun, for example, prompted a US military response on 7 April 2017 in the form of 59 Tomahawk cruise missiles directed against a Syrian air base in Homs,[97] while the Douma chemical attack was similarly met with a military response from the US, UK, and France in the form of over 100 missiles.[98] The UNSC's relevance in this respect was thus severely diminished.

94 *See* UN Doc S/2017/172 (n28); UN Doc S/2017/315 (n29); UN Doc S/2017/884 (n29); UN Doc S/2017/962 (n29); UN Doc S/2017/970 (n29); UN Doc S/2018/321 (n29).

95 UN Doc S/2017/904 (n77) Para 46; 'Dozens of Civilians Killed in Alleged "Poison Gas" Attack' (*CBS News*, 4 April 2017) <https://www.cbsnews.com/news/syria-alleged-poison-gas-chemical-attack-khan-sheikhoun-idlib-civilians/>; 'Syria Chemical Attack: Scores Killed in Douma, Rescuers Say' (*Aljazeera*, 8 April 2018) <https://www.aljazeera.com/news/2018/04/suspected-chemical-attack-kills-dozens-syria-douma-180407202906316.html>.

96 *See supra* notes 90 and 92.

97 Spencer Ackerman et al., 'Syria Missile Strikes: US Launches First Direct Military Action against Assad' (*Guardian*, 7 April 2017) <https://www.theguardian.com/world/2017/apr/06/trump-syria-missiles-assad-chemical-weapons>.

98 Julian Borger and Peter Beaumont, 'Syria: US, UK and France Launch Strikes in Response to Chemical Attack' (*Guardian*, 14 April 2018) <https://www.theguardian.com/world/2018/apr/14/syria-air-strikes-us-uk-and-france-launch-attack-on-assad-regime>.

Third, when the UNSC and other actors did choose to respond to chemical weapons use in Syria, such action was not premised upon R2P or upon protection considerations. For example, Annex I to UNSC Resolution 2118, which was adopted in response to the 2013 Ghouta chemical attack, emphasised that the OPCW's decision with respect to the destruction of chemical weapons in Syria was 'made due to the extraordinary character of the situation posed by Syrian chemical weapons and does not create any precedent for the future.'[99] Subsequent UNSC resolutions on chemical weapons use in Syria were similarly predicated upon norm enforcement (of the chemical weapons prohibition) as well as the need to uphold previous resolutions.[100] Even the US and allies (with the exceptions of the UK and Denmark[101]) refrained from referencing R2P or human protection as a basis for their threatened or actual military interventions. Instead, the US – as the primary propeller of international action in this respect – presented a string of vague arguments to justify both its potential intervention (following the 2013 Ghouta chemical attack) as well as its actual interventions (following the 2017 and 2018 chemical attacks against Khan Sheikhoun and Douma, respectively), including the need to uphold national security, norm enforcement, collective self-defence, deterrence, and degradation of the Syrian regime's capabilities.[102] The lawfulness of the strikes conducted by the US and allies in 2017 and 2018 has been debated extensively by scholars of international law, although these military operations have for the most part been deemed unlawful.[103] What is significant for the

99 UNSC Res 2118 (n52) Annex I Para 3(d).

100 *See* UN Doc S/RES/2209 (n52); UN Doc S/RES/2235 (n52); UN Doc S/RES/2314 (n52); UN Doc S/RES/2319 (n52).

101 The UK and Denmark invoked humanitarian intervention as a justification for military intervention in response to chemical weapons use in Syria. 'Chemical Weapon Use by Syrian Regime: UK Government Legal Position' (Prime Minister's Office, 29 August 2013) <https://www.gov.uk/government/publications/chemical-weapon-use-by-syrian-regime-uk-government-legal-position/chemical-weapon-use-by-syrian-regime-uk-government-legal-position-html-version>; 'Syria Action – UK Government Legal Position' (Prime Minister's Office, 14 April 2018) <https://www.gov.uk/government/publications/syria-action-uk-government-legal-position/syria-action-uk-government-legal-position>; Christian Henderson, 'The UK Government's Legal Opinion on Forcible Measures in Response to the Use of Chemical Weapons by the Syrian Government' (2015) 64 *International and Comparative Law Quarterly* 179, 192–93.

102 'Remarks by the President in Address to the Nation on Syria' (n86); Mythili Sampathkumar, 'Syria Missile Strike: Donald Trump's Speech in Full' (*Independent*, 7 April 2017) <https://www.independent.co.uk/news/world/americas/us-politics/donald-trump-latest-syria-missile-strike-tomahawk-chemical-weapons-attack-idlib-beautiful-babies-a7671471.html>; 'Statement by President Trump on Syria' (*The White House,* 13 April 2018) <https://www.whitehouse.gov/briefings-statements/statement-president-trump-syria/>.

103 *See*, for example, Anders Henriksen, 'Trump's Missile Strike on Syria and the Legality of Using Force to Deter Chemical Warfare' (2018) 23 *Journal of Conflict and Security Law* 33; Jack Goldsmith and Oona Hathaway, 'Bad Legal Arguments for the Syria Strikes' (*Just Security,* 14 April 2018) <https://www.justsecurity.org/54925/bad-legal-arguments-syria-strikes/>; Julian Ku, 'Almost Everyone Agrees that the U.S. Strikes against Syria are Illegal, Except for Most Governments'

purposes of the present analysis, however, is that despite the clear relevance of the situation to R2P and the more general imperative to safeguard human lives, international action that was forthcoming from both the UNSC and from individual States was instead premised upon more specific considerations of norm enforcement against chemical weapons use and/or the national security of vested States.

Fourth and finally, international mobilisation in response to chemical weapons use in Syria came at the exclusion of other war crimes and crimes against humanity that were long being committed throughout the conflict and which had likely left more than 100,000 people dead prior to the 21 August 2013 Ghouta chemical attack.[104] Even if it were to be argued that initiatives within and outside the UNSC succeeded in deterring the Assad regime from employing chemical weapons (which they did not[105]), it is important to bear in mind that there remained a wider and ongoing mass atrocity situation that was claiming countless civilians lives and livelihoods. This was effectively summarised by Argentina in a statement delivered to the UNSC in September 2013:

> [M]y country wishes to reiterate that the horror of chemical weapons, whose use is a war crime and a crime against humanity, should not overshadow the fact that 99 per cent of the casualties in the conflict have been from conventional weapons.[106]

As such, the international community's reaction to chemical weapons use arguably should have occurred as part of a more comprehensive strategy to address the overarching Syrian R2P situation. Had the international focus been directed towards responding to any and all mass atrocity crimes committed, the situation in Syria may have unfolded in a very different manner to the grave and horrific scenario that represents the current reality.

Overall, therefore, although the UNSC did mobilise against chemical weapons use in Syria between 2013 and 2016, such a response cannot be characterised as an R2P success. In terms of what could have been done differently at the international level with respect to the chemical weapons issue in particular, UNSC member-States should have resolved to respond to their use through the authorisation of measures under Chapter VII rather than tolerate the continued subversion of UNSC action through vague pledges to invoke

(*Opinio Juris*, 7 April 2017) <http://opiniojuris.org/2017/04/07/almost-everyone-agrees-that-the-u-s-strikes-against-syria-are-illegal-under-international-law-except-for-most-governments/>.

104 *See* 'Syria Death Toll Likely as High as 120,000, Group Says' (*Huffington Post*, 14 May 2013) <http://www.huffingtonpost.com/2013/05/14/syria-death-toll-120000_n_3272610.html>.

105 *See*, for example, 'The Syrian Regime has Used Chemical Weapons Five Times after Khan Sheikhoun Incident' (*Syrian Network for Human Rights*, 14 Aug 2017) <http://sn4hr.org/blog/2017/08/14/45499/>.

106 UN Doc S/PV.7038 (n25) 13.

Chapter VII that were never forthcoming. Had Russia or China exercised their vetoes in response to such tabled draft resolutions, a move could have been made, either by the UNSC itself or by the UNGA, to refer the situation to the UNGA as per UforP. Such a referral should not have been difficult to achieve given the intense international political will to respond to chemical weapons use in Syria. Following such a referral, the UNGA would have been justified in recommending robust measures under UforP to address chemical weapons use, up to and including the use of force. This is especially so given that the US and allies conducted two separate unauthorised military strikes against Syria in response to its employment of chemical weapons as detailed above. Here, it can at least be surmised that UforP would have offered both a legally sound and a more legitimate alternative, namely, that any force employed pursuant to UforP would have derived from a two-thirds recommendation of the UNGA, as opposed to a decision undertaken by a maximum of three States. Building upon the momentum of the chemical weapons issue, the international community should have then undertaken efforts to ensure that its response to chemical use occurred as part of a wider strategy to address the Syrian R2P situation as a whole.

7.2.5 Humanitarian access

After the 4 October 2011 UNSC draft resolution on Syria – which referenced Syria's R2P Pillar 1 responsibility – was vetoed by Russia and China due to their alleged concerns that the doctrine's invocation would provoke military intervention and regime change,[107] R2P was not cited in any UNSC resolutions or draft resolutions on the situation for over two years. Beginning in 2014, however, references to R2P returned to UNSC resolutions on Syria, primarily those that centred on the issue of humanitarian access including Resolutions 2139, 2165, 2258, 2332, 2393, and 2449.[108] These resolutions, although not adopted under Chapter VII, affirmed Syria's Pillar 1 responsibility to protect its population,[109] while references to a Pillar 3 responsibility of the international community to react were notably absent.[110]

The link between R2P and the issue of humanitarian access in Syria is that the deliberate deprivation of humanitarian aid in order to starve a civilian population can amount to a crime against humanity and perhaps also a war crime in the

107 *See supra* note 15.

108 UN Doc S/RES/2139 (n16) Para 9; UN Doc S/RES/2165 (n17) Preamble; UN Doc S/RES/2258 (n17) Preamble; UN Doc S/RES/2332 (n17) Preamble; UN Doc S/RES/2393 (n17) Preamble; UN Doc S/RES/2449 (n17) Preamble.

109 *See also* UNSC 7116th Meeting (22 February 2014) UN Doc S/PV.7116 at 9, 14 (comments of Argentina and Lithuania); UNSC 7216th Meeting (14 July 2014) UN Doc S/PV.7216, 10 (comments of Lithuania); UNSC 8423rd Meeting (13 December 2018) UN Doc S/PV.8423 at 12, 19 (comments of Poland and Côte d'Ivoire).

110 Limited affirmations of R2P's Pillar 3 were made by Chile and Argentina during the course of discussions on these resolutions. *See* UN Doc S/PV.7216 (n109) 8–9.

context of NIACs (which represents the conflict in Syria[111]). Article 7 of the ICC Statute, for example, identifies the 'deprivation of access to food and medicine, calculated to bring about the destruction of part of a population' as a form of extermination and as such prohibited as a crime against humanity.[112] The Statute furthermore lists '[i]ntentionally using starvation of civilians as a method of warfare' as a war crime, although this is notably in reference to IACs and not NIACs.[113] The International Committee of the Red Cross's (ICRC) study of customary international law, however, contends that the starvation of civilians can also constitute a war crime when committed in NIACs, justifying this conclusion through an evaluation of State practice and *opinio juris* as well as through Article 14 of Additional Protocol II (APII), which prohibits the '[s]tarvation of civilians as a method of combat' in NIACs.[114] As such, the relevance of R2P to humanitarian access in Syria can be potentially made on two different counts, both under the banner of crimes against humanity as well as war crimes.

The first resolution adopted by the UNSC on the theme of humanitarian access in Syria was Resolution 2139 in February 2014 which:

> [Demanded] that all parties, in particular the Syrian authorities, promptly allow rapid, safe and unhindered humanitarian access for United Nations humanitarian agencies and their implementing partners, including across conflict lines and across borders, in order to ensure that humanitarian assistance reaches people in need through the most direct routes.[115]

In essence, Resolution 2139 required the Assad regime and other parties to the conflict to provide UN humanitarian agencies and their implementing partners unhindered access to target communities. It fell short, however, of allowing such agencies to deliver aid if State consent was not forthcoming. In other words, if Syria denied access to UN humanitarian agencies to at-need areas following the adoption of Resolution 2139, then it would be in breach of this Resolution as well as R2P's Pillar 1. However, this would not in turn translate into a right for the relevant aid agencies to bypass Syria and conduct humanitarian relief operations within Syrian territory without State consent. Such action, if undertaken, would at face value represent a violation of Syria's territorial sovereignty.

As the Assad regime continued to restrict humanitarian access in violation of its obligations under UNSC Resolution 2139,[116] the UNSC adopted Resolution 2165 in July 2014 which:

111 *See supra* note 7.
112 ICC Statute (n79) Arts 7(1)(b) and 7(2)(b).
113 Ibid., Art 8(2)(b)(xxv).
114 'Rule 53. Starvation as a Method of Warfare' (ICRC, 2016) <https://ihl-databases.icrc.org/customary-ihl/eng/docs/v1_rul_rule53>.
115 UN Doc S/RES/2139 (n16) Para 6.
116 *See*, for example, UNSC, 'Report of the Secretary-General on the Implementation of Security Council Resolution 2139' (22 May 2014) UN Doc S/2014/365 Paras 17–40.

> [Decided] that the United Nations humanitarian agencies and their implementing partners are authorized to use routes across conflict lines and [certain border crossings] in order to ensure that humanitarian assistance … reaches people in need throughout Syria … with notification to the Syrian authorities.[117]

Unlike Resolution 2139, Resolution 2165 only required UN humanitarian aid agencies and their implementing partners to provide 'notification', but not necessarily to obtain consent from, the Assad regime in order to carry out humanitarian operations in Syria.[118] As such, this Resolution granted such entities the entitlement to enter Syrian territory through specified border crossings even if the regime's blessings were not given in order to deliver vital humanitarian aid. This mandate was renewed on an annual basis through UNSC Resolutions 2191, 2258, 2332, 2393, and 2449, so that its relevant provisions remain applicable as of this writing.[119] Nevertheless, and presumably due to security and other administrative concerns, UN and partner aid agencies continued to seek and rely upon the Assad regime's consent as a precursor to conducting a significant proportion of their aid operations in Syria. The regime in turn routinely restricted the beneficiary areas to which aid could be distributed (most notably, to deny aid to besieged or other opposition areas) as well as the types of goods to be delivered (for example, to allow only non-food items such as mosquito nets and anti-lice shampoo to be delivered to besieged populations).[120] Such actions

117 UN Doc S/RES/2165 (n17) Para 2.

118 *See* Keiichiro Okimoto, 'Humanitarian Activities Carried Out across Borders in Times of Armed Conflict in the Light of State Sovereignty and International Humanitarian Law' (2016) 17 *Yearbook of International Humanitarian Law* 121, 139–40.

119 UNSC Res 2191 (17 December 2014) UN Doc S/RES/2191 Para 2; UN Doc S/RES/2258 (n17) Para 2; UN Doc S/RES/2332 (n17) Para 2; UN Doc S/RES/2393 (n17) Para 2; UN Doc S/RES/2449 (n17) Para 3.

120 *See*, for example, Report of the Secretary-General, 'Implementation of Security Council Resolutions 2139 (2014) and 2165 (2014)' (23 October 2014) UN Doc S/2014/756 Paras 31, 48; Report of the Secretary-General, 'Implementation of Security Council Resolutions 2139 (2014), 2165 (2014), 2191 (2014), and 2258 (2015)' (20 July 2016) UN Doc S/2016/631 Paras 38–39, 46–47, 58–59; Report of the Secretary-General, 'Implementation of Security Council Resolutions 2139 (2014) and 2165 (2014), 2191 (2014), 2258 (2015) and 2332 (2016)' (25 October 2017) UN Doc S/2017/902 Paras 22–25; Report of the Secretary-General, 'Implementation of Security Council Resolutions 2139 (2014) and 2165 (2014), 2191 (2014), 2258 (2015), 2332 (2016), 2393 (2017) and 2401 (2018)' (23 October 2018) UN Doc S/2018/947 Paras 25–26; HRC, 'Report of the Independent International Commission of Inquiry on the Syrian Arab Republic' (11 August 2016) UN Doc A/HRC/33/55 Paras 34–35; Nick Hopkins and Emma Beals, 'UN Pays Tens of Millions to Assad Regime under Syria Aid Programme' (*Guardian*, 29 August 2016) <https://www.theguardian.com/world/2016/aug/29/un-pays-tens-of-millions-to-assad-regime-syria-aid-programme-contracts>; 'Syrian Aid Being Blocked by Government, Says UN Envoy' (*Middle East Eye*, 14 April 2016) <http://www.middleeasteye.net/news/syrian-aid-being-blocked-government-1714714082>.

on behalf of the regime constituted violations of relevant UNSC resolutions as well as of Syria's R2P Pillar 1 obligations.

In this scenario, UforP arguably would not have represented the most suitable means of overcoming the reluctance (or inability) of the UN and implementing partners to conduct humanitarian operations in Syria without the State's consent, because the impediment in this situation was not UNSC paralysis as a result of the veto (as required to invoke UforP),[121] but rather, the lacking implementation of existing UNSC mandates. Instead, this case presented an opportunity for other actors, inclusive of States and/or international organisations, to execute cross-border and cross-line humanitarian operations under the legal justification of third-party countermeasures as well as under the wider banner of R2P's Pillar 3.[122] These entities' violation of Syria's sovereignty would be inherently contrary to UNSC Resolution 2165 and its subsequent resolutions, which only authorised 'United Nations humanitarian agencies and their implementing partners', although not individual States and international organisations, to engage in cross-border and cross-line aid delivery in Syria without Syria's consent.[123] It would also, significantly, constitute a violation of Article 2(7) of the UN Charter's prohibition against the interference in the domestic affairs of States.[124] At the same time, however, such action would demonstrate international resolve to uphold the spirit of UNSC resolutions in R2P situations, and, in similar vein, further the case for the lawfulness of third-party countermeasures as a means by which States and international organisations can implement R2P's Pillar 3 outside the specific remit of the UNSC when action by this body is either not forthcoming or is insufficient. This, in turn, would have contributed to strengthening the enforceability of the R2P doctrine.

7.2.6 Accountability

The UNSC stressed its commitment to achieving accountability in the Syrian context within several of its resolutions, with respect to both general violations of international humanitarian law (IHL) and international human rights law (IHRL) committed throughout the course of the conflict as well for more specific crimes such as the employment of chemical weapons.[125] In general, accountability exercises represent tools of deterrence with respect to R2P and can be pursued in the context of mass atrocity situations that have already come to a conclusion, or even in the midst of ongoing atrocities.[126] In the former case, they serve to demonstrate the international community's resolve that mass atrocity crimes will not go

121 *See* Section 5.3.2.1 of this book.
122 Third-party countermeasures are discussed in Sections 2.2.1 and 5.2.
123 *See supra* notes 117 and 119.
124 UN Charter (n30) Art 2(7).
125 *See*, for example, UN Doc S/RES/2118 (n52) Para 10; UN Doc S/RES/2139 (n16) Para 13; UN Doc S/RES/2209 (n52) Para 6; UN Doc S/RES/2235 (n52) Para 4.
126 *See* Andrea Birdsall, 'The Responsibility to Prosecute and the ICC: A Problematic Relationship?' (2015) 26 *Criminal Law Forum* 51, 54; Report of the Secretary-General, 'Implementing the Responsibility to Protect' (12 January 2009) UN Doc A/63/

unpunished, which could impart deterrent ramifications with respect to other or future mass atrocity situations. In the latter case, they hold the additional effect of conveying a clear message to perpetrators or potential perpetrators of mass atrocity crimes within a particular context that the international community is invested in the outcome of justice and that the continued commission of such crimes may lead to individual criminal responsibility in this respect. As discussed within this section with focus on the Syrian R2P situation, accountability exercises represent useful means by which the international community as a whole can respond to an R2P situation. Pursued alone, however, they are incapable of bringing an end to the commission of mass atrocity crimes, and as such, must be accompanied by other non-military and/or military measures to ensure the outcome of human protection as per R2P.

In Syria, concrete efforts by the UNSC to establish accountability were quashed when both Russia and China vetoed a UNSC Chapter VII draft resolution in May 2014 to refer the situation to the ICC.[127] Given that Syria is not a party to the ICC Statute, such a UNSC referral represented the only means through which to grant the Court jurisdiction over the situation.[128] Another avenue for the centralised and international pursuit of accountability lie in the creation of a special international tribunal on Syria, although this also would have required the adoption of a UNSC Chapter VII resolution, which would expectedly face similar Russian and Chinese opposition.

On a more positive note, however, other international actors including the UNGA and individual States mobilised around the issue of accountability to seek justice for the victims of Syria's conflict, each actor undertaking measures in line with its respective mandate and jurisdiction. Although these actors were not successful in bringing to justice most or even a substantial proportion of perpetrators of international crimes, their collective efforts outside the purview of the UNSC demonstrated a capacity to overcome, at least to some extent, UNSC deadlock in R2P situations.

The UNGA, for example, adopted Resolution 71/248 on 21 December 2016 which established the International, Impartial and Independent Mechanism to Assist in the Investigation and Prosecution of Persons Responsible for the Most

677 Para 18 [hereinafter Implementing R2P]. *See*, however, Kurt Mills, 'R2P and the ICC: At Odds or in Sync?' (2015) 26 *Criminal Law Forum* 73 at 77, 80.

127 UN Doc S/2014/348 (n28).

128 The ICC could invoke jurisdiction over crimes committed in Syria through the nationals of member-States to the ICC Statute, although this would not translate to a jurisdiction over all crimes committed in the Syrian R2P situation. *See*, in general, Mark Chadwick, 'Justice in Syria: Five Ways to Prosecute International Crime' (*The Conversation*, 10 July 2017) <http://theconversation.com/justice-in-syria-five-ways-to-prosecute-international-crime-75908>. As a novel development on the issue, *see* 'The Guernica Centre for International Justice Files Article 15 Communication with the ICC Office of the Prosecutor on the Situation in the Syrian Arab Republic' (The Guernica Centre for International Justice, 4 March 2019) <https://pro-justice.org/wp-content/uploads/2019/03/Microsoft-Word-190301-Syria-Press-Statement-Final-Version-EL-.doc.pdf>.

Serious Crimes under International Law Committed in the Syrian Arab Republic since March 2011 (IIIM or 'the Mechanism').[129] This came over two years after Russia and China exercised their vetoes to defeat the referral of the Syrian situation to the ICC in 2014, and also subsequent to the Syrian and Russian military assault against Eastern Aleppo in the second half of 2016 (discussed further in the next section). The purpose of the IIIM was to:

> [C]ollect, consolidate, preserve and analyse evidence of violations of international humanitarian law and human rights violations and abuses and to prepare files in order to facilitate and expedite fair and independent criminal proceedings, in accordance with international law standards, in national, regional or international courts or tribunals that have or may in the future have jurisdiction over these crimes, in accordance with international law.[130]

In essence, the IIIM was mandated with preparing case files against perpetrators of IHL and IHRL in the context of the Syrian R2P situation, which could then be used in future domestic or international court proceedings. It did not, importantly, represent the creation of an international court or tribunal, which would arguably lie outside the UNGA's competencies, and thus did not directly bring perpetrators to justice.[131]

It is unclear from the contents of UNGA Resolution 71/248 the legal basis for the establishment of the IIIM. The Resolution, for example, was adopted by a vote of 105-15-52 (an 87.5% voting margin), which lies well within the two-thirds (roughly 66.67%) voting margin required to issue UNGA recommendations with respect to the maintenance of international peace and security, including as per UforP.[132] The President of the UNGA certainly seemed to suggest that the Resolution was adopted pursuant to the UNGA's residual right to maintain international peace and security. Responding to challenges advanced by several States regarding the Resolution's legal basis (including by Syria, Iran, Russia, Venezuela, Ecuador, Cuba, South Africa, Iran, and Algeria[133]), in particular whether the UNGA could issue recommendations with respect to a situation that threatens international peace and security with which the UNSC is actively dealing, he stated the following:

129 UNGA Res 71/248 (11 January 2017) UN Doc A/RES/71/248.
130 Ibid., Para 4.
131 *See* Christian Wenaweser and James Cockayne, 'Justice for Syria? The International, Impartial and Independent Mechanism and the Emergence of the UN General Assembly in the Realm of International Criminal Justice' (2017) 15 *Journal of International Criminal Justice* 211, 214–15.
132 The UNGA's competencies to issue recommendations pertaining to international peace and security, including through UforP, is discussed in Section 5.3.2.1 of this book.
133 UNGA, '66th Plenary Meeting' (21 December 2016) UN Doc A/71/PV.66 at 21, 23–28, 37.

> Article 12 does not prevent the General Assembly from generally considering, discussing and making recommendations on items that are on the agenda of the Security Council, in particular when the item before the Council and the Assembly are not identical.
>
> I would also like to clarify that the words 'is exercising' in Article 12 have consistently been interpreted as meaning exercising at this moment, and consequently the Assembly has made recommendations on matters that the Security Council was also considering. The accepted practice of the General Assembly to consider, in parallel with the Security Council, the same matter concerning the maintenance of international peace and security has also been noted by the International Court of Justice in its advisory opinion of 2004.[134]

The President of the UNGA thus affirmed the UNGA's right to both discuss and issue recommendations with respect to a situation that threatens or breaches international peace and security (such as in Syria) even when the UNSC is actively dealing with this case. It was implied in his response, although not overtly stated, that the IIIM was established pursuant to this right.[135] UforP was not specifically invoked, although it should be recalled that the mechanism embodies the very same Charter provisions alluded to by the UNGA President.[136] With that said, however, a stronger indication of the UNGA's legal basis for establishing the IIIM both within Resolution 71/248 and within the UNGA President's response, including through a specific reference to UforP, if applicable, would have been helpful in making a bolder statement regarding the UNGA's historic move and in setting a stronger precedent for the UNGA's future assumption of a similar role in R2P situations that witness the UNSC veto.

In addition to the UNGA, individual States, particularly those in Europe, contributed to the pursuit of accountability in Syria through prosecuting, in their domestic courts, international crimes committed within the conflict. Such convictions have been achieved under the banner of universal jurisdiction rather than R2P, although the relevance to R2P can be established in that universal jurisdiction, albeit a contested notion under international law,[137] is exercised with respect to international crimes encompassing of genocide, war crimes, and crimes against humanity (i.e. three of R2P's four mass atrocity crimes).[138] To date, convictions against Syrian war criminals have been secured in German, Swedish, and Austrian courts,[139] and have been

134 Ibid., 28–29.

135 *See also* Alex Whiting, 'An Investigation Mechanism for Syria' (2017) 15 *Journal of International Criminal Justice* 231, 234 (suggesting that the creation of IIIM may have been undertaken pursuant to the UNGA's right under Article 22 of the Charter to 'establish such subsidiary organs as it deems necessary for the performance of its functions').

136 *See* Section 5.3.2.1 of this book.

137 *See* Breau (n76) 133–37.

138 *See* Mills (n126) 78–79.

139 'Syria: First Atrocities Trials Held in Europe' (*Human Rights Watch*, 3 October 2017) <https://www.hrw.org/news/2017/10/03/syria-first-atrocities-trials-held-europe>;

helpful in highlighting that each State can play a role in responding to R2P situations as per its unique capabilities and links to the situation. With that said, however, it should be cautioned that the practical effects of these trials and convictions are limited. For example, State prosecutions are largely restricted to cases in which either the perpetrator or the victim hold physical presence within the State.[140] When it is the victim bringing such a case forward, additional difficulties arise if the accused is outside the country. As a result, and as rightly pointed out by Elliot, States' accountability pursuits with respect to Syria do not necessarily reflect the overall crimes committed in the R2P situation nor do they bring to justice the most serious perpetrators.[141]

Generally, efforts by the UNGA and individual States to achieve accountability in the Syrian context have been constructive in mobilising the international community to take concrete action with respect to the R2P situation which has been otherwise faced with implacable UNSC paralysis. However, and despite these very welcomed moves, implementing actors may have in the process unnecessarily constrained themselves to the issue of accountability at the exclusion of other compelling dimensions to the conflict. Importantly, accountability alone has been insufficient to shift the dynamics of the R2P situation or to alleviate the atrocities that continue to be committed. This is not to mention that such efforts have fallen short of achieving justice for the majority or even a substantial number of victims of the Syrian conflict, or from serving as a credible deterrent for perpetrators. Therefore, in parallel with their efforts to achieve accountability, these international actors arguably should have pursued further initiatives aimed at addressing the wider Syrian mass atrocity situation, including, for example, those detailed in the previous and upcoming sections (pertaining to general measures, chemical weapons use, humanitarian access, and civilian protection). Such efforts would have assumed a more comprehensive approach to overcoming UNSC deadlock on Syria and may have left a more tangible impact in terms of alleviating the R2P situation.

7.2.7 Civilian protection

Throughout the Syrian R2P situation, civilian-populated areas that opposed the Assad regime's rule politically and/or militarily were subjected by the regime and its allies to relentless aerial bombardments, starvation sieges, chemical attacks, and the targeting of infrastructure including hospitals, bakeries, and power and water sources, with view to bringing such areas back under regime control.[142] This

'Austria Convicts Asylum Seeker of Syria War Crimes' (*BBC News*, 11 May 2017) <https://www.bbc.co.uk/news/world-europe-39879305>.

140 *See* Ingrid Elliott, '"A Meaningful Step towards Accountability"? A View from the Field on the United Nations International, Impartial and Independent Mechanism for Syria' (2017) 15 *Journal of International Criminal Justice* 239, 246.

141 Ibid.

142 *See*, for a brief overview, Holly Yan, 'Why Syrian Civilians Get Killed with Barrel Bombs and Chemical Attacks' (*CNN*, 6 April 2017) <https://edition.cnn.com/2017/04/06/middleeast/syria-weapons-against-civilians/index.html>.

included systematic, indiscriminate, and unrestrained military offensives against Daraya, Eastern Ghouta, Homs, Madaya, Zabadani, Eastern Aleppo, Idlib, and more,[143] and by default entailed the commission of numerous mass atrocity crimes on behalf of the regime.[144] Mass atrocity crimes were also committed by other sides to the conflict, including by terrorist groups such as ISIS and ANF as well as by opposition and Kurdish groups.[145] Those committed by ISIS and ANF were met with concerted international action in the form of a US-led military intervention, which commenced in September 2014,[146] while no similar action has been forthcoming to address the atrocities committed by the regime or other groups. This is despite the fact that the carnage inflicted by the Assad regime in particular has affected a much wider segment of the civilian population, has been more sustained, and has been responsible for significantly higher death tolls, forcible displacement of the civilian population, and destruction of infrastructure as compared to any other actor involved within the conflict.[147]

The UNSC's response to the gross and sustained attacks on civilians and civilian-populated areas comprised of either inaction or the adoption of resolutions that were ambitious in scope although narrow in effectiveness (due to lacking enforcement). Resolution 2254, adopted in December 2015, for example, proposed a mechanism for settling the Syrian R2P situation once and for all, in contrast to previous UNSC resolutions, which had focused only upon specific dimensions of the conflict such as the cessation of violence, chemical weapons use, or humanitarian access.[148] This Resolution called for the initiation of talks between regime and opposition representatives by January 2016 for the purpose of negotiating a political transition in Syria, and fixed six- and 18-month targets for the establishment of transitional governance and for the convening of UN-supervised elections, respectively.[149] In order to facilitate

143 *See* Mohammed Alaa Ghanem, 'Assad's Lethal Peace Deals' (*Hoover Institution*, July 2018) <https://www.hoover.org/sites/default/files/research/docs/ghanem_assadslethalpeacedeals_revised_webreadypdf.pdf>; 'The Demographic Change & Forced Displacement in Syria' (Assistance Coordination Unit, 20 June 2017) <https://www.acu-sy.org/en/wp-content/uploads/2017/06/Force-displacement-June-2017-En.pdf>.

144 *See supra* note 9 and accompanying text.

145 *See supra* note 10.

146 This military campaign was initially justified under the premise of collective self-defence of Iraq, and received subsequent UNSC endorsement through Resolution 2249. For further discussion, *see* Section 7.5 of this chapter.

147 *See*, for example, 'A Total of 217,764 Civilians Killed, Including 27,296 Children, 93% of Them Killed at the Hands of the Syrian–Russian Alliance: Toll of Most Notable Violations of Human Rights on the Seven Anniversary of the Popular Uprising in Syria' (*Syrian Network for Human Rights*, 14 March 2018) <http://sn4hr.org/wp-content/pdf/english/Harvesting_the_most_prominent_human_rights_violations_on_the_seventh_anniversary_of_the_popular_movement_in_Syria_en.pdf> [hereinafter SNHR 7th Anniversary Statistics].

148 *See*, for example, UN Doc S/RES/2042 (n36); UN Doc S/RES/2118 (n52); UN Doc S/RES/2139 (n16).

149 UN Doc S/RES/2254 (n17) Paras 2 and 4.

the most conducive environment for the implementation of these initiatives, Resolution 2254 called for a nation-wide ceasefire to commence with the requisite political talks.[150]

Needless to say, the six- and 18-month targets to achieve a political transition and to convene UN-supervised elections were not met. Instead, the adoption of UNSC Resolution 2254 was followed by a spike in violence throughout Syria, which prompted the opposition to threaten in early February to boycott political talks if such attacks persisted.[151] The UNSC responded with a further demand for the cessation of violence in February 2016 through the adoption of Resolution 2268, which, although it succeeded in temporarily reducing the level of hostilities, was unable in the long term to salvage the political process.[152] In an almost ludicrous manner, however, this Resolution, as well as five subsequent ones adopted by the UNSC between December 2016 and December 2018, reaffirmed the body's support for the political transition process outlined in Resolution 2254, by which time the six- and 18-month deadlines to establish transitional governance as well as to convene UN-supervised elections had long passed.[153] As yet another indicator of the sheer ineffectiveness of UNSC initiatives on Syria, the penultimate such Resolution (2401) adopted in February 2018 called for another cessation of hostilities, as well as the lifting of sieges in Eastern Ghouta and Yarmouk (besieged by regime forces) as well as Foua and Kefraya (besieged by opposition forces).[154] Neither of these provisions was complied with by the parties involved.[155] UNSC initiatives and demands, because they were not given any teeth, were thus completely out of touch with developments on the ground.

In this situation, the role of other international actors, inclusive of States and international organisations, became especially vital in terms of responding to the Syrian R2P situation. International efforts that did transpire outside the purview of the UNSC – including through a US–Russian ceasefire agreement in September 2016 or through a Turkish–Russian–Iranian agreement in September 2017 to establish four de-escalation zones across Syria[156] – achieved only limited results

150 Ibid., Para 5.
151 *See* 'Syria Opposition Threatens to Walk out of Geneva Talks' (*Aljazeera*, 2 February 2016) <https://www.aljazeera.com/news/2016/01/syria-opposition-threatens-withdrawal-geneva-talks-160130212030871.html>.
152 *See* UN Doc S/RES/2268 (n53) Para 1.
153 *See* ibid., Para 2; UN Doc S/RES/2332 (n17) Para 4; UNSC Res 2336 (31 December 2016) UN Doc S/RES/2336 Para 2; UN Doc S/RES/2393 (n17) Para 4; UN Doc S/RES/2401 (n54) Para 3 (affirming UNSC Resolution 2268, which in turn affirmed Resolution 2254); UN Doc S/RES/2449 (n17) Para 5.
154 UN Doc S/RES/2401 (n54) Paras 1, 10.
155 *See* 'Oral Report to the Security Council on the Implementation of Security Council Resolution 2401' (United Nations Secretary-General, 12 March 2018) <https://www.un.org/sg/en/content/sg/speeches/2018-03-12/report-security-council-implementation-resolution-2401>.
156 Julian Borger, 'Russia and US Reach Tentative Agreement for Syria Ceasefire' (*Guardian*, 10 September 2016) <https://www.theguardian.com/world/2016/sep/10/syria-ceasefire-deal-tentative-negotiate-kerry-lavrov-us-russia>; 'Final De-escalation Zones Agreed on Astana' (*Aljazeera*, 15 September 2017) <https://www.aljazeera.

and consistently broke down. It is not difficult to see why: Russia, as a key party within most if not all of these agreements, was directly vested in the conflict on the side of the Assad regime, having intervened militarily in Syria in September 2015 in its support.[157] Furthermore, Syria and its allies were cognisant that they were shielded at the UNSC by the Russian veto and thus held no incentive to restrain their military campaigns through which they were making visible gains to re-assert their dominance over the country. Finally, Syria and its allies consistently justified their military engagements under the pretext of combating terrorism, a loophole within the various brokered agreements which they exploited to their own ends.

Rather than, or at least in addition to, pursuing such endless political talks and agreements that were demonstrably destined to fail, international actors should have focused upon employing other tools at their disposal to exert genuine and concerted pressure upon perpetrators of mass atrocity crimes in Syria, the foremost of them the Assad regime, to bring such atrocities to an end. This could have included, for example, the utilisation of a range of non-forceful measures reflective of those suggested within earlier sections (e.g. sanctions, arms embargoes, asset freezes, severing of diplomatic relations, and humanitarian aid drops), undertaken as a combination of lawful measures, third-party countermeasures, or UNGA recommendations as per UforP. The use of military force also could have been prompted through UforP. Here, it should be recalled that the mechanism can be invoked only when the UNSC is paralysed due to the veto from responding to a situation that threatens or breaches international peace and security. In this respect, it is interesting to note that with the exceptions of Eastern Aleppo and Eastern Ghouta, not a single UNSC draft resolution was tabled to address the various military campaigns waged by the Assad regime in Syria, perhaps given the knowledge of the impending Russian veto. Furthermore, the draft resolution considered by the UNSC on Eastern Ghouta was adopted as Resolution 2401, meaning that there was no veto exercised in this context.[158] Seemingly, therefore, only the assault against Eastern Aleppo was eligible for UNGA consideration as per UforP. However, this obstacle to the mechanism's invocation could have been easily overcome, namely, through the tabling of UNSC draft resolutions by vested UNSC member-States that called for international action in response to the other regime military offensives. Following the expected Russian (and perhaps Chinese) veto, States within either the UNSC or the UNGA could have initiated efforts to invoke UforP, namely through calling for a UNSC procedural vote or a UNGA majority vote in this respect.

Using the example of Eastern Aleppo to build a case for the recommendation of military force in Syria by the UNGA as per UforP, a Syrian and Russian

com/news/2017/09/final-de-escalation-zones-agreed-astana-170915102811730.html>.

157 *See supra* note 45.

158 *See* UN Doc S/Res/2401 (n54).

onslaught commenced against the city in July 2016 (after roughly four years of siege) and persisted until a deal was brokered by Russia in December 2016 between the Assad regime and opposition groups for the complete evacuation (or more precisely, forced displacement[159]) of the city's inhabitants (both civilian and combatant).[160] Two draft resolutions that aimed to bring an end to the violence in Eastern Aleppo and to grant full humanitarian access to the city were defeated in October and December 2016, respectively, by Russian and/or Chinese vetoes.[161] By this point, diplomatic routes had arguably been exhausted, and it was unlikely that international efforts short of military force would have induced the Assad regime and its allies to desist from their military campaign, at least within a reasonable timeframe. Indeed, although the situation in Eastern Aleppo was ultimately 'resolved', a brief glimpse into the final outcome reveals that it fell shamefully short of upholding IHL and IHRL standards and did not, overall, achieve human protection or otherwise further the principles of R2P.[162] Namely, following the almost-complete annihilation of the city by Assad and Russian forces, the regime struck a deal with the city for the complete evacuation of its residents in return for their safety.[163] In other words, the price that civilians had to pay for their safety was their forced displacement, a war crime under international law.[164] Furthermore, many of these civilians were 'evacuated' (i.e. forcibly displaced) to opposition-controlled areas in northern Syria (in particular, Idlib province) that lacked minimum IHRL protections and basic services such as the provision of aid, medical care, and housing.[165] This is not to mention that such areas remained subject to regular bombardment by Assad and Russian forces given that they were under the control of opposition groups.[166] This outcome

159 This represented the official conclusion of the Independent International Commission of Inquiry on Syria in its February 2017 report. HRC, 'Report of the Independent International Commission of Inquiry on the Syrian Arab Republic' (2 February 2017) UN Doc A/HRC/34/64 Para 93.
160 On the 2016 military offensive against Eastern Aleppo and the subsequent evacuation agreement, *see* ibid.; Breaking Aleppo' (*Atlantic Council*, February 2017) Paras 32–35, 44–45 <http://www.publications.atlanticcouncil.org/breakingaleppo/wp-content/uploads/2017/02/BreakingAleppo.pdf>.
161 *See* UN Doc S/2016/846 (n29); UN Doc S/2016/1026 (n28).
162 For legal analysis on the evacuation agreement from Eastern Aleppo, *see* Yasmine Nahlawi, 'Forcible Displacement as a Weapon of War in the Syrian Conflict: Lessons and Developments' in Elena Katselli Proukaki (ed.), *Armed Conflict and Forcible Displacement: Individual Rights under International Law* (Routledge 2018) 203–11 [hereinafter Nahlawi Forcible Displacement].
163 Ibid., 203–04.
164 *See* ICC Statute (n79) Art 8(2)(e)(viii).
165 Nahlawi Forcible Displacement (n162) 216–17.
166 *See*, for example, Nazih Osseiran, 'Syrian, Russian Strikes Renew Fears of Offensive to Recapture Rebel Stronghold' (*Wall Street Journal*, 3 May 2019) <https://www.wsj.com/articles/syrian-russian-strikes-renew-fears-of-offensive-to-recapture-rebel-stronghold-11556906582?fbclid=IwAR2F3W5FytsqFL5TuQJOYeyh3xRIltAGo6BjEy-UivyuXYCOOSougK7U1rw>; Martin Chulov, 'Russia and Syria Step Up Airstrikes against Civilians in Idlib' (*Guardian*, 22 July 2019) <https://www.theguardian.com/world/

for Eastern Aleppo, most unfortunately, reflected the fate of numerous other Syrian cities and villages,[167] serving only to strengthen the case for the UNGA's recommendation of the use of force pursuant to UforP as a last resort to bring an end to these atrocities.

Two potential limitations for the pursuit of UforP in the Syrian R2P context should be addressed here. First, even if the mechanism had been invoked with respect to Syria, the reality is that it may have failed to garner a two-thirds UNGA majority vote for recommending the use of force as argued for in this section. The repercussions for R2P in such a case are unclear, namely, whether it would justify resorting to unauthorised humanitarian intervention by individual or coalitions of States, or simply connote the doctrine's failure. Second, even if the UNGA had succeeded in adopting a two-thirds recommendation for the use of force in Syria, this would not have necessarily provoked the desired military efforts to protect the population. UNGA recommendations remain, after all, non-binding, and it is therefore up to States whether or not to enforce them. If no State stood ready to implement a UNGA recommendation for the use of force in Syria, therefore, then the mere invocation of UforP would have made no tangible difference on the ground in terms of human protection.

Relevant to these concerns, it should be pointed out that even outspoken critics of the Assad regime, most notably the US, UK, and France, did not seem intent on intervening militarily in Syria to end the mass atrocity situation, even if granted a legal mandate in this respect. This can be gleaned, for example, from their decision not to respond militarily to the Ghouta chemical attack of August 2013 despite threats that they would do so irrespective of a UNSC mandate.[168] When they did employ military force against the regime, as in April of 2017 and 2018, respectively, to respond to the Khan Sheikhoun and Douma chemical attacks,[169] their involvement was limited and non-recurring, signifying that they were not vested in tackling the wider Syrian mass atrocity situation through military force. Furthermore, it is significant that the lack of UNSC authorisation in both cases did not deter them from responding militarily in the least, indicating that their inaction in the wider Syrian context was not entirely premised upon the absence of a UNSC mandate. Taking these factors into account, it is questionable whether the US, UK, and France would have exerted their diplomatic leverage to secure a UNGA recommendation for the use of force in Syria, or, had such a UNGA recommendation been somehow adopted without their active lobbying, it is unclear that they (or any other States for that matter) would have mobilised to act upon it.

2019/jul/22/russia-and-syria-step-up-airstrikes-against-civilians-in-idlib>, accessed 23 July 2019.

167 *See*, for example, 'No Going Back: Forced Displacement in the Syrian Conflict' (Syrian American Council, February 2017) <https://d3n8a8pro7vhmx.cloudfront.net/sacouncil/pages/167/attachments/original/1486567664/Displacement_Paper_Version_by_Julie_F.pdf?1486567664>; 'No Return to Homs: A Case Study on the Demographic Engineering in Syria' (*PAX*, 21 February 2017) <https://www.paxforpeace.nl/publications/all-publications/no-return-to-homs>.

168 *See* Section 7.2.4 of this book.

169 Ibid.

The first concern regarding the feasibility of obtaining a two-thirds UNGA recommendation for the use of force in Syria, particularly without the backing of the US, UK, and France, can be addressed by moving back a step with respect to UforP. Importantly, it should be stressed that the mechanism could have been invoked in the Syrian context as early as October 2011 following Russia and China's first exercise of the veto,[170] far before the conflict had escalated to the point where military force may have been necessary. Had the UNGA's involvement been established in such a timely manner, its member-States could have initially coalesced around recommending less controversial non-military measures such as sanctions and arms embargoes, and incrementally increased the intensity of recommended measures as and when needed. There are clear indications that such an approach could have facilitated the UNGA's successful recommendation of non-military measures at the very least. For example, the referral of the Syrian situation to the UNGA via a UNSC procedural vote, which requires nine affirmative votes, arguably would not have been difficult to achieve, given that each of the vetoed UNSC draft resolutions was met with a vote of at least nine member-States (see Table 7.1). A UNGA simple majority vote as an alternative means of referral, and subsequently a two-thirds UNGA majority vote to issue recommendations as per UforP, were equally attainable given that the UNGA resolutions mentioned in Section 7.2.2 of this book that condemned UNSC inaction in Syria as were adopted by voting margins that well exceeded the required two-thirds majority range:[171] UNGA Resolution 66/253B was adopted by a vote of 133-12-31 (representing roughly a 92% voting margin[172]), UNGA Resolution 68/182 was adopted by a vote of 127-13-47 (roughly a 91% margin), and UNGA Resolution 71/130 was adopted by a vote of 122-13-36 (roughly a 90% margin). Finally, it is worth noting that the Canadian government, on behalf of 69 UN member-States, submitted a letter to the President of the UNGA on 13 October 2016 advocating for the body to assume a greater role in the Syrian conflict through the convening 'of a plenary meeting of the current General Assembly … in accordance with the UN Charter … [which] would also assist Member States in determining whether to call for an Emergency Special Session of the General Assembly'.[173] Although the letter did not specifically invoke UforP, the mechanism that it proposed was essentially the same.

170 *See supra* note 28.

171 *See supra* notes 62–65 and accompanying text.

172 As per Rule 86 of the UN's rules of procedure, a two-thirds majority of members 'present and voting' refers to 'members casting an affirmative or negative vote. Members which abstain from voting are considered as not voting.' 'Rules of Procedure' (General Assembly of the United Nations) <http://www.un.org/en/ga/about/ropga/plenary.shtml>.

173 'Letter from the Permanent Mission of Canada to the President of the Seventy First Session of the UN General Assembly' (Permanent Mission of Canada to the United Nations, 13 October 2016) <https://assets.documentcloud.org/documents/3142789/LETTER-to-the-PGA-on-SYRIA-2016-10-13.pdf>.

States' widespread and repeated displays of dissatisfaction with the UNSC's paralysis towards the Syrian R2P situation, including through clear indications of their willingness for the UNGA to assume a greater role in this respect, reveals a latent potential that existed within the UNGA to respond to the Syrian R2P situation under UforP. Had the body assumed a timely role in addressing the mass atrocity situation, it could have initially moved to recommend non-military measures that may well have succeeded in stalling or ending the mass atrocity situation without requiring the use of force. Had the situation deteriorated in spite of these non-forceful recommendations, however, then UNGA member-States, given their direct and continued involvement with the R2P situation, may have felt more justified in recommending the use of force as a necessary and last resort. As such, the recommendation of the use of force need not have represented the UNGA's default response to the Syrian R2P situation, but rather, the case for military force could have been built up gradually within the body if and as required to respond to developments on the ground.

As for the second concern regarding the invocation of UforP in Syria, it is indeed conceivable that even if UNGA member-States managed to adopt a two-thirds recommendation for the use of force, States may have chosen not to act upon it. With that said, however, a UforP mandate in this respect would have applied considerable political pressure upon world powers to mobilise in response to the atrocities taking place, and thus would have made it extremely difficult for them to cite Russian and Chinese vetoes as an excuse for their inaction. At a minimum, such pressure may have compelled these powers to exert more serious non-military efforts to alleviate the Syrian R2P situation. It also would have made it increasingly challenging for them to justify a lack of military involvement in the face of an ever-deteriorating mass atrocity situation. In other words, the mere exercise of UforP would have helped to close a gap that otherwise exists within R2P, whereby States can cite the absence of a legal mandate as an excuse for failing to react to a mass atrocity situation as per Pillar 3.

These arguments admittedly do not entirely placate concerns regarding the potential pitfalls of UforP. Ultimately, the mechanism remains, like the veto, a tool that States can exercise at will. This means that States may ultimately vote down proposed recommendations under UforP or may choose not to give effect to them in the case that they are adopted. However, one of the central arguments of this chapter has been that UNSC inaction in Syria need not have entirely constrained the international response to the R2P situation, but that rather, lawful and legitimate means exist within the current international legal framework to circumvent the body when it is paralysed from responding to a mass atrocity situation, including, importantly, through UforP. In the longer term, however, the concerns raised with respect to the pursuit of UforP underscore the pressing need for R2P's Pillar 3 to acquire a legally binding status so that it becomes an obligation, and not merely a right, to be exercised by the international community in mass atrocity situations, and thus to overcome the element of discretion that plagues the international community's current responses to such cases.

7.2.8 Concluding thoughts on the UN Security Council

Overall, the UNSC's response to the Syrian R2P situation can be characterised as lacking and ineffective. Largely as a result of 12 abusive vetoes exercised by Russia and/or China, as well as of various ineffective UNSC initiatives, the mass atrocity situation has been unrelenting. However, as detailed within this section, this chain of events does not reflect a shift in international discourse towards R2P as compared to the Libyan case. Rather, although references to the doctrine were slow to manifest within the UNSC with respect to Syria, when they did make their debut, States continued to affirm the Pillar 1 responsibility as an obligation upon host States (i.e. the Syrian State), while refraining from articulating any such obligation with respect to Pillar 3, in line with the conclusions made in Chapter 6 on Libya. The distinction from the Libyan situation, however, was that there was no political will on behalf of the UNSC to take robust and enforceable action to end the mass atrocity situation in Syria.

Given the UNSC's paralysis and ineffectiveness on Syria, this section argued that other international actors inclusive of States and international organisations should have stepped up to employ a range of means at their disposal to counter the R2P situation, including through their pursuit of lawful measures, third-party countermeasures, and UNGA recommendations as per UforP. The employment of third-party countermeasures in particular – such as sanctions, asset freezes, arms embargos, and conducting unauthorised humanitarian aid drops – could have encouraged the emergence of such a right under customary international law, in the process strengthening the enforceability of R2P by supporting third-States' rights to undertake more extensive measures against violating host States as per Pillar 3. There are also clear indications that had UforP been triggered in the Syrian context, it could have succeeded in facilitating some sort of international action (non-military and/or military) to alleviate the atrocities that were being committed.

Bearing the above in mind, the failure of international actors to bypass the UNSC given its overwhelming paralysis and otherwise ineffectiveness on Syria imparts two principal repercussions. First, it tragically facilitated the prolongation of the Syrian conflict, to which no just peace seems in sight more than eight years down the line. Second, it squandered an opportunity to further develop the R2P doctrine to make it more effective in combating mass atrocity crimes: although R2P has attracted significant international attention since its conception and has reasonably succeeded in shifting discourse on State sovereignty to represent a responsibility of States to protect their populations (rather than a tool of control),[174] it has yet to overcome one of the major weaknesses of the international legal system in this respect, namely, the UNSC voting mechanism and the potential of the body's inaction to obstruct international mobilisation towards mass atrocity situations. In this manner, the

174 *See*, for example, 'Key Developments on the Responsibility to Protect at the United Nations from 2005–2017' (*International Coalition for the Responsibility to Protect*, 2018) <http://www.responsibilitytoprotect.org/index.php/about-rtop/the-un-and-rtop>.

pursuit of lawful measures, third-party countermeasures, and UforP by other actors within the Syrian context could have brought to the fore compelling means of overcoming UNSC deadlock in R2P cases.

7.3 League of Arab States

The LAS initially adopted a creative range of lawful measures and third-party countermeasures to respond to the Syrian R2P situation, illustrating that individual and collective responses to mass atrocity situations need not conform to any particular methodology or protocol. In terms of lawful measures, the LAS devised a Plan of Action on 2 November 2011 to bring an end to the violence, to which Syria consented.[175] It furthermore negotiated a Protocol on 19 December 2011 – which Syria signed – which established an observer mission to monitor Syria's compliance with the Plan of Action.[176] On 23 February 2012, the LAS, in coordination with the UN (and with Syria's approval), appointed a Joint Special Envoy to Syria who was mandated with promoting a peaceful political solution to the conflict.[177] The LAS did not justify these initiatives through R2P, nor did it promote these actions as endorsing a third-party obligation to intervene or react to the situation (as per R2P's Pillar 3).[178] Nevertheless, it was obvious that these measures were undertaken with the central aim of civilian protection which reflects R2P's essence. For example, the LAS Plan of Action demanded an end to the violence in order to 'protect Syrian civilians'.[179] The LAS Protocol similarly affirmed that the observer mission would be tasked with 'verifying the Syrian government's implementation of the LAS Plan of Action to resolve the Syrian crisis and to *ensure civilian protection*'.[180] These initiatives adopted by the LAS and are thus illustrative of a range of lawful and non-forceful methods that can be used to implement R2P as per Pillar 3.

As the above measures failed to impart a tangible difference in alleviating the R2P situation in Syria, the LAS resorted to employing third-party countermeasures against the State. For example, in order to pressure Syria to abide by the 2 November 2011 Plan of Action, the LAS imposed a series of economic

175 The Plan of Action called for an end to all hostilities, the release of political detainees arrested as a result of the conflict, and an allowance for LAS observers to move freely throughout Syria to observe and monitor the situation. 'LAS Resolution 7436' (American University in Cairo, 2 November 2011) Para 1 and Annex <https://documents.aucegypt.edu/SyriaReader/Documents/2-LAS%20Action%20Plan%20November%202011.pdf>.

176 'LAS Protocol' (Carnegie Middle East, 19 December 2011) <https://carnegie-mec.org/2011/12/19/ar-pub-48430>.

177 *See supra* note 69.

178 *See* El Hassan bin Talal and Rolf Schwarz 'The Responsibility to Protect and the Arab World: An Emerging International Norm?' (2013) 34 *Contemporary Security Policy* 1, 7.

179 LAS Resolution 7436 (n175) Annex. *See also* 'LAS Resolution 7438' (12 November 2011) Para 2 <http://www.eafit.edu.co/estudiantes/grupos-estudiantiles/unsociety/eafitmun/Documents/Arab%20League.pdf>.

180 LAS Protocol (n176) Para 1 (emphasis added).

sanctions, asset freezes, and a ban on civil aviation through Resolutions 7438 and 7442.[181] Notably, the Pact of the League of Arab States (LAS Pact) contains no such provision that permits the body to adopt such measures against a member-State,[182] nor was there any prior LAS practice to suggest that the body has acquired such a right (for example, as an implied or an inherent power).[183] Instead, the employment of these measures was intrinsically unlawful and thus contributed State practice and *opinio juris* in favour of a right to undertake third-party countermeasures to address R2P situations.[184]

In addition to the above, the LAS suspended Syria's seat from the organisation on 12 November 2011 through Resolution 7438 due to its failure to comply with the 2 November Plan of Action.[185] It is recalled from Chapter 6 of this book that Article 18 of the LAS Pact allows for the expulsion, but not suspension, of member-States through a unanimous vote.[186] While a strong case can be made in favour of the lawfulness of suspending States under this Article (given the LAS's prior suspensions of Egypt and Libya),[187] Syria's suspension was not adopted through a unanimous vote as stipulated under Article 18: Lebanon and Yemen voted against Resolution 7438 and Iraq abstained.[188] This is not to mention that human rights abuses do not constitute a basis for member-State expulsion within the LAS Pact.[189] Syria directly protested its suspension along these lines although its cries fell on deaf ears.[190] The LAS's suspension of Syria's seat, undertaken in violation of its founding Pact, offers State practice and *opinio juris* in favour of a right to impose third-party countermeasures against States that violate fundamental international legal norms owed to the international community as a whole (including, notably, through the commission of mass atrocities against their population).[191]

181 LAS Resolution 7438 (n179) Para 4; 'LAS Resolution 7442' (27 November 2011) <https://issuu.com/openbriefing/docs/resolution7442>.
182 Pact of the League of Arab States (adopted 22 March 1945, entered into force 10 May 1945) 70 UNTS 241 [hereinafter LAS Pact].
183 *See* 'Syria Unrest: Arab League Adopts Sanctions in Cairo' (*BBC News*, 27 November 2011) <http://www.bbc.co.uk/news/world-middle-east-15901360>. *See also* Philippe Sands and Pierre Klein, *Bowett's Law of International Institutions* (Thomson Reuters 2009) 329.
184 *See* Martin Dawidowicz, 'Third-Party Countermeasures: A Progressive Development of International Law?' (2016) 4 *Questions of International Law* 3, 7–8.
185 LAS Resolution 7438 (n179) Para 1.
186 *See* Section 6.2.1 of this book. *See also* LAS Pact (n182) Art 18.
187 *See* Section 6.2.1.
188 No formal declaration was offered by these States in explanation of their vote. LAS Resolution 7438 (n179); Neil MacFarquhar, 'Arab League Votes to Suspend Syria over Crackdown' (*New York Times*, 12 November 2011) <http://www.nytimes.com/2011/11/13/world/middleeast/arab-league-votes-to-suspend-syria-over-its-crackdown-on-protesters.html?pagewanted=all&_r=0>.
189 As discussed in Section 6.2.1 of this book.
190 *See* MacFarquhar (n188).
191 *See* Dawidowicz (n184) 7–8. *See also* Section 6.2.1 on the legal framework pertaining to the employment of third-party countermeasures by international organisations.

The LAS's positive engagement with the Syrian R2P situation through a range of lawful measures and third-party countermeasures, however, must be evaluated with a degree of scepticism given ensuing developments in Syria. The observer mission established pursuant to the 19 December 2011 LAS Protocol, for example, was suspended only the following month in January 2012, after several LAS member-States withdrew their observers to protest what they perceived to be a lack of impartiality among the mission's leadership.[192] Most of the other aforementioned measures also failed to be enforced either in part or in whole by LAS member-States.[193] Following these setbacks, the LAS assumed a backseat on the Syrian conflict and thus delegated the primary role of responding to the mass atrocity situation to the UNSC, which was problematic in that this body was itself paralysed from addressing the situation due to the permanent veto.[194] Moving forward to 2019, the LAS, in a dramatic reversal of its policy, now seems keen to readmit Syria to the body, and several Arab States have re-established or are poised to re-establish diplomatic relations with the State.[195] This is despite the fact that Syria has failed to comply with demands of the LAS – or of any other international body for that matter – to protect its population.

From a legal standpoint, these subsequent developments pertaining to the LAS's backtracking from Syria do not necessarily diminish the significance of its initial undertakings to respond to the mass atrocity situation, particularly with respect to the utilisation of lawful measures and third-party countermeasures as means of implementing R2P's Pillar 3. They do, however, help to contextualise the role that regional organisations can or should play in defining the overall international reaction to an R2P situation. In essence, such bodies are, similar to the UNSC, themselves politicised, and thus reflect the individual and collective interests of their member-States. Küçükkeleş, for example, points out that the LAS's composition of mostly 'authoritarian state systems', some of which themselves embarked in the repression of similar non-violent uprisings within their own borders, '[makes] it difficult to regard Arab League decisions as steps supporting democracy'.[196] She furthermore identifies some of the LAS member-States' motivations for advocating human protection in Syria, namely, safeguarding from uprisings within their own borders as well as Gulf States' interests in countering Iranian influence.[197] These observations underscore that

192 'Arab League Suspends Syria Mission – Nabil el-Arabi' (*BBC News*, 28 January 2012) <https://www.bbc.co.uk/news/world-middle-east-16774171>.

193 TM, 'The Arab League's Role in the Syrian Civil War' (2014) 6 *Inquiries Journal* 1, 3.

194 As discussed in Section 7.2 of this chapter.

195 *See* Bethan McKernan and Martin Chulov, 'Arab League Set to Readmit Syria Eight Years after Expulsion' (*Guardian*, 26 December 2018) <https://www.theguardian.com/world/2018/dec/26/arab-league-set-to-readmit-syria-eight-years-after-expulsion>.

196 Müjge Küçükkeleş, 'Arab League's Syrian Policy' (*Foundation for Political, Economic and Social Research*, April 2012) at 4 <http://www.scpss.org/libs/spaw/uploads/files/Policy/04-10-2012_SETA_Policy_Brief_No_56_Arab_Leagues_Syrian_Policy.pdf>.

197 Ibid., 14–15.

regional organisations, although uniquely positioned to understand and respond to events on the ground, can themselves be politicised. As such, an over-reliance upon their stances in dictating the international response to a mass atrocity situation should be avoided, but rather, their voices should represent only one of a multitude of efforts to shape the international community's Pillar 3 response to an R2P situation.

7.4 Non-State actors

Non-State armed groups emerged in Syria as early as July 2011 with the formation of the Free Syrian Army – an anti-government armed resistance faction – by defectors from the Syrian national army (i.e. Assad's army). Several NSAs in the Syrian context became implicated in mass atrocity crimes over the next several years,[198] giving rise to questions pertaining to the applicability of R2P to such groups, more specifically regarding what, if any, host and third-State obligations arise when such groups commit genocide, war crimes, crimes against humanity, or ethnic cleansing. This question is significant because, while mass atrocity crimes are increasingly committed by NSAs on a global scale,[199] R2P remains largely State-centric. The 2005 World Summit Outcome document, for example, did not acknowledge the role that NSAs can assume in perpetrating mass atrocity situations.[200] The Global Network of Responsibility to Protect Focal Points,[201] in a 2015 meeting of over 50 States, conceded that 'conceptual gaps remain in our collective understanding of how [R2P] relates to [NSAs] and of how to respond effectively to the atrocities they perpetrate'.[202] Even then, however, this meeting failed to address these issues from a legal standpoint, focusing instead upon delineating policy measures to prevent NSAs' capabilities to commit mass atrocity crimes.[203] This section attempts to fill this gap by offering a suggested framework through which R2P can apply to NSAs. While not purporting to engage in a comprehensive examination of the legal regimes applicable to NSAs,[204] it instead

198 *See supra* note 10.

199 *See* Sandesh Sivakumaran, 'Binding Armed Opposition Groups' (2006) 55 *International and Comparative Law Quarterly* 369, 369.

200 *See* 2005 World Summit Outcome, UNGA Res 60/1 (24 October 2005) UN Doc A/RES/60/1 Paras 138–39 [hereinafter 2005 World Summit Outcome].

201 The Global Network of Responsibility to Protect Focal Points represents a network of States launched in 2010 that aims to create a 'community of commitment' to R2P. 'Global Network of R2P Focal Points' (*Global Centre for the Responsibility to Protect*) <http://www.globalr2p.org/our_work/global_network_of_r2p_focal_points>.

202 UNSC, 'Letter Dated 22 October 2015 from the Permanent Representatives of Chile and Spain to the United Nations Addressed to the President of the Security Council' (26 October 2015) UN Doc S/2015/815, 4.

203 Ibid., 5–6.

204 *See*, instead, Tilman Rodenhäuser, *Organizing Rebellion: Non-State Armed Groups under International Humanitarian Law, Human Rights Law, and International Criminal Law* (Oxford University Press 2018) [hereinafter Rodenhäuser Organizing Rebellion]; Daragh Murray, *Human Rights Obligations of Non-State Armed Groups* (Hart Publishing Ltd 2016); Andrew Clapham, *Human Rights Obligations of Non-State Actors* (Oxford University Press 2006).

undertakes a general analysis on how R2P can be employed to address the actions of NSAs and how this in turn should have been operationalised within the Syrian context.

This section and the next one focus primarily upon two NSAs in the Syrian R2P situation (although other NSAs are discussed as relevant), namely, ISIS and ANF, both because they were implicated in the commission of mass atrocity crimes and because their actions witnessed a military response from the international community.[205] To offer a brief overview of their emergence, the Islamic State of Iraq, a rebranding of the Iraqi Al-Qaeda branch, was established in 2006 out of the remnants of the 2003 US invasion of Iraq by a group of disgruntled and disenfranchised ex-Saddam elite as well as Al-Qaeda-affiliated militants.[206] With the outbreak of the Syrian uprising in 2011, the group seized an opportunity to extend its influence and control to Syria, given the collapsed security situation within the country, and thus networked with fellow militants in Syria, who consisted primarily of ex-prisoners pardoned and released by President Assad through a series of amnesties in 2011.[207] In January 2013, the Islamic State of Iraq announced a formal merger with its Syrian counterparts which led to the creation of the Islamic State of Iraq and Syria (ISIS).[208] The birth of another terrorist organisation, Al-Nusra Front (ANF), was subsequently announced by another group of fighters who rejected this merger.[209] In June 2014, ISIS renamed itself the 'Islamic State' and declared the emergence of a Caliphate with a capital of the Syrian city of Al-Raqqa.[210]

In terms of R2P's applicability to the actions of these and other NSAs in Syria, it should first be clarified that the doctrine frames protection responsibilities through the State,[211] an approach that is itself anchored within the traditional international legal framework. Under international law, for example, there is general agreement that NSAs are prohibited from committing IHL and IHRL violations. Beyond this, however, Rodenhäuser observes that 'technical legal questions relating to the definition of an internationally wrongful act, the attribution of conduct, or the consequences of wrongful acts or crimes [with respect to NSAs] are rarely discussed in detail.[212] In other words, he identifies a gap in the delineation of precise legal regimes applicable to NSAs, and, indeed, in the existence of legal tools to invoke these groups' international legal responsibility or to otherwise hold them to account

205 *See supra* notes 11–13 and accompanying text.
206 *See* Martin Chulov, 'ISIS: The Inside Story' (*Guardian*, 11 December 2014) <https://www.theguardian.com/world/2014/dec/11/-sp-isis-the-inside-story>; Richard Barrett, 'The Islamic State' (*The Soufan Group*, November 2014) at 11–12 <http://soufangroup.com/wp-content/uploads/2014/10/TSG-The-Islamic-State-Nov14.pdf>.
207 *See* Gilsinan (n11).
208 *See* Chulov (n206); Barrett (n206) 12–13.
209 *See* Gilsinan (n11).
210 *See* Barrett (n206) 13.
211 *See* Antal Berkes, '*De Facto* Regimes and the Responsibility to Protect' in Richard Barnes and Vassilis Tzevelekos (eds), *Beyond Responsibility to Protect: Generating Change in International Law* (Intersentia 2016) 156–57.
212 Rodenhäuser Organizing Rebellion (n204) 307.

for their commission of international crimes. Sassòli similarly discusses the conceptual deficiencies within international legal norms governing NSAs:

> Even when rules apply to non-State actors or are claimed to apply to them, in most cases no international forum exists in which the individual victim, the injured State, an international intergovernmental or nongovernmental organization, or a third State could invoke the responsibility of a non-State actor and obtain relief.[213]

Rodenhäuser and Sassòli's observations underscore a fundamental reality of the international legal system as pertains to NSAs: rather than holding such groups directly to account for their violations of IHL or IHRL, international law instead addresses such violations through the pursuit of individual criminal responsibility of the individual perpetrators,[214] or alternatively, through invoking the responsibility of the host State.

As for the latter, which assumes particular relevance to the applicability of R2P, States are bearers of obligations to exercise due diligence to prevent violations of international law committed by any entity within their territory, including by NSAs.[215] The nature of this obligation varies across different norms,[216] although it is important to stress that a State does not necessarily incur international legal responsibility for the actual commission of these violations (for example, by NSAs), but rather, for failing to take the necessary measures to prevent them.[217] The ILC's ASR furthermore highlight that the actions of an NSA can be directly attributable to a State if the NSA exercises 'elements of governmental authority' (Articles 5 and 9), if it is 'directed or controlled by a State' (Article 8), if it represents an insurrectional movement which becomes the new government of a State (Article 10), or if its conduct is accepted by a State as

213 Marco Sassòli, 'Taking Armed Groups Seriously: Ways to Improve their Compliance with International Humanitarian Law' (2010) 1 *International Humanitarian Legal Studies* 5, 7.
214 *See* Ben Saul, 'Enhancing Civilian Protection by Engaging Non-State Armed Groups under International Humanitarian Law' (2017) 22 *Journal of Conflict and Security Law* 39, 42.
215 *See* Cedric Ryngaert, 'State Responsibility and Non-State Actors' in Math Noortmann, August Reinisch and Cedri Ryngaert (eds), *Non-State Actors in International Law* (Hart Publishing 2015) 164; Tilman Rodenhäuser, 'Human Rights Obligations of Non-State Armed Groups in Other Situations of Violence: The Syria Example' (2012) 3 *International Humanitarian Legal Studies* 263, 269–70 [hereinafter Rodenhäuser HR Obligations of NSAs]; Jan Arno Hessbruegge, 'Human Rights Violations Arising from Conduct of Non-State Actors' (2005) 11 *Buffalo Human Rights Law Review* 21, 65–66.
216 *See* Ryngaert (n215) 177.
217 *See* John Heieck, 'The Responsibility Not to Veto Revisited: How the Duty to Prevent Genocide as a Jus Cogens Norm Imposes a Legal Duty Not to Veto on the Five Permanent Members of the Security Council' in R. Barnes and V. Tzevelekos (eds), *Beyond Responsibility to Protect: Generating Change in International Law* (Intersentia 2016) 114.

its own (Article 11).[218] In this manner, States function as gatekeepers for compliance with fundamental international legal norms by all actors operating within their borders, including by NSAs.

Such an indirect manner of tackling international crimes committed by NSAs may not seem ideal and has indeed been criticised by scholars of international law.[219] Nevertheless, this approach reflects the current international legal system's State-centric nature, whereby despite advancements that have witnessed NSAs increasingly gain recognition as subjects of international law alongside States,[220] the latter remain the primary actors within the international legal sphere and continue to enjoy almost exclusive lawmaking powers. There are some indications that international law may be moving towards a model in which NSAs assume a greater degree of international legal responsibility for their actions. Rodenhäuser, for example, contends that several emerging human rights treaties can be interpreted to apply directly to NSAs.[221] The official commentary to ASR furthermore suggests that an 'insurrectional movement may itself be held responsible for its own conduct under international law' although it fails to expand on this notion, stating only that this topic 'falls outside the scope of the present articles, which are concerned only with the responsibility of States'.[222] Such a shift in international law, however, is set against a significant set of political obstacles, most notably from States who fear that it may confer legitimacy upon NSAs and in turn challenge their traditional supremacy on the international legal scene.[223] It is therefore fundamentally unclear whether or how the notion of international legal responsibility of NSAs will emerge or crystallise under international law.

For better or for worse, R2P builds upon the traditional international legal approach and thus frames human protection as a responsibility of States. In terms of Pillar 1, for example, the 2005 World Summit Outcome document affirms that '[e]ach individual State has the responsibility to protect its populations from genocide, war crimes, ethnic cleansing and crimes against humanity'.[224] Notably, this responsibility is not confined to a negative obligation for States to refrain from committing the four mass atrocity crimes, but is rather concerned with the end

218 ILC, 'Draft Articles on Responsibility of States for Internationally Wrongful Acts, with Commentaries' (2001) II *Yearbook of the International Law Commission* 26 Arts 5, 8–11 [hereinafter ASR].

219 *See*, for example, Sassòli (n213) 9; Vladyslav Lanovoy, 'The Use of Force by Non-State Actors and the Limits of Attribution of Conduct' (2017) 28 *European Journal of International Law* 536, 580.

220 *See Reparations for Injuries Suffered in the Service of the United Nations* (Advisory Opinion) [1949] ICJ Rep 174, 179; Daragh Murray, 'How International Humanitarian Law Treaties Bind Non-State Armed Groups' (2014) 20 *Journal of Conflict and Security Law* 101, 106 [hereinafter Murray How IHL Treaties Bind NSAGs].

221 Rodenhäuser Organizing Rebellion (n204) 132.

222 ASR (n218) Commentary to Art 10 Para 16.

223 *See* Andrew Clapham, 'Extending International Criminal Law beyond the Individual to Corporations and Armed Opposition Groups' (2008) 6 *Journal of International Criminal Justice* 899, 924.

224 2005 World Summit Outcome (n200) Para 138.

goal of protecting its population from these crimes irrespective of the actor committing them. This implies that the State's Pillar 1 responsibility extends to protecting its population from mass atrocity crimes that may be perpetrated by any actor within its territory, inclusive of its own agents, other States, or NSAs.[225] This is corroborated by a 2012 UN Secretary-General report on R2P which stipulates that the 'State has a responsibility to do all possible to prevent the commission of these crimes and violations on its territory, or under its jurisdiction, and to stop them when they occur'.[226] Here again, the State's Pillar 1 responsibility is linked to the end goal of protecting its population from mass atrocity crimes irrespective of the actor perpetrating such crimes.

It follows from the above that the international community's Pillar 3 responsibility entails responding to mass atrocity crimes committed not only by a host State against its own population, but also by NSAs that operate within the territory of a State. The 2009 'Implementing the Responsibility to Protect' report maintains, for example, that:

> Non-state actors, as well as States, can commit egregious crimes relating to the responsibility to protect. When they do, collective international military assistance may be the surest way to support the State in meeting its obligations relating to the responsibility to protect and, in extreme cases, to restore its effective sovereignty.[227]

This passage clarifies that the international community's Pillar 3 responsibility is triggered when States are unable or unwilling to protect their populations from mass atrocity crimes perpetrated by NSAs as per their Pillar 1 obligations. In such cases, the international community can react through assisting the host State or even through intervening directly (although not necessarily militarily), depending upon the particular circumstances of the situation.

Following this State-centric depiction of R2P, it should nevertheless be cautioned that the primary responsibility of States to protection their populations does not absolve NSAs from the R2P Pillar 1 prohibitions against mass atrocity crimes, even if their international legal responsibility cannot (at present) be directly incurred as a result of their breach. With respect to genocide, for example, Articles 4 and 5 of the Genocide Convention stipulate, respectively, that '[p]ersons committing genocide … shall be punished'[228] and that States should 'provide effective penalties for persons guilty of genocide'.[229] Bassiouni affirms that these Articles prohibit the commission of genocide upon all persons, including those affiliated

225 *See* Berkes (n211) 156–57.

226 Report of the Secretary-General, 'Responsibility to Protect: Timely and Decisive Response' (25 July 2012) UN Doc A/66/874-S/2012/578 Para 11.

227 Implementing R2P (n126) Para 40.

228 Convention on the Prevention and Punishment of the Crime of Genocide (adopted 9 December 1948, entered into force 12 January 1951) 78 UNTS 277 Art IV [hereinafter Genocide Convention].

229 Ibid., Art V.

with NSAs.[230] With respect to the NSAs themselves, however, he argues that genocide was originally defined as a State act and that international law has not yet developed to recognise the role that NSAs can hold in perpetrating it.[231] Other international legal scholars, however, disagree and deem the prohibition against genocide to be binding upon NSAs alongside individuals and States.[232] This is corroborated by the International Court of Justice's (ICJ) conclusion in the *Bosnia* case that the Srebrenica genocide was committed by NSAs that were not official Serb State organs, did not act under the direction of Serbia or fall under its effective control, nor hold any other relationship with Serbia that would otherwise make the genocide attributable to the State.[233]

In the Syrian case, the HRC's Commission of Inquiry on Syria concluded in its 15 June 2016 report that 'ISIS has committed, and continues to commit, the crime of genocide' against the Yazidi population in Syria.[234] Although Schabas expresses reservations with respect to this conclusion,[235] an evaluation of the actions that ISIS undertook towards the Yazidi people (who are defined by their religion and ethnicity as two protected characteristics under the Genocide Convention[236]), combined with displays of intent, offer support to the Commission's findings. For example, ISIS engaged in the targeted transfer of Yazidi children, in sexual slavery directed at Yazidi women and girls, and in the killing of Yazidis,[237] all of which constitute acts of genocide as per Article 2 of the Genocide Convention.[238] These actions were also committed with the apparent intent to eradicate or destroy this group,[239] as evident from an ISIS publication, quoted in a report of the Commission of Inquiry, which declared that the Yazidis' 'continual existence to this day is a matter that Muslims should question as they will be asked about it on Judgment Day'.[240] These observations reflect both the *actus reus* and *mens rea*

230 M. Cherif Bassiouni, 'The New Wars and the Crisis of Compliance with the Law of Armed Conflict by Non-State Actors' (2008) 98 *The Journal of Criminal Law and Criminology* 711, 714.
231 Ibid.
232 *See* Hessbruegge (n215) 34; Berkes (n211) 161.
233 *Case Concerning Application of the Convention on the Prevention and Punishment of the Crime of Genocide (Bosnia & Herzegovina v. Serbia & Montenegro)* (Judgment) [2007] ICJ Rep 43 Paras 413–15 [hereinafter *Bosnia* case].
234 HRC, '"They Came to Destroy": ISIS Crimes against the Yazidis' (15 June 2016) UN Doc A/HRC/32/CRP.2 Para 201.
235 William Schabas, 'Symposum: Review of John Heieck, A Duty to Prevent Genocide' (*Opinio Juris*, 13 December 2018) <http://opiniojuris.org/2018/12/13/symposium-review-of-john-heieck-a-duty-to-prevent-genocide/>.
236 The Yazidi people represent a religious community that is ethnically Kurdish. Raya Jalabi, 'Who are the Yazidis and why is Isis Hunting Them?' (*Guardian*, 11 August 2014) <https://www.theguardian.com/world/2014/aug/07/who-yazidi-isis-iraq-religion-ethnicity-mountains>. *See also* Genocide Convention (n228) Art II.
237 *See* A/HRC/32/CRP.2 (n234) Paras 33, 40, 48, 54–68, 92–94.
238 Genocide Convention (n228) Art II.
239 As required to establish the commission of genocide. *See* ibid.
240 A/HRC/32/CRP.2 (n234) Para 153.

elements of genocide and thus offer persuasive evidence that R2P's Pillar 1 was violated by ISIS through the commission of this crime.

With respect to war crimes, both Common Article 3 to the Geneva Conventions as well as APII – which detail fundamental norms of IHL that underlie some of the war crimes identified within Article 8 ICC Statute – are commonly recognised to bind all parties within NIACs, inclusive of NSAs.[241] Common Article 3, for example, stresses that 'each *Party* to the conflict shall be bound to apply, as a minimum, the following provisions'.[242] APII furthermore states that it 'shall apply to all armed conflicts … which take place in the territory of a High Contracting Party between its armed forces and *dissident armed forces or other organized armed groups*'.[243] Scholars of international law are in general agreement regarding the binding nature of the prohibition against war crimes upon NSAs.[244] They diverge, however, with respect to the precise legal basis upon which they make this claim, for example whether NSAs' obligations to abide by these norms stem from 'customary law, general principles, state succession, third-party consent [or] legislative (or prescriptive) jurisdiction'.[245]

In the Syrian context, the application of IHL, and hence NSAs' obligations not to commit war crimes, emerged after the conflict became categorised as a NIAC in an August 2012 report by the HRC's Commission of Inquiry on Syria.[246] The Commission stressed in this report that '[a]lthough not a State party to the Geneva Conventions, organized armed groups must nevertheless abide by the principles of international humanitarian law'.[247] It since documented the commission of a number of war crimes, in violation of R2P's Pillar 1, by NSAs in Syria which are detailed further below.

241 *See* Cedric Ryngaert and Anneleen Van de Meulebroucke, 'Enhancing and Enforcing Compliance with International Humanitarian Law by Non-State Armed Groups: An Inquiry into some Mechanisms' (2012) 16 *Journal of Conflict and Security Law* 443, 464; Murray How IHL Treaties Bind NSAGs (n220) 125; Berkes (n211) 162; Sassòli (n213). Norms pertaining to NSA compliance with IHL in IACs are less developed under international law, presumably because such conflicts were traditionally assumed to fall exclusively between States. *See* Saul (n214) 41.

242 Geneva Convention Relative to the Treatment of Prisoners of War (adopted 12 August 1949, entered into force 21 October 1950) 75 UNTS 13 Art 3 (emphasis added).

243 Protocol Additional to the Geneva Conventions of 12 August 1949, and Relating to the Protection of Victims of Non-International Armed Conflicts (adopted 8 June 1977, entered into force 7 December 1978) 1125 UNTS 609 Art 1(1) (emphasis added).

244 *See* Murray (n220) 101–02. Sassòli (n213) 13–14; Sivakumaran (n199) 370, 393; Ezequiel Heffes and Brian E Frenkel, 'The International Responsibility of Non-State Armed Groups: In Search of the Applicable Rules' (2017) 8 *Goettingen Journal of International Law* 39, 47–53; Jann K. Kleffner, 'The Applicability of International Humanitarian Law to Organized Armed Groups' (2011) 93 *International Review of the Red Cross* 443, 443–44.

245 Ibid.

246 UN Doc A/HRC/21/50 (n7) Para 12. *See also* Louise Arimatsu and Mohbuba Choudhury, 'The Legal Classification of the Armed Conflicts in Syria, Yemen and Libya' (*Chatham House*, March 2014) at 7–19 <http://www.chathamhouse.org/sites/files/chathamhouse/home/chatham/public_html/sites/default/files/20140300ClassificationConflictsArimatsuChoudhury1.pdf>.

247 A/HRC/21/50 (n7) Para 134.

As for crimes against humanity, Bassiouni argues, similarly to his stance on genocide, that these crimes are committed pursuant to State policy and that international law has failed to progress to acknowledge the role that NSAs can assume in perpetrating them.[248] Hessbruegge further maintains that there is very little in treaty law to suggest that NSAs are bound by international human rights norms,[249] some of which effectively underlie the prohibitions contained within crimes against humanity.[250] McCorquodale goes as far as to assert that IHRL is not applicable to NSAs at all, and that instead, responsibility for IHRL violations committed by such groups falls upon the host State if it fails to exercise the requisite due diligence to uphold these rights for its people.[251]

However, the more persuasive opinion is that NSAs are bound by IHRL, and, by default, to the prohibition against crimes against humanity. Rodenhäuser, for example, insists that any failure to extend human rights obligations to NSAs defeats the very purpose of human rights, which he defines as the protection of the inherent rights of every individual regardless of where threats to these rights may emanate from.[252] Adding to this, Clapham points out that in some contexts, grave and persistent IHRL violations may be perpetrated in the absence of armed conflict, or within an armed conflict that has not reached the threshold of a NIAC as required to trigger IHL.[253] In such cases, he emphasises, the application of IHRL to NSAs becomes all the more compelling.[254] On the prohibtion against crimes against humanity in particular, Arsanjani points out that the definition of this crime as per Article 7(2)(a) ICC Statute encompasses attacks committed 'pursuant to or in furtherance of a State *or organisational* policy'.[255] The inclusion of 'organisational policy', he

248 Bassiouni (n230) 714.

249 Hessbruegge (n215) 31.

250 The specific acts entailed under crimes against humanity (as defined within Article 7 ICC Statute) can be found within, or are at least closely related to, obligations contained within human rights instruments. *See*, for example, murder (Article 6 ICCPR); enslavement (Article 8 ICCPR); deportation and forcible transfer (Articles 12–13 ICCPR); imprisonment and severe deprivation of liberty (Article 9 ICCPR); torture and inhuman acts (Article 8 ICCPR and Article 2 CAT); persecution (Articles 2 and 26 ICCPR); and apartheid (Article 3 CERD). International Covenant on Civil and Political Rights (adopted 16 December 1966, entered into force 23 March 1976) 999 UNTS 171 Arts 2, 6, 89 12–13, 26; Convention against Torture and other Cruel, Inhuman or Degrading Treatment or Punishment (adopted 10 December 1984, entered into force 26 June 1987) 1465 UNTS 85 Art 2; International Convention on the Elimination of all Forms of Racial Discrimination (adopted 7 March 1966, entered into force 4 January 1969) 660 UNTS 195 Art 3.

251 Robert McCorquodale, 'Overlegalizing Silences: Human Rights and Nonstate Actors' (2002) 96 *American Society of International Law Proceedings* 384, 385.

252 Rodenhäuser HR Obligations of NSAs (n215) 269.

253 Andrew Clapham, 'Human Rights Obligations of Non-State Actors in Conflict Situations' (2006) 88 *International Review of the Red Cross* 491, 503–05.

254 Ibid. *See also* Rodenhäuser Organizing Rebellion (n204) 143–44, 149.

255 Mahnoush Arsanjani, 'The Rome Statute of the International Criminal Court' (1999) 93 *American Journal of International Law* 22, 31; ICC Statute (n79) Art 7 (emphasis added).

notes, extends this provision to NSAs.[256] This approach was adopted by the Commission of Inquiry on Syria, which declared that '[NSAs] may also bear responsibility for gross abuses of human rights, in particular those that amount to international crimes'.[257]

Along these lines, the Commission of Inquiry on Syria documented the commission of war crimes and crimes against humanity by various NSAs in the context of the Syrian conflict, including both war crimes and crimes against humanity of murder and torture, as well as the war crimes of extrajudicial execution, attacking civilians, and attacking protected objects.[258] The Commission furthermore concluded that ISIS committed the war crime and crime against humanity of sexual violence against women, many of whom (pursuant to a systematic policy) were taken as sex slaves, forced into marriage, raped, and forcibly impregnated.[259] Children under the age of fifteen were also regularly recruited, trained, and employed in combat by this group, constituting a war crime of child recruitment.[260]

Overall, therefore, various NSAs in Syria violated R2P's Pillar 1 through the commission of war crimes, crimes against humanity, and possibly even genocide as detailed throughout this section.[261] Following from the analysis presented thus far regarding the relationship between R2P and NSAs, this effectively triggered Syria's Pillar 1 obligation, as the host State, to protect its population from the actions of these groups. However, not only did Syria fail to exercise due diligence to prevent the commission of mass atrocity crimes by NSAs within its territory, but it furthermore indirectly enabled the actions of terrorist groups such as ISIS so as to cast itself as the only viable alternative to the rise of terrorism.[262] For example, the regime largely refrained from attacking ISIS-controlled areas in Syria and instead focused its military efforts upon non-proscribed rebel groups (including Western-backed ones), thus facilitating ISIS's expansion into territory ceded by these rebels.[263] It furthermore

256 Arsanjani (n255) 31.
257 A/HRC/21/50 (n7) Para 134.
258 *See*, for example, ibid.; UN Doc A/HRC/22/59 (n9) Paras 56–57, 64, 103, 133; HRC, 'Report of the Independent International Commission of Inquiry on the Syrian Arab Republic' (12 February 2014) UN Doc A/HRC/25/65 Paras 29–33, 61, 114; UN Doc A/HRC/27/60 (n10) Paras 38, 64; UN Doc A/HRC/27/CRP.3 (n10) Paras 46, 50–52, 63.
259 UN Doc A/HRC/27/CRP.3 (n10) Paras 51–52, 56–57; UN Doc A/HRC/32/CRP.2 (n234) 93.
260 UN Doc A/HRC/27/60 (n10) Para 95; UN Doc A/HRC/27/CRP.3 (n10) Para 60.
261 It should be noted that the prohibition for NSAs to commit ethnic cleansing is, as rightly explained by Berkes, subsumed within the prohibitions against the other three mass atrocity crimes given that acts of ethnic cleansing can in fact be reflective of genocide, war crimes, and crimes against humanity. Berkes (n211) 163.
262 *See* Gilsinan (n11); Simon Speakman Cordall, 'How Syria's Assad Helped Forge ISIS' (*Newsweek*, 21 June 2014) <http://www.newsweek.com/how-syrias-assad-helped-forge-isis-255631>.
263 *See* Aryn Baker, 'Why Bashar Assad Won't Fight ISIS' (*Time*, 26 February 2015) <http://time.com/3719129/assad-isis-asset/>. *See also* '"More than 90%" of Russian Airstrikes in Syria have not Targeted ISIS, US Says' (*Guardian*, 7 October 2015)

engaged in military and economic cooperation with ISIS.[264] Essentially, Assad employed such terrorist groups as an ultimatum to the international community: either me or the terrorists. As per R2P's Pillar 3, Syria's failure to protect its population from mass atrocity crimes committed by NSAs (not to mention that it was committing such mass atrocity crimes itself) shifted the burden of protection upon the international community. As discussed within the next section, although the international community did take military action against ISIS and ANF in Syria (as two of the NSAs that committed mass atrocity crimes), it did not do so under the pretext of human protection or under the banner of R2P.

7.5 International Coalition against ISIS

It can be reasonably argued that the international community's Pillar 3 responsibility to protect the Syrian population arose not only in relation to the mass atrocity situation inflicted by the Assad regime as discussed in Sections 7.2 and 7.3 of this chapter, but also in relation to mass atrocity crimes perpetrated by NSAs. In this respect, it is worth briefly exploring whether and how the various Pillar 3-related obligations upon States to react to mass atrocity crimes examined in Section 5.2 of this book – namely, the Article 1 Genocide Convention obligation to prevent genocide, the Common Article 1 Geneva Conventions obligation to ensure respect for the Conventions, as well as the Article 41 ASR obligation to cooperate to bring an end to serious *jus cogens* violations – apply to R2P situations perpetrated by NSAs in particular. These findings are then used to evaluate the international community's response to mass atrocity crimes perpetrated by NSAs in the Syrian context.

As for Article 1 of the Genocide Convention, which stipulates that 'genocide … is a crime under international law which [the Contracting Parties] undertake to prevent and to punish',[265] it is recalled from Section 5.2.1 that the meaning of the term 'prevent' as per the ICJ's *Bosnia* case confers a reactive element as relevant to R2P's Pillar 3. This means that the obligation to prevent does not end once genocide is actually committed, but that rather, it requires States to continue to exert efforts to cease its continued perpetration.[266] Importantly, Article 1 Genocide Convention does not specify that the obligation to prevent and to punish arises only when genocide is committed by a specific set of actors (e.g. States). As such, it can be interpreted as calling upon States to prevent and to punish genocide that is committed by any State or non-State actor. This was indeed the premise of the ICJ's *Bosnia* judgment,

<https://www.theguardian.com/world/2015/oct/07/russia-airstrikes-syria-not-targetting-isis>.

264 *See* Stuart Ramsay, 'IS Files Reveal Assad's Deals with Militants' (Sky News, 2 May 2016) <https://news.sky.com/story/is-files-reveal-assads-deals-with-militants-10267238>; Josie Ensor, 'How ISIL Colluded with Assad to Make $40m a Month in Oil Deals' (*Telegraph*, 25 April 2016) <https://www.telegraph.co.uk/news/2016/04/25/isils-deal-with-bashar-al-assad-and-the-40m-a-month-oil-profits/>.

265 Genocide Convention (n228) Art 1.

266 *See Bosnia* case (n233) Para 430.

as Serbia's failure to discharge its obligation to prevent was established with respect to a genocide that was perpetrated by NSAs rather than a State actor.[267]

Second, the Geneva Conventions' Common Article 1 requires States to 'ensure respect' for the respective Conventions. Section 5.2.2 outlined the relevance of this provision to establishing an obligation to react to war crimes, given that the Geneva Conventions delineate rules of IHL from which many of the prohibitions against war crimes derive. Section 5.2.2 furthermore noted that the more authoritative interpretation of Common Article 1 submits that contracting States are required to ensure respect for the Geneva Conventions by all parties to an armed conflict, inclusive of States and NSAs (even if the contracting States are not themselves party to this armed conflict). This encompasses an obligation to react to breaches of the Conventions and to endeavour to bring violating parties (States and non-State actors) back to a position of respect. Such a reading is consistent with both the literal meaning and the object and purpose of Common Article 1 and has been supported by scholars of international law as well as the ICRC.[268]

Finally, Article 41 ASR calls upon States to 'cooperate to bring to an end through lawful means any serious [breaches]' of peremptory norms. Section 5.2.3 detailed that this Article holds applicability to each of the four mass atrocity crimes encompassed under R2P given their strong basis in *jus cogens*, although it was noted that it is premature to assert this Article as binding under international law as it represents neither a treaty norm nor, arguably, a customary international norm. Instead, Article 41 ASR perhaps more accurately represents a statement of intent as to how international law is or should be evolving and can thus serve as a form of soft law.[269] With respect to its applicability to NSAs, it should be noted that the Article's literal text does not constrain its applicability to serious *jus cogens* breaches that are committed by a specific set of actors (e.g. States), but it rather presents an all-encompassing obligation upon States to cooperate to bring an end to serious *jus cogens* breaches in general. It is therefore reasonable to conclude that this Article's scope seeks to establish an obligation to react to serious peremptory breaches (e.g. mass atrocity crimes) that are committed by any actor, inclusive of NSAs.

With respect to Syria, therefore, existing international legal norms, albeit fragmented, reinforce elements of an emerging (although not crystallised) R2P Pillar 3 obligation for States to react to mass atrocity crimes perpetrated not only by the host State, but also by NSAs. In reality, however, human protection rhetoric was largely absent from the international response to the actions of NSAs in Syria. This becomes particularly apparent through an analysis of the US-led military campaign

267 Ibid., Para 438.

268 *See* Laurence Boisson de Chazournes and Luigi Condorelli, 'Common Article 1of the Geneva Conventions Revisited: Protecting Collective Interests' (2000) 82 *International Review of the Red Cross* 67, 70; Andrea Breslin, 'A Reflection on the Legal Obligation for Third States to Ensure Respect for IHL' (2017) 22 *Journal of Conflict and Security Law* 5, 12–13; 'Commentary of 2016, Article 1: Respect for the Convention' (*ICRC*, 2016) at Paras 153–56 <https://www.icrc.org/applic/ihl/ihl.nsf/Comment.xsp?action=openDocument&documentId=72239588AFA66200C1257F7D00367DBD>.

269 *See* Section 2.2.2 of this book.

to eradicate ISIS, which was initiated in September 2014. Namely, on 20 September, Iraq submitted a letter to the UN which declared that ISIS's establishment of a 'safe haven' beyond Iraq's borders 'has made our borders impossible to defend and exposed our citizens to the threat of terrorist attacks'.[270] As such, Iraq formally 'requested the United States of America to lead international efforts to strike ISIL sites and military strongholds, with our express consent'.[271] The letter did not mention Syria, nor did it specify where, geographically, Iraq consented to the use of force by American troops. In response to this request, however, the US initiated an air campaign on 22 September to target ISIS strongholds within both Iraq and Syria as part of an international coalition (the US-led Coalition) to eradicate the group.[272]

It is relatively uncontroversial that the US-led Coalition's anti-ISIS military operations within Iraq were legally justifiable under the premise of intervention by invitation of the host State.[273] However, scholars of international law are highly divided over the lawfulness of Coalition actions within Syria, which did not extend a similar invitation to Coalition forces to strike and eradicate ISIS within its territory.[274] Some States justified their involvement in this Coalition under the premise of individual self-defence from actual or imminent attack given that ISIS coordinated military attacks within other countries in the region such as Turkey, Lebanon, Egypt, Libya, and Tunisia, as well as on European soil, including in France and Belgium.[275] Other States, including the US, invoked the collective self-defence of Iraq,[276] including a highly contentious 'unwilling or unable' standard

270 UNSC, 'Letter Dated 20 September 2014 from the Permanent Representative of Iraq to the United Nations Addressed to the President of the Security Council' (22 September 2014) UN Doc S/2014/691, 2.

271 Ibid.

272 *See* Helen Cooper and Eric Schmitt, 'Airstrikes by U.S. and Allies Hit ISIS Targets in Syria' (*New York Times*, 22 September 2014) <https://www.nytimes.com/2014/09/23/world/middleeast/us-and-allies-hit-isis-targets-in-syria.html>.

273 *See* Karine Bannelier-Christakis, 'Military Interventions against ISIL in Iraq, Syria and Libya, and the Legal Basis of Consent' (2016) 29 *Leiden Journal of International Law* 743, 751–52; Laurie O'Conner, 'Legality of the Use of Force in Syria against Islamic State and the Khorasan Group' (2016) 3 *Journal on the Use of Force in International Law* 70, 73–74.

274 *See*, for example, Jutta Brunnée and Stephen J Toope, 'Self-defence against Non-State Actors: Are Powerful States Unable but Willing to Change International Law?' (2018) 67 *International and Comparative Law Quarterly* 263; Olivier Corten, 'The "Unwilling or Unable" Test: Has it Been, and Could it be, Accepted?' (2016) 29 *Leiden Journal of International Law* 777; Olivia Flasch, 'The Legality of Air Strikes against ISIL in Syria: New Insights on the Extraterritorial Use of Force against Non-State Actors' (2016) 3 *Journal on the Use of Force in International Law* 37; O'Connor (n273). *See*, however, Michael P. Scharf, 'How the War against ISIS Changed International Law' (2016) 48 *Case Western Reserve Journal of International Law* 15.

275 *See* Zachary Laub, 'The Islamic State' (*Council on Foreign Relations*, 10 August 2016) <https://www.cfr.org/backgrounder/islamic-state>; 'ISIS Fast Facts' (CNN, 21 January 2019) <https://edition.cnn.com/2014/08/08/world/isis-fast-facts/index.html>.

276 *See* Corten (n274) 781–83; O'Connor (n273) 85–88.

articulated within a letter submitted by US Ambassador to the UN Samantha Power to the UN Secretary-General:

> Iraq has made clear that it is facing a serious threat of continuing attacks from ISIL coming out of safe havens in Syria … For these reasons, the Government of Iraq has asked that the United States lead international efforts to strike ISIL sites and military strongholds in Syria …
>
> States must be able to defend themselves, in accordance with the inherent right of individual and collective self-defense, as reflected in Article 51 of the UN Charter, when, as is the case here, the government of the State where the threat is located is unwilling or unable to prevent the use of its territory for such attacks. The Syrian regime has shown that it cannot and will not confront these safe-havens effectively itself. Accordingly, the United States has initiated necessary and proportionate military actions in Syria in order to eliminate the ongoing ISIL threat to Iraq.[277]

In essence, the 'unwilling or unable' test cited by the US maintains that a State can invoke the right to self-defence in response to an armed attack by an NSA, which can be executed on the territory of a third State if that State is unwilling or unable to prevent such attacks emanating from its territory.[278] To be clear, this purported right does not arise as a result of the attribution of the NSA's actions to the host State *per se* (which represents the more traditional approach under international law with respect to triggering the right of self-defence in the territory of another State for attacks initiated by NSAs from within its borders[279]), but rather, because the host State is unwilling or unable to prevent attacks which are planned or executed by the NSA from within its territory.[280] Despite accumulating State practice,[281] however, the unwilling or unable standard remains highly contentious among scholars of international law, in particular because of legal ambiguities surrounding its scope, its seeming clash with the principles of State sovereignty and non-interference, as well as serious difficulties with the notion that a State's susceptibility to territorial violability can arise from a mere inability to suppress an attack emanating from within its borders.[282]

277 UNSC, 'Letter Dated 23 September 2014 from the Permanent Representative of the United States of America to the United Nations Addressed to the Secretary-General' (23 September 2014) UN Doc S/2014/695.
278 *See* Brunnée and Toope (n274) 264; Flasch (n274) 52.
279 *See* Flasch (n274) 49; Nicholas Tsagourias, 'Self-Defence against Non-State Actors: The Interaction between Self-Defence as a Primary Rule and Self-Defence as a Secondary Rule' (2016) 29 *Leiden Journal of International Law* 801, 804–05. *See also supra* note 218.
280 *See* Christian Henderson, 'Non-State Actors and the Use of Force' in Math Noortmann, August Reinisch and Cedric Rygaert (eds), *Non-State Actors in International Law* (Hart Publishing 2015) 93–95.
281 *See* ibid., 84–85; Monica Hakimi, 'Defensive Force against Non-State Actors' (2015) 91 *International Law Studies* 1, 13–14.

While a detailed examination of the legal complexities surrounding the unwilling or unable standard is unnecessary for the purposes of this section, what stands significant is that R2P rhetoric (and that of human protection more generally) was relatively absent from international discourse pertaining to the ISIS threat, despite the doctrine's clear relevance in this respect. It should be distinguished here that R2P should not have been invoked as a justification for the US-led Coalition's military operations in Syria. Given the questionable lawfulness of these operations, such a move would have served to undermine the doctrine by playing into concerns of sceptical States regarding its potentially interventionist nature and its capacity to be abused. Nevertheless, and at the very least, the threats posed by ISIS should have been framed as affecting fundamental interests of human protection owed to the international community as a whole, alongside any other applicable dimensions such as self-defence.

This imperative to highlight human protection in the context of the ISIS threat can be particularly gleaned through the UNSC's adoption of Resolution 2249 in November 2015, which characterised ISIS as a 'global and unprecedented threat to international peace and security'[283] and:

> [Called] upon Member States that have the capacity to do so to take all necessary measures ... on the territory under the control of ISIL also known as Da'esh, in Syria and Iraq, to redouble and coordinate their efforts to prevent and suppress terrorist acts committed specifically by ISIL also known as Da'esh as well as [Al-Nusra Front].[284]

Scholars of international law have pointed out that this Resolution's allowance to 'take all necessary measures' is ambiguous as to whether it authorises the use of force, especially given that Chapter VII was not specifically invoked.[285] Regardless, however, what is of interest here is that when the UNSC did respond to the ISIS (and ANF) threat, it framed the issue through the lens of counterterrorism and failed to reference R2P. The Resolution did condemn 'in the strongest terms the continued gross, systematic and widespread abuses of human rights and violations of humanitarian law ... carried out by ISIL', demonstrating that it at least noted some of the fundamental IHL and IHRL violations perpetrated by this group.[286] However, when it called upon States to 'take all necessary measures', it did so for the sole purpose of '[redoubling] and [coordinating] ... efforts to prevent and suppress terrorist acts committed specifically by ISIL ... as well as ANF'.[287] In other words,

282 *See* Flasch (n274) 53; Hakimi (n281) 12–13; O'Connor (n273) 88; Tsagourias (n279) 809–13.
283 UNSC Res 2249 (20 November 2015) UN Doc S/RES/2249 Preamble.
284 Ibid., Para 5.
285 *See* Brunnée and Toope (n274) 271–72; O'Connor (n273) 76.
286 UN Doc S/RES/2249 (n283) Para 3.
287 Ibid., Para 5.

no direct link was established between human protection and the call to take all necessary measures.

To be sure, both the self-defence of States that were subject to attacks by ISIS (which did not include the US[288]), as well as anti-terrorism norms, were certainly applicable to the international community's efforts to combat ISIS. Nevertheless, it is contended that human protection posed an equally compelling dimension to the situation, one that perhaps more accurately encapsulated the full impact and threat posed by the group. Indeed, the primary victims of ISIS's crimes were the civilian populations of Iraq and Syria. This was compounded by another – and arguably deadlier and overarching – mass atrocity situation in Syria inflicted by the Assad regime, which affected a much wider segment of the country's population, was more sustained, and was responsible for significantly higher death tolls, forcible displacement of the population, and destruction of infrastructure.[289] Such conditions in turn served only to facilitate a breeding ground for the further expansion of ISIS's network, given that terrorist elements thrive best in environments of chaos, anarchy, and deprivation.[290] As such, an R2P-centred agenda would have stressed that equally important and certainly reinforcing to the fight against terrorism was the protection of the affected Iraqi and Syrian populations from mass atrocity crimes. This approach would have rightly recognised that the emergence of ISIS within Syria and the enabling environment that facilitated its growth and projection of power abroad in fact stemmed from an underlying lack of protection, both by ISIS but also more critically by the Assad regime.

Overall, the international community's response to the ISIS threat closely mirrors that of its response to chemical weapons use in Syria discussed in Section 7.2.4 of this chapter. Specifically, the international community chose to respond to only one facet of a much wider R2P case, which, even if its efforts were argued to be successful,[291] have done little to alleviate the wider mass atrocity situation perpetrated by other parties (in particular, the Assad regime) and/or through other means. Furthermore, when this international response was forthcoming, it

288 While ISIS-inspired attacks were committed within the US, including in San Bernardino, California in December 2015 as well as in Orlando, Florida in June 2016, these attacks were not directly attributed to the group. *See* Tim Lister et al., 'ISIS Goes Global: 143 Attacks in 29 Countries have Killed 2,043' (*CNN*, 12 February 2018) <https://edition.cnn.com/2015/12/17/world/mapping-isis-attacks-around-the-world/index.html>.

289 *See*, for example, SNHR 7th Anniversary Statistics (n147).

290 *See* Daniel L. Byman, '6 Counterterrorism Lessons from the Syrian Civil War' (*Brookings Institution*, 27 February 2018) <https://www.brookings.edu/blog/order-from-chaos/2018/02/27/6-counterterrorism-lessons-from-the-syrian-civil-war/>.

291 US President Trump announced on 19 December 2018 that 'We have Won against ISIS', although the situation in Syria remains inconclusive. *See* Karen DeYoung, Louisa Loveluck, and Jane Hudson, 'U.S. Military Announces Start of Syria Withdrawal' (*Washington Post*, 11 January 2019) <https://www.washingtonpost.com/world/middle_east/us-military-announces-start-of-syria-troop-withdrawal/2019/01/11/77455bda-1585-11e9-90a8-136fa44b80ba_story.html?utm_term=.a0d45629863c>.

was not framed in accordance with R2P or human protection more generally, but rather under the banner of individual and collective self-defence as well as the need to combat terrorism.

Two major lessons can be extracted here. First, it should be stressed that irrespective of parallel dynamics existing within a mass atrocity situation (e.g. terrorism or self-defence), human protection should always remain paramount within any international response. Not only does this serve to address fundamental community interests of human protection (alongside any other fundamental community interests that may be at stake), but it furthermore ensures that international action in such a case is directed towards achieving a comprehensive and sustainable solution that tackles the roots of what may be a quagmire of problems. In Syria, for example, a focus upon human protection as the ultimate end goal would have helped to address not only the mass atrocity crimes perpetrated by both ISIS and the Assad regime (as well as by other parties), but also the enabling environment which allowed ISIS to emerge and consequently its capability to coordinate attacks abroad, thereby also contributing towards the goals of self-defence as well as combating terrorism.

Second, the international community's focus upon ISIS (and ANF) at the exclusion of the wider mass atrocity situation taking place in Syria underscores the need to overcome issues of selectivity within R2P. Although the international community admittedly pledged in the 2005 World Summit Outcome document to take action in response to mass atrocity crimes on a 'case-by-case' basis,[292] it is both illogical and contrary to the principles of R2P to focus international efforts upon protecting populations from only one aspect of a much larger mass atrocity situation. Indeed, as the military operations conducted against ISIS and ANF seem to be drawing to a close as of this writing,[293] there has been no significant alleviation of the wider mass atrocity situation in Syria. As such, R2P's Pillar 3 should be understood as allowing for differentiated international responses to mass atrocity situations based upon the specific circumstances of each case, but not as allowing for blatant selectivity – as a result of mere political will – that hinders the achievement of human protection.

7.6 Conclusion

Despite underlying similarities with respect to the historical and socioeconomic roots of the Libyan and Syrian conflicts – including a comparable initial progression of events within the respective uprisings – the international community's response to the Syrian R2P situation stood in stark contrast to that of Libya. Overall, this response can be characterised as a glaring failure to protect the population and an overt dereliction from the principles that govern R2P, attributable to the UNSC's unyielding deadlock as well as the disinclination of other actors, in particular States and international organisations, to lawfully circumvent

292 2005 World Summit Outcome (n200) Para 139.
293 *See* DeYoung, Loveluck, and Hudson (n291).

the body in this regard. Within the UNSC, for example, the exercise of the veto on 12 separate occasions by Russia and/or China obstructed the body from adopting meaningful initiatives to overcome the mass atrocity situation, particularly in the spheres of chemical weapons use, accountability, and civilian protection. Resolutions that were adopted by the body – which called for the establishment of a UN supervision mission, complete ban on the use of chemical weapons, allowance for UN aid agencies to conduct humanitarian operations through select corridors absent the consent of the Assad regime, convening of a political transition process, and instatement of ceasefires – were not followed through with credible enforcement measures and were thus set for failure. Similarly, initiatives launched outside the UNSC, albeit conferring limited advantages in terms of protecting the population, also fell short of alleviating the mass atrocity situation as a whole, either because they were lacking in teeth (for example, ceasefire agreements between major world and/or regional powers), because they failed to deter perpetrators of mass atrocity crimes (for example, accountability initiatives), or because they were not directed at achieving a comprehensive solution to the conflict (for example, the military campaign against ISIS).

Despite these failures, a number of observations can be extracted from the Syrian case with respect to R2P. First, consistent with the Chapter 6 conclusions on Libya, R2P's Pillar 1 continued to be upheld as legally binding while Pillar 3 was understood to be more aspirational rather than legal. Admittedly, references to the doctrine within the UNSC were relatively muted throughout the first three years of the Syrian conflict. However, an analysis of States' positions in this respect confirmed that this was not due to their backtracking from a Pillar 1 obligation, but rather, due to political prudence regarding the divisiveness that R2P had acquired through the implementation of the Libyan R2P mandate (which, critically, pertained to Pillar 3 rather than Pillar 1). Consistent with this, R2P's Pillar 1 made a reappearance in UNSC Resolution 2139 in February 2014, after which it was incorporated into six additional UNSC resolutions on Syria.[294] Pillar 3, on the other hand, remained contentious among States and was rejected as imposing any obligation to react to mass atrocity situations.

Second, and also consistent with the Libya conclusions, the Syrian mass atrocity situation reinforced that R2P can be implemented through a diverse range of means and by a wide set of international players. This chapter focused upon reactions that transpired or could have transpired by the UNSC, UNGA, OPCW, LAS, and by individual and coalitions of States (e.g. US-led Coalition). This affirms that R2P's implementation is not confined to the UNSC or to any other specific set of entities (including a cautionary note against an over-reliance upon regional organisations in dictating international responses to R2P situations), but that rather, various actors can react to the commission of mass atrocity crimes in line with their specific mandates and spheres of influence. The range of measures undertaken by these actors in Syria, inclusive of calling for ceasefires, establishing chemical weapons monitoring mechanisms, removing

294 *See supra* note 17.

impediments to humanitarian access, pursuing accountability in domestic and international forums, adopting sanctions and asset freezes, suspending membership from the LAS, and launching a military operation against ISIS, furthermore underscores that military intervention represents but one of a multitude of means through which R2P can be implemented.

Third, the targeted yet confined international reactions to chemical weapons use as well as the ISIS threat in Syria underscore the need for comprehensive responses to R2P situations, namely, those that are directed towards achieving human protection as a whole rather than – or at least alongside – addressing particular manifestations of such situations. Such an approach acknowledges that a range of community interests may be at play within any given mass atrocity situation (for example, the chemical weapons and terrorism prohibitions in the Syrian context). It furthermore, however, emphasises that an international response centred upon human protection is the most conducive to ensuring a comprehensive and long-term resolution of these various dimensions.

Fourth, NSAs' heavy involvement within the Syrian R2P situation provoked an examination of the doctrine's applicability to such groups. Overall, it was affirmed that R2P builds upon the traditional and State-centric international legal approach, which maintains that while NSAs may be prohibited from committing mass atrocity crimes, it is generally only individual criminal responsibility or State responsibility (for example, for failing to exercise the requisite due diligence) that can be incurred for the perpetration of these crimes by such groups. As such, R2P's Pillar 1 calls upon host States to protect their populations from mass atrocity crimes committed by any actor within their borders, including by NSAs. Should they fail in this respect, then as per Pillar 3, the international community should either provide support to the host State or intervene directly (although not necessarily militarily) to react to the mass atrocity crimes committed by NSAs. These observations extended to a finding of Syria's violation of its R2P Pillar 1 obligations not only in perpetrating mass atrocity crimes itself, but also in failing to protect its population from similar crimes committed by NSAs. This, in turn, gave rise to the international community's Pillar 3 responsibility on these two same counts.

Fifth and finally, the Syrian conflict confirmed that in its current form, R2P is ill-equipped to consistently and effectively deliver on the prevention of and reaction to mass atrocity crimes. In order to rectify existing inadequacies, R2P must evolve in at least one of two ways. The first is that it must acquire a legally binding status (in particular, with respect to its Pillar 3), inclusive of formal limitations upon the permanent veto in mass atrocity situations. The latter component is important because despite the diversity in actors that can be involved in instituting an R2P reaction, the UNSC holds a particularly sensitive role in authorising the use of force and in adopting measures that are binding upon all UN member-States. In this respect, ensuring that international reactions to R2P situations do not become hostage to the political interests of the P5 is crucial to the doctrine's effective discharge.

Should R2P fail to develop in line with the above, then it must at least come to recognise alternative means that can be pursued by States and/or international organisations during situations of UNSC paralysis. Such alternatives would serve indirectly to hold the UNSC to account for any failure to fulfil its primary responsibility to maintain international peace and security (including in mass atrocity situations), and would thus incentivise the body to ensure the proper discharge of its functions in future R2P situations or to face the prospect of other international actors stepping in to fill this void. This chapter identified three means of achieving international mobilisation outside the confines of the UNSC, namely, lawful measures, third-party countermeasures, as well as the invocation of UforP. Lawful measures were employed in the Syrian context to pursue accountability in domestic courts under the banner of universal jurisdiction, to negotiate ceasefires by regional and world powers, and to establish a Plan of Action, observer mission, and post for a Joint Special Envoy by the LAS. Third-party countermeasures were invoked by the LAS through its adoption of economic sanctions, asset freezes, and a ban against civil aviation directed against Syria as well as through its suspension of Syria from the body. It was also suggested that third-party countermeasures could have been pursued by States and international organisations in Syria to undertake unauthorised cross-border humanitarian operations to protest the UN's failure to implement existing mandates in this regard. Finally, this chapter argued that although UforP was not invoked in the Syrian context, it could (and should) have been utilised to facilitate a wide range of international responses to the R2P situation, including through the UNGA's recommendation of the use of force in response to chemical weapons use as well as Assad and/or Russian military onslaughts against civilian-populated areas such as that of East Aleppo.

Overall, the international community's failure to respond appropriately to the Syrian R2P situation imparts two primary repercussions. First, it tragically facilitated the prolongation of the Syrian mass atrocity situation, which in turn claimed the lives and livelihoods of millions of Syrians. Second, it overlooked a compelling opportunity to develop R2P in line with its central objective of eradicating mass atrocity crimes. In this respect, it should be stressed that Syria was not the first mass atrocity situation to witness UNSC paralysis, nor is it expected to be the last. As such, a strong demonstration of political will by States and international organisations to protest and counter UNSC paralysis, including through calling for formal restrictions upon the permanent veto, through employing lawful measures and third-party countermeasures, and through pursuing UforP, would have induced the UNSC to more seriously fulfil its primary role to maintain international peace and security, or alternatively, would have helped to ensure that the body's paralysis would no longer serve as an impediment for the effective discharge of R2P's Pillar 3.

8 Conclusion

This book cast R2P as an emerging umbrella norm of various underlying sub-norms pertaining to the prevention of and reaction to mass atrocity crimes which the doctrine seeks to pull together, repackage, and build upon in order to deliver one central framework that secures the promise to 'never again'. This formulation ascribes a degree of legal character to R2P even if the doctrine does not in itself represent a binding international legal norm. Indeed, many of R2P's underlying provisions derive from existing international legal frameworks that grapple directly or indirectly with the objective of human protection, including the laws of the UN, laws of international organisations, international human rights law, international humanitarian law, international criminal law, international environmental law, and laws of State responsibility. An examination of the legal underpinnings of R2P's Pillar 1 conducted in Chapter 3, for example, revealed that host State obligations to protect their populations from mass atrocity crimes for the most part already exist under international law irrespective of R2P, including as *jus cogens* norms. Chapter 5 affirmed that even third-State obligations to react to the outbreak of mass atrocity crimes when host States manifestly fail in this respect (as per Pillar 3) can be derived to a limited extent from existing international legal norms.

Beyond this, the more revolutionary aspect of R2P is that it aspires to establish an all-encompassing obligation (rather than a discretionary right) for the international community to react (militarily or non-militarily) in the event that host States are unable to protect their populations from mass atrocity crimes. This element was meant to address protection gaps that were revealed through the international community's lacking responses in the 1990s to the Rwanda and Srebrenica genocides as well as to the ethnic cleansing in Kosovo. R2P thus emerged as a vehicle for cementing obligations of host and third-party States to ensure consistent and effective human protection from mass atrocity crimes.

Despite the high hopes for R2P, however, the reality is that it has not succeeded in instigating the necessary changes within the international legal system to deliver upon its promise to 'never again'.[1] The Syrian R2P situation is a compelling

1 *See* Aidan Hehir, 'The Responsibility to Protect: "Sound and Fury Signifying Nothing"?' (2010) 24 *International Relations* 218. *See also* Robert Pape, 'When Duty Calls: A Pragmatic Standard of Humanitarian Intervention' (2012) 37 *International*

example in this respect: notwithstanding the numerous international failures to respond to this case as detailed in Chapter 7, the writing of this book was concluded in the midst of an Assad and Russian military onslaught against the country's Idlib province, which has thus far consisted of scorched earth and 'surrender or die' tactics that the Assad regime previously employed against other areas across the country such as Daraya, Eastern Aleppo, Homs, and Eastern Ghouta. The regime and its allies continue to commit war crimes and crimes against humanity through targeting hospitals, medical facilities, schools, markets, and other civilian and protected objects, and the civilian death toll increases day by day. The lives of an estimated 3 million people are at stake, and with the neighbouring Turkish border closed, these people have nowhere to flee from imminent death. Also notoriously familiar in this situation is the international community's inaction in the face of these atrocities. Russia continues to protect the regime in the UNSC, and it is not apparent that other States possess an intention or desire to circumvent the body's paralysis in any way to ensure human protection.

Elsewhere across the world, examples are rife with situations in which R2P has similarly failed to galvanise the international community to discharge its responsibility to protect. The Global Centre for the Responsibility to Protect, for example, lists seven ongoing mass atrocity situations perpetrated by government forces and/or non-State armed groups in the Democratic Republic of the Congo, Myanmar, North Korea, Afghanistan, Yemen, and Eritrea (in addition to Syria).[2] It identifies an additional three situations at 'imminent risk' of mass atrocities (Sudan, Mali and Burkina Faso, and the Cameroon), as well as eight situations of 'serious concern' (Israel and the Occupied Palestinian Territories, Nigeria, South Sudan, Libya, Central African Republic, Venezuela, Burundi, and China).[3] Despite the high hopes for R2P, therefore, the sheer number and scale of mass atrocity situations occurring globally reveals that the doctrine has thus far failed to prompt fundamental changes within the international legal system to achieve consistent and effective human protection from mass atrocity crimes, as it sought to do.

The promise of R2P, however, remains a powerful one, and its end goal of mass atrocity eradication a compelling and necessary one. This book, through its critical examination of the Libyan and Syrian cases that transpired in 2011, captured some of the doctrine's key shortcomings which render it unable in its current form to live up to its promise, coupled with concrete suggestions regarding how R2P can and should be strengthened for it to achieve its full potential, both through the future progression of international law as well as through reviving existing yet under-practiced (or inadequately enforced) international legal norms. The latter exercise in particular is critical in that it moves beyond the deadlocked discourse

Security 41; Alex J. Bellamy, 'The Responsibility to Protect: Added Value or Hot Air?' (2013) 48 *Cooperation and Conflict* 333.

2 'Populations at Risk' (*Global Centre for the Responsibility to Protect*, 2019) <http://www.globalr2p.org/regions/>.

3 Ibid.

on R2P's failings and instead thinks constructively on how to improve the doctrine's functionality.

With respect to the Syrian mass atrocity situation discussed in Chapter 7, the international community's unrelenting paralysis to this case underscored that while the doctrine retains the potential to rally the international community for the purpose of human protection (as observed in Libya), it remains selective in its application and hence fails to offer a consistent framework for tackling mass atrocity crimes. Importantly, however, this book's discussion of the Syrian case stressed that there are means through which this weakness of R2P can be overcome. The first is that R2P's Pillar 3 in particular must come to represent a legally binding obligation (rather than a discretionary right) which encompasses clear and enforceable limitations to the exercise of the permanent veto in mass atrocity situations. Chapter 5 of this book highlighted that third-State obligations to react to the outbreak of mass atrocity crimes can already be derived to a limited extent from existing and emerging international legal norms, most particularly from Article 1 of the Genocide Convention (with respect to genocide); Common Article 1 to the Geneva Conventions (with respect to war crimes); Articles 1, 2, and 24 of the UN Charter (to restrict the use of the veto in mass atrocity situations); and Article 41 of the Articles on State Responsibility (with respect to all four mass atrocity crimes, as well as the veto). At the same time, however, it was acknowledged that each of these Pillar 3-related norms suffers from key limitations such as their fragmented nature, their lack of acceptance or implementation by States, the absence of a clear due diligence standard by which to establish their breach, and/or a lack of clarity regarding the specific bearers of these obligations or of the measures through which they can be discharged. These shortcomings underscore the pressing need to achieve an overarching and binding R2P Pillar 3 norm that establishes clear and implementable obligations upon third-party States and/or other international actors to respond to the commission of mass atrocity crimes that occur anywhere in the world, and which similarly prevents the permanent veto from obstructing UNSC action in such cases.

Should R2P fail to generate such a legally binding obligation, then the Syrian case stressed that it must at least come to formally recognise means of circumventing the UNSC when the body is deadlocked from responding appropriately to a mass atrocity situation. This book identified four key alternatives that should receive serious consideration with respect to R2P's future development, namely, lawful measures, third-party countermeasures, Uniting for Peace (UforP), and regional authorisation. The first two options offer non-military means of circumventing the UNSC in R2P cases, while the latter two propose measures that encompass a right of the UNGA and regional organisations, respectively, to employ the use of force outside the body's purview.

Lawful measures, for example, consist of a wide range of non-military means that States and international organisations can draw upon to respond to R2P situations in a manner that is entirely compatible with their obligations under international law. Such measures – which can include formal protests and condemnations, severance of diplomatic ties, diplomacy, suspension or expulsion of a

State from an international body, use of positive incentives, establishment of peacekeeping forces, pursuit of accountability in domestic or international courts, and acceptance of refugees – can be employed to protest a State's failure to protect its population as per its R2P Pillar 1 obligation. However, while they may be useful in signifying States' collective outrage against potential or ongoing mass atrocity situations, they are generally not powerful enough in themselves to induce a State to abide by its Pillar 1 obligations.

Third-party countermeasures offer more robust means through which the international community can respond non-militarily to mass atrocity situations outside the purview of the UNSC. Such measures allow individual States and international organisations to violate their international legal obligations (subject to certain limitations, including the non-use of force) in order to induce a State to comply with obligations owed to the international community as a whole, which include R2P Pillar 1 protection obligations. Third-party countermeasures can encompass, for example, the adoption of sanctions or arms embargoes, the suspension or expulsion of a State from an international organisation outside stipulated rules, and the implementation of humanitarian operations within a State without its express consent. Despite extensive State practice, however, the lawfulness of third-party countermeasures remains disputed. This book argued strongly for their incorporation into R2P as part of their wider crystallisation under international law, as such an allowance would significantly enhance the doctrine's enforceability by allowing every State and international organisation to contribute more effectively to the R2P Pillar 3 response to mass atrocity situations.

The third means of circumventing a deadlocked UNSC, namely, the UforP mechanism, allows for a situation that threatens or breaches international peace and security (inclusive of R2P situations) to be referred from the UNSC to the UNGA if the former is paralysed from acting due to the permanent veto. Following such a referral, the UNGA can recommend measures up to and including the use of force which States can then implement at their discretion. UforP offers tremendous potential for strengthening R2P's enforceability and for ensuring that international action in mass atrocity situations does not become hostage to the political interests of the P5. Its primary obstacle, however, is that it is under-utilised; it has not been invoked since 1997 and has furthermore never been drawn upon to recommend the use of force.[4] Nevertheless, this book presented a strong case for its revival as a lawful and legitimate means through which international action, including through the use of force if and when necessary, can be spurred in mass atrocity situations despite UNSC paralysis.

Finally, regional authorisation for the use of force represents an emerging means of circumventing a deadlocked UNSC in R2P situations. A discussion of regional organisations' competencies in Chapter 5 concluded that these bodies do not possess a legal entitlement to authorise force – even to respond to the commission of mass atrocity crimes – as this would lie in contravention of Chapter VIII of the

4 *See* 'Emergency Special Sessions' (UNGA) <https://www.un.org/en/ga/sessions/emergency.shtml>.

UN Charter, which requires any regional military action to be preceded by UNSC authorisation. A novel challenge in this respect, however, has presented in the form of treaty-based consent to regional intervention in mass atrocity situations, as exemplified within Article 4(h) of the African Union's (AU) Constitutive Act. However, this Article it has yet to be invoked in practice so it is unclear whether States and/or international legal scholars will accept its lawfulness in sanctioning force absent UNSC authorisation.

In addition to the above lessons extracted from the Syrian R2P situation, the Libyan mass atrocity situation, discussed in Chapter 6, also revealed its own set of gaps with respect to R2P despite the international community's contrasting timely and robust reaction to the mass atrocity crimes committed by Gaddafi. The first such gap pertains to uncertainties regarding the limits to the use of force in R2P protection mandates. Specifically, NATO's pursuit of regime change in Libya, while arguably compatible with both the literal text and the object and purpose of UNSC Resolution 1973 (which authorised 'all necessary measures' to protect civilians), nevertheless evoked widespread criticisms among States – most significantly Russia and China as UNSC permanent members – that regime change exceeded the authorising Resolution's mandate. Ironically, even States that spearheaded NATO's military campaign, including the US, UK, and France, maintained that their pursuit of regime change did not stem from UNSC Resolution 1973, although they argued such an end goal to be necessary from a humanitarian perspective.

The divisiveness of NATO's implementation of UNSC Resolution 1973 in Libya underscores the need for greater clarity regarding the relationship between R2P and the use of force, including the role that regime change can or should play in discharging R2P protection mandates. In the near future, what some States (in particular, Russia and China) have perceived as an over-stepping of Resolution 1973 is likely to increase their wariness regarding the authorisation of UNSC Chapter VII protection mandates in general. Constructively, this may provoke greater clarity with respect to the specific allowances and contours of each UNSC Chapter VII authorisation so that there is less room for discretionary (and potentially abusive) implementations of these mandates by States. Conversely, however, this is also likely to restrict the UNSC's capability to adopt more robust measures under Chapter VII (e.g. military intervention) when such measures are arguably necessary to counter mass atrocity situations. This was observed in the Syrian R2P case, in which Russia in particular vetoed any draft resolutions that invoked Chapter VII, even those that clearly were not drafted in the context of authorising the use of force.

The second major revelation from the Libyan case is that the omission of a formal rebuilding requirement as part of R2P significantly constrains the doctrine's capacity to ensure long-term safeguarding from the resurgence of mass atrocity crimes within a country affected by an R2P intervention. Despite a swift and relatively successful NATO military campaign in Libya, for example, the country relapsed following Gaddafi's ousting due to the international community's insufficient engagement with Libya's rebuilding priorities. Rebuilding was highlighted as a key component of R2P in the 2001 International Commission on Intervention and State Sovereignty report (which introduced R2P as a concept), although it was excluded from the 2005 World Summit Outcome document, which offers the more authoritative formulation of the doctrine. Without formal rebuilding obligations as part of R2P, however, it is difficult to see how the doctrine can secure long-term protection from mass atrocity crimes. As such, it is argued that the doctrine's future progression should include reinstating a rebuilding component that is grounded within international legal obligations.

Overall, this book presented R2P as a tool to propel the further development of international law with respect to combating mass atrocity crimes, but also one which has thus far failed to do so. It furthermore branded the doctrine as a concept anchored within existing international legal norms while falling short of representing a legal norm in itself. Through its analysis of the two very contrasting international responses to the Libyan and Syrian mass atrocity situations, this book pinpointed R2P's key limitations which hinder the doctrine's effective discharge and simultaneously offered specific means through which these limitations can be overcome. It is now up to the international community to commit to achieving the necessary changes at the normative level in order to transform R2P's promise of mass atrocity eradication into a reality.

Bibliography

Ademola Abass, 'Consent Precluding State Responsibility: A Critical Analysis' (2004) 53 *International and Comparative Law Quarterly* 211

Ademola Abass and Mashood A. Baderin, 'Towards Effective Collective Security and Human Rights Protection in Africa: An Assessment of the Constitutive Act of the New African Union' (2002) 49 *Netherlands International Law Review* 1

Dapo Akande, 'The International Court of Justice and the Security Council: Is there Room for Judicial Control of Decisions of the Political Organs of the United Nations?' (1997) 46 *International and Comparative Law Quarterly* 309

Philip Alston and Gerard Quinn, 'The Nature and Scope of States Parties' Obligations under the International Covenant on Economic, Social and Cultural Rights' (1987) 9 *Human Rights Quarterly* 156

Jose E. Alvarez, 'Revisiting the ILC's Draft Rules on International Organization Responsibility' (2011) 105 *American Society of International Law Proceedings* 344

Juraj Andrassy, 'Uniting for Peace' (1956) 50 *American Journal of International Law* 563

Kwesi Aning and Frank Okyere, 'The African Union' in Alex J. Bellamy and Tim Dunne (eds), *The Oxford Handbook of the Responsibility to Protect* (Oxford University Press 2016)

Mahnoush Arsanjani, 'The Rome Statute of the International Criminal Court' (1999) 93 *American Journal of International Law* 22

Sydney D. Bailey, 'Veto in the Security Council' (1968) 37 *International Conciliation* 1

Karine Bannelier-Christakis, 'Military Interventions against ISIL in Iraq, Syria and Libya, and the Legal Basis of Consent' (2016) 29 *Leiden Journal of International Law* 743

Alicia L. Bannon, 'The Responsibility to Protect: The U.N. World Summit and the Question of Unilateralism' (2005–2006) 115 *Yale Law Journal* 1157

Mauro Barelli, 'Preventing and Responding to Atrocity Crimes: China, Sovereignty and the Responsibility to Protect' (2018) 23 *Journal of Conflict and Security Law* 173

Richard Barnes and Vassilis Tzevelekos, 'Beyond Responsibility to Protect: Ceci n'est pas Une Pipe' in Richard Barnes and Vassilis Tzevelekos (eds), *Beyond Responsibility to Protect: Generating Change in International Law* (Intersentia 2016)

M. Cherif Bassiouni, 'Crimes Against Humanity: The Case for a Specialized Convention' (2010) 9 *Washington University Global Studies Law Review* 575

M. Cherif Bassiouni, 'International Crimes: Jus Cogens and Obligations Erga Omnes' (1996) 59 *Law and Contemporary Problems* 63

M. Cherif Bassiouni, 'The New Wars and the Crisis of Compliance with the Law of Armed Conflict by Non-State Actors' (2008) 98 *The Journal of Criminal Law and Criminology* 711

Ed Bates, 'History' in Daniel Moeckli, Sangeeta Shah and Sandesh Sivakumaran (eds), *International Human Rights Law* (2nd edn, Oxford University Press 2014)

Alex J. Bellamy, 'The Responsibility to Protect: Added Value or Hot Air?' (2013) 48 *Cooperation and Conflict* 333

Alex J. Bellamy and Paul D. Williams, 'The New Politics of Protection? Côte d'Ivoire, Libya and the Responsibility to Protect' (2011) 87 *International Affairs* 825

Antal Berkes, 'De Facto Regimes and the Responsibility to Protect' in Richard Barnes and Vassilis Tzevelekos (eds), *Beyond Responsibility to Protect: Generating Change in International Law* (Intersentia 2016)

Sari Bernstein, 'The Responsibility to Protect after Libya: Humanitarian Prevention as Customary International Law' (2012) 38 *Brooklyn Journal of International Law* 305

Andrea Bianchi, 'Human Rights and the Magic of Jus Cogens' (2008) 19 *European Journal of International Law* 491

El Hassan bin Talal and Rolf Schwarz, 'The Responsibility to Protect and the Arab World: An Emerging International Norm?' (2013) 34 *Contemporary Security Policy* 1

Annie Bird, 'Third State Responsibility for Human Rights Violations' (2011) 21 *European Journal of International Law* 883

Andrea Birdsall, 'The Responsibility to Prosecute and the ICC: A Problematic Relationship?' (2015) 26 *Criminal Law Forum* 51

Ariela Blätter and Paul D. Williams, 'The Responsibility Not to Veto' (2011) 3 *Global Responsibility to Protect* 301

Michael Bothe, 'War Crimes' in Antonio Cassese, Paola Gaeta and John R.W.D. Jones (eds), *The Rome Statute of the International Criminal Court: A Commentary* (Oxford University Press 2002)

Auriane Botte, 'Redefining the Responsibility to Protect Concept as a Response to International Crimes' (2015) 19 *The International Journal of Human Rights* 1029

Susan Breau, *The Responsibility to Protect in International Law: An Emerging Paradigm Shift* (Routledge 2016)

Andrea Breslin, 'A Reflection on the Legal Obligation for Third States to Ensure Respect for IHL' (2017) 22 *Journal of Conflict and Security Law* 5

Ian Brownlie, 'International Law and the Use of Force by States Revisited' (2000) 21 *Australian Yearbook of International Law* 21

Ian Brownlie, *Principles of Public International Law* (7th edn, Oxford University Press 2008)

Jutta Brunnée and Stephen J. Toope, 'Self-Defence against Non-State Actors: Are Powerful States Willing but Unable to Change International Law?' (2018) 67 *International and Comparative Law Quarterly* 263

Michael Byers, 'Abuse of Rights: An Old Principle, A New Age' (2002) 47 *McGill Law Journal* 389

Stephen Carley, 'Limping toward Elysium: Impediments Created by the Myth of Westphalia on Humanitarian Intervention in the International Legal System' (2008–2009) 41 *Connecticut Law Review* 1741

Andrew J. Carswell, 'Unblocking the UN Security Council: The Uniting for Peace Resolution' (2013) 18 *Journal of Conflict and Security Law* 453

Jonathan I. Charney, 'Universal International Law' (1993) 87 *American Journal of International Law* 529

Christine Chinkin, 'Sources' in Daniel Moeckli, Sangeeta Shah and Sandesh Sivakumaran (eds), *International Human Rights Law* (2nd edn, Oxford University Press 2014)

Ethan Chorin, 'NATO's Libya Intervention and the Continued Case for a "Responsibility to Rebuild"' (2013) 31 *Boston University International Law Journal* 365

Andrew Clapham, 'Extending International Criminal Law beyond the Individual to Corporations and Armed Opposition Groups' (2008) 6 *Journal of International Criminal Justice* 899

Andrew Clapham, *Human Rights Obligations of Non-State Actors* (Oxford University Press 2006)

Andrew Clapham, 'Human Rights Obligations of Non-State Actors in Conflict Situations' (2006) 88 *International Review of the Red Cross* 491

Elise Anne Clark, 'Strengthening Regional Fisheries Management – An Analysis of the Duty to Cooperate' (2011) 9 *New Zealand Journal of Public and International Law* 223

Olivier Corten, 'The "Unwilling or Unable" Test: Has it been, and Could it be, Accepted?' (2016) 29 *Leiden Journal of International Law* 777

Olivier Corten and Vaios Koutroulis, 'The Illegality of Military Support to Rebels in the Libyan War: Aspects of Jus Contra Bellum and Jus in Bello' (2013) 18 *Journal of Conflict and Security Law* 59

Michael Cottier, 'Preliminary Remarks on Subparagraphs (xvii)–(xx): Prohibited Weapons: Drafting History' in Otto Triffterer (ed.), *Commentary on the Rome Statute of the International Criminal Court* (Nomos Verlagsgesellschaft Baden-Baden 1999)

Matthew Craven, *The International Covenant on Economic, Social and Cultural Rights: A Perspective on its Development* (Oxford University Press 1995)

James Crawford, *The International Law Commission's Articles on State Responsibility: Introduction, Text, and Commentaries* (Cambridge University Press 2002)

James Crawford, 'The Rights of Peoples: "Peoples" or "Governments"?' in James Crawford (ed.), *The Rights of Peoples* (Clarendon Press 1988)

Jason W. Davidson, 'France, Britain and the Intervention in Libya: An Integrated Analysis' (2013) 26 *Cambridge Review of International Affairs* 310

Martin Dawidowicz, 'Public Law Enforcement without Public Law Safeguards? An Analysis of State Practice on Third-party Countermeasures and Their Relationship to the UN Security Council' (2006) 77 *British Yearbook of International Law* 333

Martin Dawidowicz, 'Third-party Countermeasures: A Progressive Development of International Law?' (2016) 29 *Questions of International Law* 3

Laurence Boisson de Chazournes and Luigi Condorelli, 'Common Article 1 of the Geneva Conventions Revisited: Protecting Collective Interests' (2000) 82 *International Review of the Red Cross* 67

Emer de Vattel, *Law of Nations; or Principles of the Law of Nature, Applied to the Conduct and Affairs of Nations and Sovereigns* (6th American edn, Merriam and Cooke 1884)

Alex de Waal, 'African Roles in the Libyan Conflict of 2011' (2013) 89 *International Affairs* 365

Zsuzsanna Deen-Racsmány, 'A Redistribution of Authority Between the UN and Regional Organizations in the Field of the Maintenance of Peace and Security?' (2000) 13 *Leiden Journal of International Law* 297

Yoram Dinstein, *War, Aggression and Self-Defence* (4th edn, Cambridge University Press 2005)

Rodney Dixon, 'Crimes against Humanity: "Chapeau"' in Otto Triffterer (ed.), *Commentary on the Rome Statute of the International Criminal Court* (Nomos Verlagsgesellschaft 1999)

Frédéric Dopagne, 'Sanctions and Countermeasures by International Organizations: Diverging Lessons for the Idea of Autonomy' in Richard Collins andNigel D. White (eds), *International Organizations and the Idea of Autonomy: Institutional Independence in the International Legal Order* (Routledge 2011)

Bart Duijzentkunst, 'Interpretation of Legislative Security Council Resolutions' (2008) 4 *Utrecht Law Review* 188

Ingrid Elliott, '"A Meaningful Step towards Accountability"? A View from the Field on the United Nations International, Impartial and Independent Mechanism for Syria' (2017) 15 *Journal of International Criminal Justice* 239

Gareth Evans, *The Responsibility to Protect: Ending Mass Atrocity Crimes Once and for All* (Brookings Institution Press 2008)

Olivia Flasch, 'The Legality of the Air Strikes against ISIL in Syria: New Insights on the Extraterritorial Use of Force against Non-State Actors' (2016) 3 *Journal on the Use of Force and International Law* 37

Carlo Focarelli, 'Common Article 1 of the 1949 Geneva Conventions: A Soap Bubble?' (2010) 21 *European Journal of International Law* 125

Giorgio Gaja, 'The Position of Individuals in International Law: An ILC Perspective' (2010) 21 *European Journal of International Law* 11

Adrian Gallagher, 'The Promise of Pillar II: Analysing International Assistance under the Responsibility to Protect' (2015) 91 *International Affairs* 1259

Andrew Garwood-Gowers, 'The Responsibility to Protect and the Arab Spring: Libya as the Exception, Syria as the Norm?' (2013) 36 *University of New South Wales Law Journal* 594

Andrea Gattini, 'Breach of the Obligation to Prevent and Reparation Thereof in the ICJ's Genocide Judgment' (2007) 18 *American Journal of International Law* 695

Mark Gibney, 'Genocide and State Responsibility' (2007) 7 *Human Rights Law Review* 760

Jess Gifkins, 'The UN Security Council Divided: Syria in Crisis' (2012) 4 *Global Responsibility to Protect* 377

T. D. Gill, 'Legal and Some Political Limitations on the Power of the UN Security Council to Exercise its Enforcement Powers under Chapter VII of the Charter' (1995) 26 *Netherlands Yearbook of International Law* 33

Luke Glanville, 'Intervention in Libya: From Sovereign Consent to Regional Consent' (2013) 14 *International Studies Perspectives* 325

Luke Glanville, *Sovereignty and the Responsibility to Protect: A New History* (University of Chicago Press 2014)

Christine Gray, 'The Charter Limitations on the Use of Force: Theory and Practice: The Evolution of Thought and Practice since 1945' in Vaughan Lowe et al. (eds), *The United Nations Security Council and War* (Oxford University Press 2008)

Christine Gray, 'The Use of Force for Humanitarian Purposes' in Nigel D. White and Christian Henderson (eds), *Research Handbook on International Conflict and Security Law* (Edward Elgar Publishing Limited 2013)

Christopher Greenwood, 'International Law and the NATO Intervention in Kosovo' (2000) 49 *International and Comparative Law Quarterly* 926

Andrew T. Guzman, 'Saving Customary International Law' (2005–2006) 27 *Michigan Journal of International Law* 115

Nabil Hajjami, 'The Institutionalisation of the Responsibility to Protect' in Richard Barnes and Vassilis Tzevelekos (eds), *Beyond Responsibility to Protect: Generating Change in International Law* (Intersentia 2016)

Monica Hakimi, 'Defensive Force against Non-State Actors' (2015) 91 *International Law Studies* 1

Monica Hakimi, 'To Condone or Condemn? Regional Enforcement Actions in the Absence of Security Council Authorization' (2007) 40 *Vanderbilt Journal of Transnational Law* 643

Monica Hakimi, 'Toward a Legal Theory on the Responsibility to Protect' (2014) 39 *Yale Journal of International Law* 247

Lauri Hannikainen, *Peremptory Norms (Jus Cogens) in International Law: Historical Development, Criteria, Present Status* (Finnish Lawyers' Pub. Co. 1988)

Ezequiel Heffes and Brian E. Frenkel, 'The International Responsibility of Non-State Armed Groups: In Search of the Applicable Rules' (2017) 8 *Goettingen Journal of International Law* 39

Aidan Hehir, 'The Permanence of Inconsistency: Libya, the Security Council, and the Responsibility to Protect' (2013) 38 *International Security* 137

Aidan Hehir, 'The Responsibility to Protect: "Sound and Fury Signifying Nothing"?' (2010) 24 *International Relations* 218

John Heieck, 'The Responsibility Not to Veto Revisited: How the Duty to Prevent Genocide as a Jus Cogens Norm Imposes a Legal Duty Not to Veto on the Five Permanent Members of the Security Council' in R. Barnes and V. Tzevelekos (eds), *Beyond Responsibility to Protect: Generating Change in International Law* (Intersentia 2016)

Christian Henderson, 'International Measures for the Protection of Civilians in Libya and Cote d'Ivoire' (2011) 60 *International and Comparative Law Quarterly* 767

Christian Henderson, 'Non-State Actors and the Use of Force' in Math Noortmann, August Reinisch and Cedric Rygaert (eds), *Non-State Actors in International Law* (Hart Publishing 2015)

Christian Henderson, 'The UK Government's Legal Opinion on Forcible Measures in Response to the Use of Chemical Weapons by the Syrian Government' (2015) 64 *International and Comparative Law Quarterly* 179

Lois Henkin, 'Human Rights and State "Sovereignty"' (1995–1996) 25 *Georgia Journal of International and Comparative Law* 31

Louis Henkin, 'Kosovo and the Law of "Humanitarian Intervention"' (1999) 93 *American Journal of International Law* 824

Anders Henriksen, 'Trump's Missile Strike on Syria and the Legality of Using Force to Deter Chemical Warfare' (2018) 23 *Journal of Conflict and Security Law* 33

Jan Arno Hessbruegge, 'Human Rights Violations Arising from Conduct of Non-State Actors' (2005) 11 *Buffalo Human Rights Law Review* 21

James E. Hickey Jr, 'Challenges to Security Council Monopoly Power Over the Use of Force in Enforcement Actions: The Case of Regional Organizations' (2004) 10 *Ius Gentium* 77

Peter Hilpold, 'Jus Post Bellum and the Responsibility to Rebuild – Identifying the Contours of an Ever More Important Aspect of R2P' (2015) 6 *Journal of International Humanitarian Legal Studies* 284

Wayne Hudson, 'Fables of Sovereignty' in Trudy Jacobsen, Charles Sampford and Ramesh Thakur (eds), *Re-Envisioning Sovereignty: The End of Westphalia?* (Ashgate Publishing Limited 2008)

Margo Kaplan, 'Using Collective Interests to Ensure Human Rights: An Analysis of the Articles on State Responsibility' (2004) 79 *New York University Law Review* 1902

Elena Katselli, 'Commentary: R2P as a Transforming and Transformative Concept in the Context of Responsibility as Liability' in Richard Barnes and Vassilis Tzevelekos (eds), *Beyond Responsibility to Protect: Generating Change in International Law* (Intersentia 2016)

Elena Katselli, 'Countermeasures by Non-Injured States in the Law on State Responsibility' (*European Society of International Law 2005*) <http://www.esil-sedi.eu/fichiers/en/Katselli_874.pdf>

Elena Katselli, 'Holding the Security Council Accountable for Human Rights Violations' (2007) 1 *Human Rights and International Legal Discourse* 301

Hans Kelsen, *The Law of the United Nations: A Critical Analysis of its Fundamental Problems* (Frederick A. Praeger 2011)

Outi Keranen, 'What Happened to the Responsibility to Rebuild?' (2016) 3 *Global Governance: A Review of Multilateralism and International Organizations* 331
Müge Kinacioğlu, 'Forcing Democracy: Is Military Intervention for Regime Change Permissible?' (2012) 1 *All Azimuth* 28
Ben Kioko, 'The Right of Intervention under the African Union's Constitutive Act: From Non-interference to Non-intervention' (2003) 85 *International Review of the Red Cross* 807
Frederic L. Kirgis, 'Book Review and Note: Book Reviews: Exclusion from Participation in International Organisations: The Law and Practice Behind Member States' Expulsion and Suspension of Membership. By Konstantinos D. Magliveras' (2001) 95 *American Journal of International Law* 734
Phillippe Kirsch and John Holmes, 'The Rome Conference on an International Criminal Court: The Negotiating Process' (1999) 93 *American Journal of International Law* 2
Jann K. Kleffner, 'The Applicability of International Humanitarian Law to Organized Armed Groups' (2011) 93 *International Review of the Red Cross* 443
Pierre Klein, 'Responsibility' in Jacob Kantz Cogan, Ian Hurd, and Ian Johnstone (eds) *The Oxford Handbook of International Organizations* (Oxford University Press 2016)
Harold Koh, 'The War Powers and Humanitarian Intervention' (2016) 53 *Houston Law Review* 971
Robert Kolb, *International Law on the Maintenance of Peace* (Edward Elgar 2018)
Dan Kuwali, 'From Stopping to Preventing Atrocities: Actualisation of Article 4(h)' (2015) 24 *African Security Review* 248
Dan Kuwali, 'Protect Responsibly: The African Union's Implementation of Article 4(h) Intervention' (2010) 11 *Yearbook of International Humanitarian Law* 51
Vladyslav Lanovoy, 'The Use of Force by Non-State Actors and the Limits of Attribution of Conduct' (2017) 28 *European Journal of International Law* 536
Christina Leb, 'One Step at a Time: International Law and the Duty to Cooperate in the Management of Shared Water Resources' (2015) 40 *Water International* 21
Thomas H. Lee, 'The Law of War and the Responsibility to Protect Civilians: A Reinterpretation' (2015) 55 *Harvard International Law Journal* 251
Brian D. Lepard, *Customary International Law: A New Theory with Practical Applications* (Cambridge University Press 2010)
Richard B. Lillich, 'Forcible Self-Help by States to Protect Human Rights' (1967–1968) 53 *Iowa Law Review* 325
Richard B. Lillich, 'The Role of the UN Security Council in Protecting Human Rights in Crisis Situations: UN Humanitarian Intervention in the Post-Cold War Era' (1995) 3 *Tulane Journal of International and Comparative Law* 1
Marco Longobardo, 'Genocide, Obligations Erga Omnes, and the Responsibility to Protect: Remarks on a Complex Convergence' (2015) 19 *International Journal of Human Rights* 1199
Vaughan Lowe, *International Law* (Oxford University Press 2007)
T M, 'The Arab League's Role in the Syrian Civil War' (2014) 6 *Inquiries Journal* 1
Konstantinos D. Magliveras, *Exclusion from Participation in International Organisations: The Law and Practice behind member States' Expulsion and Suspension of Membership* (Kluwer Law International 1999)
Eyal Mayroz, 'The Legal Duty to "Prevent": After the Onset of "Genocide"' (2012) 14 *Journal of Genocide Research* 79
Emma McClean, 'The Responsibility to Protect: The Role of International Human Rights Law' (2008) 13 *Journal of Conflict and Security Law* 123

Robert McCorquodale, 'Overlegalizing Silences: Human Rights and Nonstate Actors' (2002) 96 *American Society of International Law Proceedings* 384

Graham Melling and Anne Dennett, 'The Security Council Veto and Syria: Responding to Mass Atrocities through the "Uniting for Peace" Resolution' (2017) 57 *Indian Journal of International Law* 285

Theodor Meron, *War Crimes Law Comes of Age: Essays* (Oxford University Press 1998)

Jason Dominguez Meyer, 'From Paralysis in Rwanda to Boldness in Libya: Has the International Community Taken "Responsibility to Protect" from Abstract Principle to Concrete Norm Under International Law?' (2011–2012) 34 *Houston Journal of International Law* 87

Kurt Mills, 'R2P and the ICC: At Odds or in Sync?' (2015) 26 *Criminal Law Forum* 73

Mirka Möldner, 'Responsibility of International Organizations – Introducing the ILC's DARIO' (2012) 16 *Max Planck Yearbook of United Nations Law* 281

Justin Morris, 'Libya and Syria: R2P and the Spectre of the Swinging Pendulum' (2013) 89 *International Affairs* 1265

John F. Murphy, 'Responsibility to Protect (R2P) Comes of Age? A Sceptic's View' (2011–2012) 18 *International Law Students' Association Journal of International and Comparative Law* 413

Sean D. Murphy, 'Crimes Against Humanity and Other Topics: The Sixty-Ninth Session of the International Law Commission' (2017) 111 *American Journal of International Law* 970

Daragh Murray, 'How International Humanitarian Law Treaties Bind Non-State Armed Groups' (2014) 20 *Journal of Conflict and Security Law* 101

Daragh Murray, *Human Rights Obligations of Non-State Armed Groups* (Hart Publishing Ltd 2016)

Yasmine Nahlawi, 'Forcible Displacement as a Weapon of War in the Syrian Conflict: Lessons and Developments' in Elena Katselli Proukaki (ed.), *Armed Conflict and Forcible Displacement: Individual Rights under International Law* (Routledge 2018)

Yasmine Nahlawi, 'The Legality of NATO's Pursuit of Regime Change in Libya' (2018) 5 *Journal on the Use of Force and International Law* 295

Yasmine Nahlawi, 'The Responsibility to Protect and Obama's Red Line on Syria' (2016) 8 *Global Responsibility to Protect* 76

Yasmine Nahlawi, 'Self-Determination and the Right to Revolution: Syria' (2014) 8 *Human Rights and International Legal Discourse* 84

Faustin Ntoubandi, *Amnesty for Crimes against Humanity under International Law* (Martinus Nijhoff Publishers 2007)

Laurie O'Conner, 'Legality of the Use of Force in Syria against Islamic State and the Khorasan Group' (2016) 3 *Journal on the Use of Force in International Law* 70

Chris O'Meara, 'Should International Law Recognize a Right of Humanitarian Intervention?' (2017) 66 *International and Comparative Law Quarterly* 441

Keiichiro Okimoto, 'Humanitarian Activities Carried Out across Borders in Times of Armed Conflict in the Light of State Sovereignty and International Humanitarian Law' (2016) 17 *Yearbook of International Humanitarian Law* 121

L. Oppenheim and Hersch Lauterpacht, *International Law: A Treatise, vol* I, *Peace* (8th edn, Longmans, Green 1955)

Alexander Orakhelashvili, *Collective Security* (Oxford University Press 2011)

Alexander Orakhelashvili, *Peremptory Norms in International Law* (Oxford University Press 2006)

S. Pandiaraj, 'Sovereignty as Responsibility: Reflections on the Legal Status of the Doctrine of Responsibility to Protect' (2016) 15 *Chinese Journal of International Law* 795

Efthymios Papastavridis, 'Interpretation of Security Council Resolutions under Chapter VII in the Aftermath of the Iraqi Crisis' (2007) 56 *International and Comparative Law Quarterly* 83

James Pattison, 'Perilous Noninterventions? The Counterfactual Assessment of Libya and the Need to be a Responsible Power' (2017) 9 *Global Responsibility to Protect* 219

Jordan Paustet al., *International Criminal Law: Cases and Materials* (Carolina Academic Press 1996)

Mehrdad Payandeh, 'The United Nations, Military Intervention, and Regime Change in Libya' (2011–2012) 52 *Virginia Journal of International Law* 355

Pärtel Piirimäe, 'The Westphalian Myth and the Idea of External Sovereignty' in Hent Kalmo and Quentin Skinner (eds), *Sovereignty in Fragments: The Past, Present and Future of a Contested Concept* (Cambridge University Press 2010)

S. Pandiaraj, 'Sovereignty as Responsibility: Reflections on the Legal Status of the Doctrine of Responsibility to Protect' (2016) 15 *Chinese Journal of International Law* 795

Anne Peters, 'The Security Council's Responsibility to Protect' (2011) 8 *International Organizations Law Review* 1

Jean Pictetet al., *Commentary: Geneva Convention for the Amelioration of the Condition of the Wounded and Sick in Armed Forces in the Field*, vol. I (ICRC 1952) 26

Fausto Pocar, 'To What Extent is Protocol I Customary International Law?' (2002) 78 *International Law Studies* 337

Catherine Powell, 'Libya: A Multilateral Constitutional Moment?' (2012) 106 *American Journal of International Law* 298

Elena Katselli Proukaki, *The Problem of Enforcement in International Law: Countermeasures, the Non-Injured State and the Idea of International Community* (Routledge 2009)

Helen Quane, 'The United Nations and the Evolving Right to Self-Determination' (1998) 47 *International and Comparative Law Quarterly* 537

John Quigley, 'State Responsibility for Ethnic Cleansing' (1999) 32 *University of California Davis Law Review* 341

Patrick Quinton-Brown, 'Mapping Dissent: The Responsibility to Protect and its State Critics' (2013) 5 *Global Responsibility to Protect* 260

Michael Ramsden, '"Uniting for Peace" and Humanitarian Intervention: The Authorising Function of the U.N. General Assembly' (2016) 25 *Washington International Law Journal* 267

Michael D. Ramsey, 'Reinventing the Security Council: The U.N. as a Lockean System' (2003–2004) 79 *Notre Dame Law Review* 1529

Harry Reicher, 'The Uniting for Peace Resolution on the Thirtieth Anniversary of its Passage' (1981) 20 *Columbia Journal of Transnational Law* 1

August Reinisch, 'Developing Human Rights and Humanitarian Law Accountability of the Security Council for the Imposition of Economic Sanctions' (2001) 95 *American Journal of International Law* 851

Theresa Reinold, 'The "Responsibility Not to Veto", Secondary Rules, and the Rule of Law' (2014) 6 *Global Responsibility to Protect* 269

W. Michael Reisman, 'Sovereignty and Human Rights in Contemporary International Law' (1990) 84 *American Journal of International Law* 866

Geoffrey Robertson, *Crimes against Humanity: The Struggle for Global Justice* (New Press 1999)

Darryl Robinson, 'Defining "Crimes Against Humanity" at the Rome Conference' (1999) 93 *American Journal of International Law* 43

Tilman Rodenhäuser, 'Human Rights Obligations of Non-State Armed Groups in Other Situations of Violence: The Syria Example' (2012) 3 *International Humanitarian Legal Studies* 263

Tilman Rodenhäuser, *Organizing Rebellion: Non-State Armed Groups under International Humanitarian Law, Human Rights Law, and International Criminal Law* (Oxford University Press 2018)
Sophie Rondeau, 'The Responsibility to Protect Doctrine, and the Duty of the International Community to Reinforce International Humanitarian Law and Its Protective Value for Civilian Populations' in Richard Barnes and Vassilis Tzevelekos (eds), *Beyond Responsibility to Protect: Generating Change in International Law* (Intersentia 2016)
Sheri P. Rosenberg, 'Responsibility to Protect: A Framework for Prevention' (2009) 1 *Global Responsibility to Protect* 442
Robert Rosenstock, 'The Declaration of Principles of International Law Concerning Friendly Relations: A Survey' (1971) 65 *American Journal of International Law* 713
Cedric Ryngaert, 'State Responsibility and Non-State Actors' in Math Noortmann, August Reinisch and Cedric Ryngaert (eds), *Non-State Actors in International Law* (Hart Publishing 2015)
Cedric Ryngaert and Anneleen Van de Meulebroucke, 'Enhancing and Enforcing Compliance with International Humanitarian Law by Non-State Armed Groups: An Inquiry into some Mechanisms' (2012) 16 *Journal of Conflict and Security Law* 443
Leila Nadya Sadat, 'A Contextual and Historical Analysis of the International Law Commission's 2017 Draft Articles for a New Global Treaty on Crimes against Humanity' (2018) 16 *Journal of International Criminal Justice* 683
Leila Nadya Sadat, 'Crimes against Humanity in the Modern Age' (2013) 107 *American Journal of International Law* 334
Philippe Sands and Pierre Klein, *Bowett's Law of International Institutions* (Thomson Reuters 2009)
Danesh Sarooshi, *The United Nations and the Development of Collective Security: The Delegation by the UN Security Council of its Chapter VII Powers* (Clarendon Press 1999)
Marco Sassòli, 'State Responsibility for Violations of International Humanitarian Law' (2002) 84 *International Review of the Red Cross* 401
Marco Sassòli, 'Taking Armed Groups Seriously: Ways to Improve their Compliance with International Humanitarian Law' (2010) 1 *International Humanitarian Legal Studies* 5
Ben Saul, 'Enhancing Civilian Protection by Engaging Non-State Armed Groups under International Humanitarian Law' (2017) 22 *Journal of Conflict and Security Law* 39
William Schabas, *Genocide in International Law: The Crime of Crimes* (2nd edn, Cambridge University Press 2009)
William Schabas, *An Introduction to the International Criminal Court* (2nd edn, Cambridge University Press 2004)
William Schabas, *The International Criminal Court: A Commentary on the Rome Statute* (Oxford University Press 2010)
Michael P. Scharf, 'How the War against ISIS Changed International Law' (2016) 48 *Case Western Reserve Journal of International Law* 15
Michael N. Schmitt, 'Wings over Libya: The No-fly Zone in Legal Perspective' (2011) 36 *Yale Journal of International Law Online* 45
Albrecht Schnabel, 'The Responsibility to Rebuild' in W. Andy Knight and Frazer Egerton (eds) *The Routledge Handbook of the Responsibility to Protect* (Routledge 2012)
Malcolm Shaw, *International Law* (6th edn, Cambridge University Press 2008)
Bruno Simma, *The Charter of the United Nations: A Commentary*, vol. I (2nd edn, Oxford University Press 2002)
Bruno Simma, 'NATO, the UN and the Use of Force: Legal Aspects' (1999) 10 *European Journal of International Law* 1

Bruno Simma and Philip Alston, 'The Sources of Human Rights Law: Custom, Jus Cogens, and General Principles' (1988–1989) 12 *Australian Yearbook of International Law* 82

Bruno Simma and Andreas S. Paulus, 'The "International Community": Facing the Challenge of Globalization' (1998) 9 *European Journal of International Law* 266

Sandesh Sivakumaran, 'Binding Armed Opposition Groups' (2006) 55 *International and Comparative Law Quarterly* 369

Sandesh Sivakumaran, *The Law of Non-International Armed Conflict* (Oxford University Press 2012)

Michael Small, 'An Analysis of the Responsibility to Protect Program in Light of the Conflict in Syria' (2014) 13 *Washington University Global Studies Law Review* 179

Lois B. Sohn, 'The New International Law: Protection of the Rights of Individuals Rather than States' (1982–1983) 32 *American University Law Review* 1

Gary D. Solis, *The Law of Armed Conflict* (Cambridge University Press 2010)

Carsten Stahn, 'Between Law-breaking and Law-making: Syria, Humanitarian Intervention and "What the Law Ought to be"' (2013) 19 *Journal of Conflict and Security Law* 25

Carsten Stahn, 'Marital Stress or Grounds for Divorce? Re-thinking the Relationship between R2P and International Criminal Justice' (2015) 26 *Criminal Law Forum* 13

Ekkehard Strauss, 'A Bird in the Hand is Worth Two in the Bush – On the Assumed Legal Nature of the Responsibility to Protect' (2009) 1 *Global Responsibility to Protect* 291

Christian Tams, *Enforcing Obligations Erga Omnes in International Law* (Cambridge University Press 2005)

Heidarali Teimouri and Surya P. Subedi, 'Responsibility to Protect and the International Military Intervention in Libya in International Law: What Went Wrong and What Lessons Could be Learnt from It?' (2018) 23 *Journal of Conflict and Security Law* 3

Ruti Teitel, *Humanity's Law* (Oxford University Press 2011)

Fernando R. Tesón, 'Collective Humanitarian Intervention' (1995–1996) 17 *Michigan Journal of International Law* 323

Pierre Thielbörger, 'The Status and Future of International Law after the Libya Intervention' (2012) 4 *Goettingen Journal of International Law* 11

Daniel Thürer, *International Humanitarian Law Theory, Practice, Context* (Brill 2011)

Vito Todeschini, 'The Place of Aggression in the Responsibility to Protect Doctrine, in Richard Barnes and Vassilis Tzevelekos (eds), *Beyond Responsibility to Protect: Generating Change in International Law* (Intersentia 2016)

Mark Toufayan, 'The World Court's Distress When Facing Genocide: A Critical Commentary on the Application of the Genocide Convention Case (Bosnia and Herzegovina v. Yugoslavia (Serbia and Montenegro))' (2005) 40 *Texas International Law Journal* 233

Nicholas Tsagourias, 'Self-defence against Non-State Actors: The Interaction between Self-defence as a Primary Rule and Self-defence as a Secondary Rule' (2016) 29 *Leiden Journal of International Law* 801

Oscar M. Uhleret al., *Commentary: Geneva Convention Relative to the Protection of Civilian Persons in Time of War*, vol. IV (ICRC 1958)

Geir Ulfstein and Hege Føsund Christiansen, 'The Legality of the NATO Bombing in Libya' (2013) 62 *International and Comparative Law Quarterly* 159

Matthias Vanhullebusch, 'Regime Change, the Security Council and China' (2015) 14 *Chinese Journal of International Law* 665

Joe Verhoeven, 'Jus Cogens and Reservations or <<Counter-Reservations>> to the Jurisdiction of the International Court of Justice' in Karel Wellens (ed.), *International Law: Theory and Practice* (Martinus Nijhoff Publishers 1998)

Jure Vidmar, 'Norm Conflicts and Hierarchy in International Law: Towards Vertical International Legal System?' in Erika de Wet and Jure Vidmar (eds), *Hierarchy in International Law: The Place of Human Rights* (Oxford University Press 2012)

Santiago Villalpando, 'The Legal Dimension of the International Community: How Community Interests are Protected in International Law' (2010) 21 *European Journal of International Law* 387

Colin Warbrick, 'British Policy and the National Transitional Council of Libya' (2012) 61 *International and Comparative Law Quarterly* 247

Christian Wenaweser and James Cockayne, 'Justice for Syria? The International, Impartial and Independent Mechanism and the Emergence of the UN General Assembly in the Realm of International Criminal Justice' (2017) 15 *Journal of International Criminal Justice* 211

Nigel D. White, 'Commentary: International Institutions and their Role in R2P' in Richard Barnes and Vassilis Tzevelekos (eds), *Beyond Responsibility to Protect: Generating Change in International Law* (Intersentia 2016)

Nigel D. White, 'Due Diligence Obligations of Conduct: Developing a Responsibility Regime for PMSCs' (2012) 31 *Criminal Justice Ethics* 233

Nigel D. White, 'The Legality of Bombing in the Name of Humanity' (2000) 5 *Journal of Conflict and Security Law* 27

Alex Whiting, 'An Investigative Mechanism for Syria: The General Assembly Steps into the Breach' (2017) 15 *Journal of International Criminal Justice* 231

Paul R. Williams and Colleen Popken, 'Security Council Resolution 1973 on Libya: A Moment of Legal & Moral Clarity' (2011) 44 *Case Western Reserve Journal of International Law* 225

Gary Wilson, 'Applying the Responsibility to Protect to the "Arab Spring"' (2014) 35 *Liverpool Law Review* 157

Michael C. Wood, 'The Interpretation of Security Council Resolutions' (1998) 2 *Max Planck Yearbook of United Nations Law Online* 73

Michael C. Wood, 'The Interpretation of Security Council Resolutions, Revisited' (2017) 20 *Max Planck Yearbook of United Nations Law Online* 1

Jan Wouters and Sten Verhoeven, 'The Prohibition of Genocide as a Norm of Ius Cogens and its Implications for the Enforcement of the Law of Genocide' (2005) 5 *International Criminal Law Review* 401

Sienho Yee, 'The Dynamic Interplay between the Interpreters of Security Council Resolutions' (2012) 11 *Chinese Journal of International Law* 613

Margaret Young and Sebastian Sullivan, 'Evolution through the Duty to Cooperate: Implications of the Whaling Case at the International Court of Justice' (2015) 16 *Melbourne Journal of International Law* 311

Dominik Zaum, 'The Security Council, the General Assembly, and War: The Uniting for Peace Resolution' in Vaughan Lowe et al. (eds), *The United Nations Security Council and War* (Oxford University Press 2008)

Spencer Zifcak, 'The Responsibility to Protect after Libya and Syria' (2012) 13 *Melbourne Journal of International Law* 59

Andreas Zimmermann, 'Crimes within the Jurisdiction of the Court' in Otto Triffterer (ed.), *Commentary on the Rome Statute of the International Criminal Court* (Nomos Verlagsgesellschaft 1999)

Index

For Product Safety Concerns and Information please contact our EU representative GPSR@taylorandfrancis.com
Taylor & Francis Verlag GmbH, Kaufingerstraße 24, 80331 München, Germany

www.ingramcontent.com/pod-product-compliance
Ingram Content Group UK Ltd.
Pitfield, Milton Keynes, MK11 3LW, UK
UKHW022128190926
475702UK00013B/1699
* 9 7 8 1 0 3 2 2 3 9 7 1 2 *